HURRY UP AND WAIT!

War Stories My Dad (and Others) Told to Kill the Boredom and Bury the Terror

by James K. Turner

Lambert Hill

Hurry Up and Wait!
War Stories My Dad (and Others) Told
to Kill the Boredom and Bury the Terror

Copyright © 2023 by James K. Turner

Lambert Hill, Brea, CA 92821
Books@LambertHill.com

ISBN: 9781737428527

To all 503rd troopers,
past, present, and future.

Cpl. Thomas E. Turner. 1941

Contents

Introduction

Among my fondest and most vivid memories as a boy growing up in Anaheim, California, are the nights "Uncle" Max and "Aunt" Irene would come to visit from Long Beach. Max and my father had served together in the 503rd Parachute Infantry Regiment. Not only was it the United States Army's first airborne regiment, but it was also one of only a handful of such units which spearheaded General Douglas MacArthur's "leapfrogging" strategy (he preferred this term to "island hopping" which he contended was just a series of frontal assaults) and enabled the fulfillment of his laconically eloquent vow: "I shall return." They never mentioned the unsightly horrors and dreadful fear of being in battle. Rather, the war stories they recounted, as my brother and I snuck out of our bedrooms and down the hall to listen, were hilarious incidents that happened to them during boot camp, parachute school, Australian jungle training, and even firefights with the enemy.

The idea for this book took root when I attended some of my father's regimental association meetings and reunions. The conversations followed the same vein Dad's and Max's had. The vets would agree that the worst fight was on Negros Island, or that the war had been at least "ninety percent" against the elements and maybe "ten percent" against the enemy, but that was the end of it.

Humorous stories would resurface, and laughter would resume. Sometimes the old troopers would allude to their always off-color marching songs or sing tunes that were popular on the radio then. Dad's comrades-in-arms rehashed inanity on the islands or told of the pranks they pulled, all the while suppressing the nightmarish battle memories which haunted most of them. It was not till many years later, long after Dad was gone, that they opened up to interviewers who wrote many of the books cited in the bibliography for this one.

My goal, set thirty-five years ago, when the stories and memories were fresher, was to get their anecdotes—no matter how exaggerated they had become—recorded before they were lost. The time grew shorter as career and family pushed the project onto the back burner. All the while the list of players dwindled. Finally, the Covid-19 Pandemic and subsequent lockdown gave me an entire year devoid of any excuse for not writing the book which had been in the back of my head and on sheets of paper in a drawer for a long time.

Almost immediately, questions popped up: involved units, strengths, and casualties; weapons and equipment used; specific locales and timelines. For the most part, I had to conjecture where and when each story occurred, since many had been prefaced with something like, "Once on a run" or "In a foxhole somewhere" or "On some island...." Dad and his friends were no longer here to ask. An invaluable find, at the bottom of a trunk in my mother's garage, was her scrapbook of the war years. Here were headlines with first-hand reports from the theaters of war and the home front. These concurrent events provided background context typically beyond the enlisted man's immediate "need to know" frontline viewpoint but relevant to the local and global campaigns or to the units and commanders with whom the paratroopers fought arm-in-arm.

It also became clear that Army conversations were well-seasoned with cursing, even in the retellings years later, especially when emotions were rekindled. Additionally, "the enemy" was dehumanized during the war in public forums and throughout military training by racial slurs and caricatures. Inexcusably, racism spilled over into our own leadership, citizenry, and armed forces as attested to by Relocation Camps and segregated Army units. To his credit, my father never engaged in either practice. He called the enemy just that, and he limited his expletives to "darn" and "heck" in his anecdotes. While I wanted my father's progeny to be aware of his experiences, I was leery of exposing them to harsh language inappropriate for their ages. I decided to tell the stories as Dad would have, so I [bracketed] and deleted or softened words which I thought were particularly vulgar or degrading. The reader can substitute liberally for a more historical version.

This book is not meant to be a history of the 503rd Regiment. That task has been admirably handled by historians and the men who were there. Their expert and eye-witness accounts have been included in the bibliography. As noted by Wellington, Grant, and Patton, no one soldier sees the whole battlefield, let alone the whole war. Rather, this is the journey of one man, who, like all the others in what Tom Brokaw called *The Greatest Generation*, did his duty when called, lived a life that honored those who didn't get to come home, and thanked the Lord Who gave him the chance to do both.

Despite the pervasive death, debilitating disease, and inescapable discomfort, my father's service was the pinnacle of his life. His regiment's climactic battle and ensuing Presidential Unit

Citation were as significant to Tom Turner as an All-State trophy or a World Series ring would be to other men. The 503rd was his championship team.

My hope remains that others like me, my children, and my grandchildren, who weren't there and never experienced the fraternity that comes from surviving life-and-death desperation together, can understand how these farm hands, factory workers, college kids, shop keepers, longshoremen, garage mechanics, and tenement dwellers, who wanted nothing more than a taste of the American dream after the decade-long Depression, could keep their sanity during and following the gruesome duty they were assigned. Perhaps those yellow news clippings and the vets' reunion snippets will reveal that these citizen soldiers, who were expected to hurry up and win a war they didn't start but were constantly required to wait for the resources and opportunities to do it, are more than anonymous names on letters and faces on faded snapshots. MacArthur lauded them as "splendid" and "extraordinary" soldiers, who displayed "magnificent courage" and "heroism in the highest degree." Tom Turner called them his friends.

Prologue

Sunday, February 13, 1977, was a warm balmy day, even by Southern California standards. Tom and Betty Turner decided to take a drive in the unusually good weather and headed for a favorite place, Walter Knott's Berry Farm in Buena Park. In those days, before the security wall was built around the replica ghost town and its attractions, one could park, wander, and shop for free, watch the horse-drawn stagecoach and working 4-4-0 steam locomotive, see a shootout in front of the saloon, have a chicken dinner, and take home one of Cordelia Knott's famous boysenberry pies. Knott's was never as busy as Disneyland, some six or seven miles away, and it was a pleasant, relaxing, inexpensive way to spend an afternoon.

As the Turners exited the park along Grand Avenue, they passed the Buena Park Hotel (later the Grand and now the Knott's Berry Farm Hotel). Tom suddenly slammed on the brakes; Betty lurched forward and flopped back in her seat. "What's the matter?" she blurted, seeing nothing but pavement ahead of them.

"Geez, that's my old army outfit!" Tom was backing up, arm over the back of Betty's seat. She could see now behind her on the hotel marquis the greeting, "Welcome 503rd Parachute Regimental Combat Team." He turned into the hotel parking lot, found a space, and hopped out. She followed quickly, but Tom was a six-footer on a mission.

As he bounded into the lobby, he exchanged glances with a man coming out of the cocktail lounge. Across the lobby, they peered at each other through thirty-some years of wrinkles, added weight, and graying, receding hair. "Ollie!"

"Tom!" They ran towards each other and hugged and slapped each other's back as they had not since V-J Day, when they had realized they would not have to make a planned jump into Japan with a projected 90% casualty rate. "Come on, Tom, the guys are all in the hospitality room. Glad you could make it to the reunion."

Betty was just now catching up. "Betty, this is Ollie Patterson. We were in the Philippines together." She followed the two, arms around each other's shoulders, into the adjoining room where ice cubes rattled in glasses, cigarette smoke clouded the air, and laughs accented the buzz of conversation.

"Holy mackerel, Turner's here! Where the [heck] ya been?"

"I didn't even know. I was just driving by and saw the sign outside."

"Hey Tom, dj'eet?" hollered Andy Amaty, a fellow sergeant and native New Yorker.

No, Andy, dj'oo?

Chapter 1

THE PACIFIC
Rise of the Imperial Sun

E lizabeth Dockter, a twenty-two-year-old Russell Sage student and Albany State Laboratory technician, was writing a letter to her fiancé, Thomas Turner. He had been drafted in February 1941, as the United States sluggishly responded to the rapidly accelerating European and Sino-Japanese wars. Tom was currently in the Advanced Infantry Training program at Fort Benning, Georgia, and was nearly through with his one-year commitment to the Army.

She wrote to him of wedding plans. She'd found a dress, she said, on a second-hand rack downtown. The service would be, of course, at the Albany West End Presbyterian Church, officiated by her father, the Reverend Albert Dockter. Tom's family had been long-time members and he a deacon at West End before the recent arrival of Reverend Dockter and his red-headed daughters. Her sister, Dorothy, and a couple college chums had agreed to be bridesmaids.

Betty and Dotty had just cleaned up from the family's late lunch after their long morning at church. Hits of the Big Bands—

Benny Goodman, Tommy Dorsey, Harry James, and Duke Ellington—wafted through the manse from the radio downstairs in the living room. Then there was breaking news. The United States military base at Pearl Harbor, Hawaii, had just been attacked. Numerous ships and airplanes had been damaged or destroyed, including all but one of the battleships in the US Navy's (USN) Pacific Fleet.[1] There were hundreds, perhaps thousands, of civilian and military casualties. The early morning surprise attack had been carried out by Japanese carrier-based aircraft. Hawaii and the West Coast were now bracing for a possible invasion. President Franklin Roosevelt was assuming a state of war now existed and would address Congress and the nation the next morning. There was little doubt Congress would declare war on Japan. Betty tore up the letter.

That evening, she wrote in her diary, "A 'state of war'? What does that mean? It doesn't sound like Merry Christmas." Next day her entry read, "The President is declaring war on Japan today. We're really in it. I went to bed crying, woke up crying and been at it all day. And it's not just Tom now, it's all the boys...."

Prior to the Pearl Harbor attack, England's Prime Minister, Winston Churchill, had been prodding President Roosevelt and hoping for US entry into the war on the side of the Allies. Due to America's overriding isolationist policy, the best Churchill had been able to get was the Lend-Lease program, wherein the United States sent planes, tanks, and ships (mostly obsolete) to the UK in exchange for use of British naval and air bases at strategic locations. The surprise attack would, at last, give Churchill his wish.

Within ten hours of the Pearl Harbor attack, Japanese bombers from Formosa (modern day Taiwan) bombed Clark Field northwest of Manila, the capital of the Philippine Islands and site of General Douglas MacArthur's Pacific headquarters. Devoid of information since the initial warnings from Hawaii, he assumed the glut of sea and air power at Pearl Harbor had severely defeated the Japanese. Even though he scrambled planes as a precaution against the anticipated air attack, it coincided with their being lined up on the ground ("like sitting ducks," according to one Japanese pilot) refueling as their crews ate lunch and studied maps for a reconnaissance over Formosa. The few outgunned and inexperienced pilots who made it into the air were overwhelmed. Half of MacArthur's air force was easily destroyed. Fortunately, he had moved the other half to Mindanao, at the southern end of the Philippines and out of range of Formosa's air bases. MacArthur said of a proposed counterattack against Formosa later reported in the news that it would have been suicide: his bombers lacked the fighter support that aircraft carriers had provided the enemy. Simultaneously with the Manila raid, the Japanese bombed Guam and Wake Islands to the east. They stormed and captured Guam on December 10. Wake's defenders staved off one attack, but when the Japanese beefed up their assault on the twenty-third with Imperial Marines, two carriers, and two battleships, Wake finally succumbed.

The day Guam fell, the Japanese invaded the Philippines. MacArthur's mobile reserve and remaining planes repelled several diversionary landings along the northern and southern coasts of Luzon. The Japanese Sixteenth Army invaded Mindanao on the twentieth. Three days before Christmas, most of General Masaharu Homma's Fourteenth Army, 28,000 troops battle-hardened in China, landed in Lingayen Gulf along the northwest coast of Luzon. The other 15,000 landed southeast of Manila at Rosario.

The two forces, which had armored and artillery support, began to converge on Manila. MacArthur's army outnumbered Homma's, but only his "Philippine Division" of 30,000 American soldiers and Philippine Scouts[2] were regulars. The vast majority were recently called up untrained Filipino reservists who had WWI weapons if any at all. Moreover, Homma was able to replace his losses but MacArthur could not: President Roosevelt had made it clear that all resources were to be used against Germany, which had declared war on the United States within days of the Pearl Harbor attack.

On Christmas Day the US and Filipino forces began retreating before the relentless Japanese, who seemed to be able to breach any defensive line. By January 6, MacArthur had declared Manila—"The Pearl of the Orient"—an open city to avoid its destruction and pulled all his forces into the Bataan Peninsula, whose jungles, mountains, swamps, and bamboo forests he had mapped during his first tour of duty in the islands. This withdrawal was according to War Plan Orange (WPO), a defensive strategy for the peninsula which he had also drafted earlier. Some critics say he waited too long, leaving stockpiled supplies behind. Whether the General didn't want to foment panic, thought he could knock the Japanese back into the ocean, or believed Washington would send help, not even former staff members could say. However, the war plan's one contingency—relief within six months—would never be met. American and Filipino budget slashes in the 1930s and the President's decree doomed the defenders. Per WPO protocol, MacArthur moved his headquarters, Philippine President Manuel Quezon's office, their staffs, and their families to Corregidor, one of the small but heavily fortified islands sitting between Manila Bay and the South China Sea. Because he now lived and operated in tunnels beneath the island, soldiers and news reporters derisively began to call MacArthur "Dugout Doug."

On Bataan, new enemies reared their heads: malaria, malnutrition, and exhaustion. The few American supply attempts were thwarted. Quinine, used to suppress malaria symptoms, ran out. Faced with feeding 20,000 refugees as well, the defenders were cut to half and then three-eighths rations. One officer noted his soldiers looked "like walking dead men." Still the "Battling Bastards of Bataan" held out through February and into March. At 7:30 PM on March 11, having been ordered[3] to Australia to command what he had been led to believe was the necessary relief force, MacArthur left Corregidor with his family and staff on patrol torpedo (PT) boats, whose sharp prows, flat hulls, and triple Packard engines made rooster tails as they sped to Mindanao, where 25,000 Americans and Filipinos were stiffly resisting the Japanese.[4]

B-17s flew the group 1600 miles over the East Indies and New Guinea, now all enemy territory, to Darwin, Australia, where DC-3s took off for Alice Springs just ahead of Japanese pursuit planes. From there the entourage rode a thousand miles on wooden benches in narrow-gauge railroad cars to Adelaide. Finally, they boarded the standard-gauge Australian Railroad (the General got the commissioner's private car) for the last leg to Melbourne. It was not until after this "trip in a cement mixer," at his new headquarters as Supreme Commander of Allied Forces in the South West Pacific Area, that MacArthur found out there was no relief force.[5] There were more troops in Bataan than in all of Australia. In fact, Australia, fearing to be the next target as Japan invaded New Guinea, had recalled its three divisions from North Africa and the Levant. The British were left with the dilemma of abandoning or trying to hold on to their protectorates in the Mediterranean.

General Homma faced his own problems. Tropical diseases thinned his ranks. His crack 48th Division was withdrawn to assault the Dutch East Indies. He'd nearly called off his stalled Luzon invasion when the Imperial Japanese Army (IJA) reinforced him with 20,000 fresh troops late in March. He began a non-stop bombardment and renewed the attacks along the crumbling line. On April 9, a few days after Easter, Major General (Maj. Gen.) Edward King, Jr., surrendered the sick, starving forces on the Bataan Peninsula. Maj. Gen. Jonathan Wainwright, left in charge on Corregidor, held out for another month against constant artillery barrages and air bombardments. After Wainwright's heavy naval guns and mortars had been knocked out, Homma landed troops and tanks on Corregidor. Wainwright, fearing a slaughter of not only the remaining garrison but the many nurses, civilians, and wounded soldiers on the island, wired Roosevelt and MacArthur his decision to surrender Corregidor. Homma insisted that he surrender *all* the Philippine Islands to avoid the slaughter. This was the first, and only, surrender of an entire American Army—over 100,000 men—in US history. In the brief lull, thousands of American and Filipino soldiers slipped into the jungles and hills on the islands from where they would lead the resistance movement against the Japanese occupation. The infamous Bataan Death March followed. General Homma, having exceeded the fifty days in which he had been expected to conquer the Philippines, was recalled to Japan and relieved of command.

The defenders of the Philippines, though defeated and about to endure three and a half years of brutal imprisonment if not perish miserably, were celebrated as heroes. They had diverted Japanese resources from the attacks on Borneo and Java. They had slowed the advance towards New Guinea and the Solomon Islands.

They had bought Australia time to prepare a defense. Nevertheless, the Japanese Empire had neutralized the Allied presence in Asia and the Pacific. Besides the beating they'd given Pearl Harbor, the Imperial Japanese Navy (IJN) had sunk England's largest battleships, *Prince of Wales* and *Repulse*, off the coast of Malaya. Japanese armies had captured Bangkok on December 9, Hong Kong on Christmas Day, and Singapore—according to Churchill, "the worst disaster and largest capitulation" in Britain's history— on February 13, 1942. The Dutch had surrendered Java on March 8, and the rest of the East Indies the next day. The Empire of Japan now controlled most of southeast Asia, threatened India from Burma, and possessed an island buffer zone ranging from Sumatra through New Guinea to the Mariana Islands.

Only the Midway Islands, so named for being equidistant from Japan and California, remained as the last outpost between the Japanese surge and the US Pacific coast. While the Japanese invaded the Aleutian Islands as a deception on June 3, an invasion fleet under Admiral Isaroku Yamamoto, bigger than his fleet for Pearl Harbor, steamed towards Midway with the intent of taking out the Pacific Fleet's only three aircraft carriers while conquering the islands. Midway's Army garrison and the Navy, forewarned by code breakers, patrol planes, and the submarine *USS Nautilus*, sent out seven waves of bombers and fighters (like MacArthur's, outmoded) on the morning of the fourth. A handful of planes came back. They had scored not a single hit on the IJN. Then a five-minute window of opportunity opened while the Japanese carriers had their decks packed with Mitsubishi "Zero" fighters, which had fought off the American planes, and "Val" dive bombers and "Kate" torpedo bombers, which had just returned from early morning attacks on Midway. They were refueling and rearming, unable to take off because the ships were still harassed by a few dogged US fighters. The last wave of two dozen American SBD "Dauntless" dive bombers appeared and swooped in on the carriers, sinking all four. Three hundred Japanese airplanes had been sunk with the flat tops or shot down. The US Air Corps and Navy lost half as many planes and only the carrier *Yorktown*, which had to be scuttled. This battle, one of the first where enemy ships never came within shooting range of each other (about 150 to 200 miles apart and as far from Midway), crippled the IJN and at last gave the United States some breathing space and a much-needed morale boost. Upon leaving Corregidor, General MacArthur had sworn to return to the Philippines. The long road back began.

1 *USS Colorado* was being refitted in Puget Sound. The USN immediately dispatched *Mississippi*, *New Mexico*, and *Idaho* from the Atlantic to guard the West Coast. Fortunately, the three aircraft carriers of the Pacific Fleet were ferrying planes to island outposts. Several others remained in the Atlantic.

2 Filipinos and Filipino-Americans trained and commanded by American officers. Originally formed in 1901 by MacArthur's father, then the military governor of the Philippines, to help suppress the Philippine Revolution, they were the first US ground units involved in WWII. They had their own infantry, cavalry, and artillery regiments. The veterans of Bataan heralded them as the "backbone" of the defense.

3 MacArthur had ignored Army orders to leave the Philippines and had even threatened to resign and fight to the death as a private alongside his men. He at last gave in only to the Commander-in-Chief, Roosevelt.

4 PT-41, which evacuated MacArthur's family, was skippered by Lieutenant John "Buck" Bulkeley, who became an early war hero by successfully evading the Japanese naval screen 600 miles from Corregidor to Mindanao. He would later win the Medal of Honor as Lieutenant Commander of a PT squadron and eventually retire as a Rear Admiral, having been promoted by another former PT

skipper, President John F. Kennedy.

5 Though their relationship remained respectful and cordial, the General never forgave the President for this perceived perfidy. Another general said MacArthur "despised" Roosevelt, and there is evidence that he considered running against FDR for President in 1944. MacArthur refuted any such plans, but described Roosevelt to a staff officer as "a man who would never tell the truth when a lie would serve him just as well."

Chapter 2

CAMP WOLTERS
Boot Camp

Mineral Wells, Texas, is forty-eight miles west of Fort
Worth. Three miles north of Mineral Wells lies the
site of Camp Wolters, originally a fifty-acre Texas
National Guard base. When Tom Turner stepped off the bus in
mid-March 1941, Camp Wolters was a small city, covering 7500
acres and billeting 15,000 recruits and conscripts. Brigadier
General (Brig. Gen.) William H. Simpson ran the camp. New
buildings were going up by the week; headquarters even sported
new awnings. White clapboard two-story barracks were arranged
in "company streets" so that the men who trained together lived
together. Camp facilities included a hospital, fire station, gas
station, bakery, three theaters, and classrooms (not just for military
lessons; undereducated troops were taught the three Rs). There
were chapels for several faiths, guest cottages for visiting families,
officers' housing and clubs, and battalion area recreation rooms
offering ping pong, pool, magazines, books, and soda pop
machines. Baseball diamonds, a football field, and a swimming
pool were available for physical recreation and competition. A

sports arena was under construction, slated to open the next January, which would offer three basketball courts, a boxing ring, and gymnastics equipment.

For some time before and after the Pearl Harbor attack, Camp Wolters was the largest Infantry Replacement Training Center (IRTC) in the United States, with as many as 30,000 soldiers on-post at a time and 200,000 passing through during the war. The mess halls ordered 7,200,000 eggs a year, and the Postal Exchange (PX) processed 75,000 letters a day. Later in the war Camp Wolters was used as a Prisoner of War (POW) camp for German prisoners. After the war it lay dormant for a while, then became an Air Force base for a few years, and finally reverted back to the Army. Renamed Fort Wolters in 1963, it housed the Army's fledgling helicopter school. The program expanded throughout the Vietnam War, until 1973, when the helicopter training center was relocated to Fort Rucker, Alabama.[1] Fort Wolters was then deactivated and the land gifted or sold for development. A branch of Weatherford College, a state park, a heliport, an industrial complex, and a newer National Guard center replaced the fort. The only reminders of the post's military history are a few decaying buildings and the entrance archway off Highway 180 which reads, "US Army Primary Helicopter Center Fort Wolters Texas."

The new recruits and conscripts lined up for preliminary physical and dental exams. After the doctor checked over the first man in Turner's group (nothing in the Army was private), he told him to "urinate in a cup."

The recruit responded, "What?"

The doctor pointed to a counter lined with small cups. "Urinate in a cup," he repeated.

Quizzically, the man queried, "What?"

The doctor sighed. "I want you to [pee] in a cup."

With an incredulous look, the man asked, "From here?"

Next, the new arrivals were issued uniforms: khaki and denim fatigues with a "cotton field (forage) cap with visor" for everyday wear; Class "A" cotton khakis for summer dress wear; and serge olive drabs (ODs), for winter. Dress uniforms were topped off with the newly adopted fore-and-aft overseas cap (one khaki and one OD), better known as the "go-to-hell hat"—so named for the message implied by nonconformists who blatantly wore it too far forward or too far to the side. For enlisted men (EM), this flat-folding cap replaced the garrison hat with circular crown and leather peak, still worn by officers and jokingly referred to as a "bus driver's hat." Of the ODs, Tom Turner said, "The woolies were itchy. We tried to smooth out the fabric by wrapping the coat or pants around a post and yanking on the legs and sleeves. Of course, after a while you'd tear something and have to go back to Supply, trade them in, and start over." 1938 lace-and-hook leggings had replaced the old-style WWI wrap-around type, but "dishpan" combat helmets were still part of the infantry uniform. Their fathers had gotten the name "doughboys" for wearing them.

Each man was assigned to a training battalion numbered from the 51st to 67th. Each battalion was comprised of Companies A through D. Between 200 and 250 men filled out a company, led by half a dozen officers and thirty staff members and instructors. At some point in the first few weeks, all troops took mechanical and clerical aptitude tests which, along with former occupations listed on their induction cards, might qualify them for staff work or maintenance companies. Some were assigned to heavy weapons (i.e., heavier than a rifle—machine gun or mortar), artillery, armored, transportation, or engineer companies.

For thirteen weeks, at $21 a month, the battalion trainees underwent Basic Infantry Training (BIT), or more commonly, "Boot Camp." They learned how to stow their belongings, press their uniforms, salute their officers, and even make their beds: if the sergeant couldn't bounce a quarter on the corner of the bed, you remade it. Their lives now ran on military time. A typical day started with first call at 0630 (6:30 AM), *Reveille* at 0645, and breakfast at 0700. Everything was geared towards physical conditioning and performing as part of a unit. Morning routines included calisthenics, marching, close order drill, weapons training, and manual of arms drill. Each battalion had its own obstacle course with ropes and walls to climb, balance beams to walk across and mud holes to fall into, pipes to crawl through, and barbed wire to slither under. Lunchtime (called "dinner") varied, depending upon the daily activity. There were afternoon hikes and runs, always several miles, eventually in full gear and with weapons. Finally, at 1745 (5:45 PM), the companies were dismissed to barracks with supper following at 1845. Lights were out at 2200 (10 PM).

Within a few weeks, Turner's battalion was issued Springfield Model 1903 .30-06-caliber (cal.) bolt-action rifles. Like the helmets, they were left over from the last war. While the men learned to shoot, the drill and training continued, but now with their own rifles. A man's rifle became his constant companion —not just on the firing line but during calisthenics, and on the hikes and runs. If one were not drilling, firing, or running with the rifle, he was constantly cleaning it (along with one's boots, which always accumulated mud despite the hot dusty Texas climate) so as to pass equipment inspection the next morning. On March 31, Turner scored high enough on the firing range to merit the Marksman's badge, just missing Expert.

There were field manuals to memorize, along with one's Army, rifle, and bayonet serial numbers. Drill Instructors (DIs) expected recitation of this information at any time. Should one forget a number or regulation, the typical DI response was, "Give me ten!"—pushups, that is—or maybe twenty, if the infraction had been serious enough. In addition to the conditioning and training, assigned duties were rotated throughout the camp: guard duty, kitchen police (KP), latrine orderly, table waiting, paint detail, and grounds crew. There were extra duties for missing bed check, showing up late for assembly, or failing inspection. Turner sent Betty a magazine cartoon showing how the duties were assigned. A sergeant was pointing and barking at some soldiers sitting on a barracks stoop, "I want four volunteers...you, you, you, and you!" Tom added, "This is actually what happens at Camp Wolters."

The men housed together in a company barracks helped, chastised, and exhorted each other, mostly to avoid platoon or company punishment for an infraction by any one of them. Self-policing became a group effort that was not discouraged by officers or instructors. One backwoods fellow in Turner's barracks didn't see any point to taking a shower; all his life he had had a bath on an occasional Saturday. Despite the sweat and grime of physical exertions for days on end and the pleas of those in nearby bunks, he held to his Elizabethan view of not needing to bathe. One night the men dragged him kicking and yelling into the showers and scrubbed him with a vegetable brush. He never needed another reminder to shower.

Another night found a recruit staggering back into the

barracks well after curfew and lights out. He plopped onto his bed and passed out. Where he'd gotten the booze at that hour nobody knew. What they did know was there would be the devil to pay in the morning, so they decided to exact restitution. "We got a couple ropes," my dad said, "passed them under the bed and threw the ends over the rafters. Then we hoisted him up to the ceiling. In the middle of the night he woke up, figured out where he was, and yelled, 'Hey get me down from here!' Somebody yelled back, 'Get down yourself!' We all laughed and rolled over and went back to sleep."

When they were off duty, the battalions formed baseball, basketball, and football teams, along with marching and jazz bands. The companies competed to have the best boxers. The camp radio station played swing hits and gave local news and updates on the wars in Europe and China. The theaters showed movies (which cost fifteen cents) several times a day and evening. But the best place to hang out, besides the battalion rec center, was the Service Club, which featured a soda fountain, where guys could get snacks, and a stage, where concerts, plays, and USO shows were performed. Some weekends there were dances with young ladies bussed in from the nearby communities. For these, the battalion bands, or sometimes professional bands, would play.

The young men were not beyond creating their own entertainment outside of sports and music. Before long they would begin to publish a biweekly post newspaper, *The Camp Wolters Longhorn*, that GIs[2] could buy for a nickel and for which General Simpson gave his blessing and a "call for 15,000 editors." It gave post news, announcements and deadlines, more war updates, and daily highlights. According to later clippings from *The Longhorn*, Judy Garland visited Camp Wolters in February of 1942. Another article for that month announced that Herr Hitler showed up at the paymaster's office to collect his $21. After the paymaster jumped out of his chair, Private (Pvt.) Joseph Neuhaus of the 55th Battalion, whose hobby was making celebrity masks, removed his latest creation—Adolf. The paper proclaimed that Army strength in mid-1941 was 1,477,000.

Newspaper headlines and movie theater newsreels reported German tanks blasting Belgrade, their paratroopers landing in Crete, and the Afrika Korps besieging Tobruk. At sea, British biplanes sank the *Bismarck,* and Midway's scanty forces repulsed Yamamoto's fleet. The 99th Pursuit Squadron transferred from Illinois to Alabama and started training its first African-American pilots—the future Tuskegee Airmen. Baseball star Lou Gehrig, famous teammate of Babe Ruth, died two weeks before his thirty-eighth birthday of amyotrophic lateral sclerosis—a little-known disease soon to be identified with his name. "When we heard that news," Turner said of his boyhood hero, "we couldn't believe it."

BIT neared its end as summer began, and Texas warmed up even more. Advanced Infantry Training (AIT) loomed as the next phase. Some vets say there was no distinct line: one just morphed into the other. The soldiers would practice hand-to-hand combat with bayonets and jiu-jitsu, set up defenses, team up to fire mortars, machine guns, and grenade launchers, and learn map-reading and camouflaging techniques. Calisthenics, cross-country runs, obstacle courses, and rifle range practices would continue ubiquitously and unabated. Eventually, like the battalions further along in their training, the men would climb down rope netting on a simulated transport (the "USS Yardbird") into landing craft, ride them across a lake, and establish beachheads. Those in engineering companies would learn to build bridges, set explosive charges, and plant or disarm mines. Platoons would learn how to attack with and against tanks (jeeps transformed by covering them with large sheets of plywood). There would be an extra week for a regimental-sized field exercise with real tanks and artillery.

Men in Turner's company started getting orders telling them when and where to report for AIT. Many were moving on to other posts for specialized training in armored, artillery, engineer, or Air Corps units. When he queried the company commander about what his orders might entail, he was told he would not be among those moving on: he had done so well in BIT that he was to be assigned as a DI at Camp Wolters. He had no intention of spending the rest of his time yelling at young men in the middle of Texas, but that was the Army's prerogative.

A poster calling for volunteers had recently caught his eye. The young parachute training program at Fort Benning was looking for men to fill out new battalions. Besides the raise in regular pay to $30 at the end of boot camp (making them dollar-a-day "buck" privates), the Army would add a $50 per month "hazardous duty" bonus.[3] Equally enticing to Turner was that some of the outfits were training in New Jersey, near his home state of New York, for anticipated action in Europe.

Turner's father and uncles had all worked for the New York Central Railroad and thus were spared from WWI and survived the Depression. But his mother's father had been in the British Army before immigrating to America, and his father's uncle had fought in the New York cavalry in the Civil War. Originally, Turner felt he might carry on a family tradition by joining the cavalry. Although there actually would be a last cavalry charge, by Philippine Scouts on the Bataan Peninsula in the Philippines, by 1941 mechanization had taken over for horses. Parachuting seemed like an exciting alternative. Furthermore, if he volunteered, the Army would have to give him his chance. He told his captain, "OK. I'll join the airborne."

Applicants to the parachute program had to be single, between 5'6" and 6'2", and under 185 pounds. Turner topped out just under the maximums. He applied. Of the selection process he said, "One guy looked in one of your ears. Another guy looked in the other. If they didn't see each other, you were in."[4] He soon received orders to report to the commander of the Provisional Parachute Group at Fort Benning by June 18, 1941.

1 Turner's great-grandson, Christian Turner, would learn to fly UH-60 Black Hawk helicopters at Fort Rucker forty-five years after the relocation.

2 Acronym for Government (or General) Issue, used as a slang term for an American soldier.

3 Even though the US was not yet in the war, thousands of men answered this call. As my dad's friends told me, when I asked what could make them want to jump out of a plane with the likelihood of people shooting at them, "To a bunch of guys coming out of The Depression, that extra fifty bucks was a [heck] of a lot of money."

4 Not so: applicants for the parachute program took the same test as officer candidates—the Army General Classification Test—and had to score as high as those who qualified for Officer Candidate School.

Chapter 3

FORT BENNING
Parachute School

King David surrounded himself with his Mighty Men. The Hypaspists anchored the flanks of Alexander the Great's phalanxes. Napoleon's Imperial Guard was feared and undefeated before Waterloo. The Navy's Marines have been lauded since the Revolution. The United States Army only established its own elite fighting force, the Airborne, at the beginning of World War II.

Billy Mitchell had proposed the formation of an airborne infantry unit to General John Pershing during WWI. George Marshall, then an aide-de-camp for Pershing, was intrigued by Mitchell's proposal, but the war soon ended, and the idea was shelved until May of 1939, when the US War Department took note of the development of European and Japanese parachute units. Even though Italy had made the first successful drops of men and supplies in the 1920s, the United States' interest only perked up when the Russians used airborne soldiers against Finland—actually dropping them into snowbanks without parachutes—and the Germans employed them against Norway and the Low Countries to capture canals, bridges, and seemingly impregnable fortresses. Now Army Chief of Staff, Gen. Marshall rekindled the concept of "vertical envelopment" as a cutting-edge tactic. After France fell in June 1940, Marshall had the Army Chief of Infantry, George Lynch, form a Parachute Test Platoon (PTP) of forty-eight volunteers from the 29th Infantry Regiment at Fort Benning.

General Lynch requested nine planes—and received two—for training at Fort Benning and put Lieutenant Colonel (Lt. Col.) William Lee (NCSU '16 ROTC), a company commander in WWI and a like-minded airborne advocate since, in charge of training and equipping the platoon. To lead the platoon, Lee selected the officer with the highest written test score—and who had finished the two-hour test in less than half the time—First Lieutenant (1st Lt.) William Ryder (West Point '36). It was no wonder: Ryder had researched the foreign airborne developments and had submitted papers from which many of the test questions came. He would later move on to command the 542nd Parachute Regiment before becoming the airborne advisor on MacArthur's general staff. In the event that Ryder might be injured, Second Lieutenant (2nd Lt.) James Basset (who would rise to lieutenant colonel) was designated assistant platoon leader. Lee chose Hobert Wade, an eleven-year career soldier, to be platoon sergeant.

Lee assigned a team of the most experienced parachutists from the Army Air Corps to rigorously train the PTP. On August 16, 1940, the platoon members made their initial individual parachute jumps—with Ryder first out the door, of course.[1] One man who failed to jump and a couple others who gave up along the way were immediately reassigned and replaced by eagerly waiting volunteers. Two weeks later, on the twenty-ninth, Gen. Marshall and the Secretary of War, Henry Stimson, watched the final massed parachute jump whereby the PTP's two lieutenants and forty-six enlisted men qualified as the United States' first officially certificated paratroopers.

Initially visualizing the use of paratroopers in small raider-like units to disrupt enemy communication and supply centers, the War Department revised their thinking and proposed larger units. In mid-September, the PTP became the cadre[2] for the newly activated 1st Parachute Battalion (PB) by dispersing the platoon members amongst the battalion's three companies. Volunteers were added from regular divisions to bring the companies up to strength. Before the month was up, to avoid confusion with the Marines' parachute battalions (likewise numbered 1st, 2nd, 3rd, etc.), the Army decided to redesignate the 1st as the 501st Parachute Battalion.[3] So that Lee could concentrate on the development of the airborne program at Ft. Benning, he appointed Major William "Bud" Miley (West Point '18) to be the commanding officer (CO) of the battalion. At forty-two, Miley was old for a paratrooper, but having been a star gymnast at West Point, he was in superb shape and not only kept up with but outperformed many of his men.

The Army would award Lee the Distinguished Service Medal for his work as the "Father of the American Airborne" and appoint him the first commander of the 101st "Screaming Eagles" Parachute Infantry Division. Major (Maj.) Miley, who would later command the 17th Airborne Division, got authorization for qualified jumpers to wear their trousers bloused over their boots, a "501" emblem to wear above their infantry insignia, and a round sky blue patch with white embroidered parachute to attach to their overseas caps. He had 1st Lt. William Yarborough of his staff (an Academy classmate of Ryder, later commander of the 509th Parachute Infantry Battalion, and eventually a lieutenant general) design and order silver paratrooper badges, which became known as "jump wings." These details would become the earmarks and source of *esprit de corps* for the elite American Airborne forces.

On March 21, 1941, Brig. Gen. Omar Bradley, currently the CO for the US Infantry School at Fort Benning (and who took Parachute Training there), joined Miley to observe as the 501st PB got the last of its men jump qualified. They handed out 276 of Yarborough's silver badges. Assisting them were Captains Ryder, now on Miley's staff, and Yarborough himself, now a company commander. Shortly thereafter, in May, Miley received orders to prepare a company for deployment. At the end of June, Company C, Miley's most experienced, boarded a train to New Orleans and then a ship to Panama, where the 550th Airborne Infantry Battalion, intended to be neither parachute nor glider but air-landing (requiring a captured or constructed airfield for delivery), was being formed.

While Company C was preparing for its departure, Hitler broke his Nazi-Soviet pact with Josef Stalin by launching Operation "Barbarossa," the invasion of Russia. Finland and Hungary joined the Germans by declaring war as well. The same week, Private First Class (Pfc.) Thomas Turner arrived at Ft. Benning. Col. Lee assigned him, by reason of his aptitude testing, experience as a stockroom clerk, and some accounting coursework, to Headquarters Company of the 501st as S-1 (Personnel) Clerk. After reporting to company headquarters, acquainting himself with the staff, taking the base tour, getting billeted, and learning his new tasks, he found he had a week to kill until his duties began. A couple days later, on June 26, Betty was writing a report for a class she was taking when she got a phone call from Tom: he was at the Greyhound station. Ecstatic, she dropped everything and raced downtown to pick him up. They had only two "swell" days together before he had to get back on the bus, but having fretted along with him about his posting, she was relieved he was at least back on the east coast.

Fort Benning, near Columbus, Georgia, was an old camp flaunting a few new facilities. There were wide tree-lined streets and brick barracks with reading rooms. The white buildings of the main camp had manicured lawns bordered by white pebble paths. Except for the guards at the entrance, Tom could imagine he was on an Ivy League campus. The new trainees, however, were housed on the other side of some football-field-high towers near Lawson Field where practice jumps would be made. There were rows of unpainted "tar paper" barracks (rectangular bunkhouses, built on pylons, with pine siding covered with tar paper), meant to be temporary but used for decades. At one end of each barracks was the latrine, and at the other end, the mess hall. They sat at the edge of a depression which, because of the summer heat, was called the "Frying Pan."

There was a high degree of morale and enthusiasm at Fort Benning. The food was better than in Basic, much like home cooked. The men were the most physically fit and confident in the Army. They were issued high-top lace-up brown Corcoran boots (also designed by Yarborough), which were fancier than they'd had in Basic, but more functional for jumping. The boots were expected to shine like glass every day. The parachute trainees tucked their pants into them "straight-legged" but were spared the leggings of the regular Army. They sewed Miley's circular parachute patches onto their go-to-hell caps.

A week before the 501st got their wings, the War Department had constituted three more parachute battalions and used cadres of trained paratroopers, NCOs (non-commissioned officers—corporals and sergeants), and commissioned officers (lieutenants and above) from the 501st to create them at Fort Benning. On July 1, 1941, just five weeks after the Germans had parachuted and air-landed onto Crete, the Army created the 502nd Parachute Infantry Battalion (PIB).[4] Maj. George Howell, Jr. (West Point '19), who had been the Executive Officer (XO) of the 501st, was given command. On August 22, months earlier than planned and despite Lee's protest for lack of men and equipment, the 503rd PIB was activated[5] "by order of the Chief of Infantry." Maj. Robert Sink (West Point '27) moved up from company command in the 501st to CO of the 503rd. Volunteers from Fort Jackson, South Carolina, and Fort Bragg, North Carolina, formed both battalions.

Having begun AIT with the 501st only two months before, Pfc. Turner now found himself in the cadre for the 503rd. The day the battalion was activated, Maj. Sink promoted him to corporal and transferred him laterally to be Personnel Clerk for Headquarters and Headquarters Company (HHQ), 503rd PIB. Turner hooked up quickly with two men in 503rd Headquarters Company who would remain lifelong friends with him—Walt Hudyma and Bill Ryle. George Clay, who had transferred into the airborne from the 9th Division just the previous month, joined them. A pal of Tom's from the 501st, Pete Komer, was now in Company A. Two other privates, Charles Rambo in HHQ and Donald Abbott in Company A, would become "mustangs"— enlisted men who worked their ways up through the ranks to the officer corps—and play important roles, as would young lieutenants John Britten and Robert Woods of Companies B and C.

Major Sink's XO in the 503rd PIB was Captain (Cpt.) Richard Chase (Syracuse U '27 ROTC), who had been a volunteer from the 29th and Miley's supply officer in the 501st. 1st Lt. James Hite, the Personnel (often referred to as "Adjutant") and Intelligence officer, was Turner's immediate boss. Other staff members were Cpt. Joe Lawrie (LSU '36 ROTC), Planning and Training officer, 2nd Lt. Francis Donovan, Assistant Adjutant, and 1st Lt. Cameron Knox, Headquarters Company commander. These last three were to become mainstays for the 503rd and would advance as the unit trained, grew, deployed, and campaigned.

Hundreds of men of diverse backgrounds and from IRTCs all over the country filled out the new battalions throughout the summer of 1941. Four hundred NCOs even agreed to be "busted" (demoted in rank) to start the new training as privates. Battalion strengths were increased to nearly 400 officers and EM by volunteers from Selective Service conscripts. Companies A and B of the 501st, having been stripped of cadres to form the new battalions, were partially replenished by September, when they followed Company C to Panama.

On October 5, the 504th PIB was activated under newly promoted Maj. Chase from the 503rd. Cpt. Gerald Higgins took over Chase's duties as XO of the 503rd. Higgins would one day be Assistant Commander for the 101st Airborne Division. The Army having run out of cadres, the 504th PIB would be the first airborne unit to have all its men enlist, volunteer, undergo Basic, Advanced, and Parachute Training, and graduate Jump School together.[6] Col. Lee's battalions collectively constituted the First Provisional Parachute Group, which had been organized at the end of March to oversee training in, provide resources for, and facilitate the expansion of the parachute school in order to deliver a battle-ready airborne force.

At the end of AIT and before Parachute Training began,

there were a few free days to spend in the swimming pool or otherwise unwind. After that, there were occasional weekend passes to be had if one's boots glistened and he had no demerits. At night and on weekends, the PX beer gardens were packed with paratroopers stacking up empty beer cans, learning paratrooper songs, or provoking each other into fistfights. They particularly disliked being arrested by *non*-paratroop Military Police (MP) for drunkenness, disorderly conduct, or property damage. MPs learned the easiest way was to bop them on the head first, then cuff them.

On one weekend pass, Turner and a carload of his pals drove to Atlanta to see a re-released showing of Oscar-winning *Gone with the Wind.* Before the movie they ate in a diner. When the bill came, they discussed how to split it up. One of them said, "I'll take care of it. I'll meet you at the car." He headed for the bathroom.

"From the parking lot," Tom said, "we could see him walk back to the lunch counter. He talked to the waitress...picked his teeth...helped himself to a mint. Finally, he waved goodbye to her and came out to the car. On the way to the theater, I asked him, 'So how'd you take care of the bill?'

"The guy told me, 'I flushed it.'"

The Parachute Infantry Training (PIT) Program was another thirteen weeks spent further developing the muscle tone, mobility, and stamina required specifically for parachute units and their unique role as crack troops. Physical Training (PT), with its calisthenics, obstacle courses, drills, and marches, often lasted till dinner. PIT took on a new dimension: double-time. You ran everywhere—to assembly, the mess hall, the latrine, the rifle range, the guard shack, up and down hills, from the back of the formation to the front. Paratroopers never walked. Many days there were five-mile runs before breakfast. Ten- to twenty-five-mile runs—sometimes overnight, often in step with NCOs calling out a cadence—were extremely taxing and came to be known as "rat races." Another added facet was having live ammunition fired over the men's heads as they crawled through mud and barbed wire, and in and out of trenches. The ten or twenty pushups demanded by the DIs in basic became as many as a hundred here. It backfired once. Frank Boginski, who had played briefly for the Green Bay Packers, made some misstep, and his instructor yelled, "Give me fifty!" The former Packer yelled back, "Left or right?"

As summer waned and Fort Benning's trees began to turn colors, the Japanese Army spread throughout Indochina and wrested complete control from the Vichy French puppet administration. Operation Barbarossa rolled towards Moscow, Kharkov, and Leningrad. Parachute Training intensified. Besides the expected hand-to-hand, jiu-jitsu, bayonet, mortar and machine gun practice, there were parachute training films and lectures on all conceivable weapons, explosives, and small unit tactics, aircraft recognition exercises, and longer runs, often without water, with weapons and packs despite the lingering heat and rain. Those who couldn't keep up were transferred to Company W ("Washout") and assigned to menial camp duties before returning to regular Army units.

Several thousand men had originally volunteered for the 503rd Battalion. Fewer than 500 of them would become certified jumpers. Richard Winters, of *Band of Brothers* fame, noted that of the 400 officers who later went through the parachute training camp with the 506th Parachute Infantry Regiment at Camp Toccoa, Georgia, 148 got their wings. Only 1800 out of 5300 enlisted men completed the airborne training. The 511th Regiment, which would deploy to the Pacific, screened 12,000 applicants. Of 3000 selected trainees, only 2000 got their wings. These figures were not abnormal: it had taken 200 volunteers to boil down to the original four dozen in the PTP.

In early September, Tom got a weekend pass. Betty took Pennsylvania Railroad's *Southerner* from Penn Station, New York City, to Atlanta, where he met her. On the train ride down, Betty had gotten her first experience with segregation. When the train was going through the Carolinas, a conductor suggested she might want to move to a different car. She insisted she was fine in this one. He became adamant that she move. It was then that she noticed the car was full of African-Americans. She had played and gone to school with Black children, worked in fully integrated jobs, and communed with her father's African-American parishioners. She had thought nothing of riding in the coach, but not wanting to make a scene, she acquiesced and slipped out into another car.

They stayed at the Piedmont Hotel on Peachtree Street (separate rooms, of course) and visited the Ocmulgee National Monument in Macon. She later glued her ticket, the hotel bill (each room was $3 a night!), and the park brochure into a scrapbook she kept throughout the war—mostly articles to try to keep track of her future husband's whereabouts, but also headlines of significant events and operations as well as telegrams and cartoons Tom sent her.[7]

As the month wore on, Leningrad came under siege, and the Russians lost Kiev and a million men to the Panzers. General Hideki Tojo—a descendent of samurai warriors—would soon replace pacifist Fumimaro Konoe as Prime Minister of Japan and push for all-out war against American and British embargoes.

Meanwhile, groups of the 503rd PIB began to take turns leaving PIT and entering the Parachute, or "Jump," School. This four-week course progressed rapidly from ground training and tower training to the final test: qualifying jumps from planes. After completing Parachute School, each group would resume PIT. Rotation of small units through Jump School allowed an entire battalion to graduate the Provisional Parachute Group's program simultaneously.

At the beginning of the first week of Jump School, "Stage A," students were issued one-piece jumpsuits[8] (the same as those issued to Air Corps mechanics) and leather football-style aviator helmets. Besides doing more strenuous calisthenics specific to parachuting, men learned to tumble backwards, forwards, and sideways to enable their bodies to absorb the shock of landing. They practiced these summersaults from raised platforms of various heights and from the backs of moving trucks. They bounced on trampolines and shinnied up ropes (hand-over-hand waist high, not overhead) to the ceiling of an old, corrugated metal hangar. They twisted their bodies through a maze of galvanized pipe, much like a playground jungle gym but the size of a house with ropes, catwalks, and ladders to boot. This "plumber's nightmare" was copied from the German parachute-training handbook, but its use was later deemed unnecessary and discontinued after the first few battalions finished training. Richard Clarke, an American who had joined the Canadian Air Force and transferred to the US Airborne, wrote in an *American Magazine* article that between getting "banged up" in the jiu-jitsu practice, having one's teeth "rattled" with every tumble, roll, or twist, and suffering "assorted broken bones," thirty-five of his group's 200 men had already dropped out by week's end.

In "Stage B" the students were taught how to exit correctly

from the door of a cutaway plane fuselage section (also copied from the Germans) by jumping into a sand pit, first singly and then in a group (called a "stick") of five, ten, up to twenty men, like they would in action. They hung with their harnesses connected to a scaffolding instead of parachutes to learn how different pulls on the risers (the four straps which gathered the suspension lines from the canopies) would turn their bodies, quell body oscillation—one's body often swung like a pendulum depending on its position when the canopy opened—and "spill (partially collapse) the chute" for quicker descent and safer landing. Movie studio wind machines blew the men in their parachutes across the field to simulate "prop (propeller) blast" and give them practice controlling and collapsing their chutes while getting out of them in a stiff wind.

They climbed thirty-four-foot towers. Standing in another mock door on the platform atop the four telephone poles, each trainee in turn had his jump harness hooked to a trolley on an overhead zip line which was attached to the top of a shorter pole sixty yards away. After the instructor on the platform checked for proper jump stance and gave a clearance warning, each soldier kicked out and off the platform as he would later from a plane. Bennett Guthrie, in *The Three Winds of Death*, called the second or so till the slack in the harness played out from the cable "the longest fifteen foot drop you'll ever have." When their harnesses tightened upon jumping (simulating the shock of the parachute opening), many men got bruises on their shoulders and legs called "strawberries." As each man traveled down the diagonal cable towards the short pole, instructors on the ground shouted suggestions about his approach and facing in the few seconds he had before tumbling with a Parachute Landing Fall (PLF) near the end of the cable. Afterwards, while another student ran the trolley back to the tower, an instructor reviewed with the jumper both how to and how *not* to be in control of one's chute. The former ensured a good chance of landing uninjured. The latter could be deadly. The men appropriately came to call this apparatus "the Lulu," or "the Separator." More men quit parachute training on the Lulu tower than at any other stage.

"Stage C" took the soldiers to the 250-foot towers they had first noticed when they got to the fort. They looked like something from an amusement park, and in fact they had been built by the company which installed a similar ride at the New York World's Fair. Huge metal hoops hung parallel to the ground from booms on top of the towers. First, a winch hoisted pairs of men together on a bench to a boom where they were dropped—faster than a real drop from a plane—but with brakes to slow down and stop near the bottom. This Coney Island ride got them used to heights and the sensation of falling.

On one of the booms, four guide cables were attached to the hoop and concrete anchors in the ground. Grommets on the outer edge of the parachute kept it connected to the cables for a "controlled" individual drop. When a man was lifted by his harness, the parachute was expanded beneath the hoop by the cables while he got a sky-scraper view. He was then released from the pulley, to feel the effects of the parachute filling and to practice a safe PLF, all the while remaining within the confines of the guide cables. While visiting one day, Gen. Lynch—who had convinced Gen. Marshall that the Parachute Test Platoon ought to be an Army, rather than an Air Corps or Engineering endeavor—decided he wanted a crack at the controlled descent. Scrapping protocol, the troopers cheered and applauded the sixty-something-year-old general during the drop. After landing awkwardly, he stood up ramrod straight and exclaimed, "By God, men, I haven't had that much fun since I was a kid!" They cheered again.

From another tower, with booms on all sides but no guide cables, the parachutists were let loose from the hoops and dropped free-fall in their chutes. In the eleven seconds they were in the air, they practiced facing, approach angles, and their PLFs, which were affected by airspeed and severity of oscillation. Sometimes they were at the mercy of gusts of wind. They practiced a couple night drops from the towers. Throughout these first three weeks, if the men were not marching, running, perfecting weaponry skills, or practicing handling and getting out of the chutes quickly, they were learning how to pack their own parachutes in the corrugated hangars, which doubled as classrooms. Eventually, a parachute maintenance company would do the packing, allowing the trainees more practice time.

At last "Stage D," the most exciting week, came. The students made five "qualifying" jumps from C-47s (Douglas DC-3s with canvas "jump" seats along each side of the fuselage, facing each other, instead of rows of upholstered seats), with the men repacking their own chutes for the next day's jump. The first was from 1500 feet, the next from 1000 feet, and three from 750 feet. The first three of these were individual jumps (one man dropped on each pass over the field), one being at night. For the fourth, men jumped in pairs. The fifth and final jump was a simulated combat jump, with sticks of ten in full gear. Men who completed all five qualifying jumps earned their "wings" as accredited paratroopers. Those who froze or refused wound up in Company W.

During the first week of October, Group #1 of exuberant paratroopers from the 503rd celebrated with silver wings on their chests and smiles on their faces. Turner and the others anticipated their rotation turns, but instead of emptying beer cans at the PX, he, Bill Ryle, and a couple others got weekend passes and drove to Pine Mountain State Park,[9] some fifty miles north of Fort Benning.

After the short furlough, everyone listened to the "Subway" World Series on the camp radio. Despite having the National League batting champ, Pete Reiser, slugging MVP, Dolph Camilli, and 22-game winner, Kirby Higbe, the Dodgers dropped two of the first three games to the Yankees. A passed ball negated a Dodger lead in the ninth inning that would have tied the series at two wins each but instead took the wind out of Brooklyn's sails. The Bronx Bombers rallied to win the game and beat the Dodgers the next day as well for the championship. "Joltin' Joe" Dimaggio earned MVP honors by leading the American League in Runs Batted In and by eclipsing "Wee Willie" Keeler's record hitting streak with his own of fifty-six straight, even though Ted "the Thumper" Williams led in homers and overall hitting—and was the last major leaguer to hit over .400![10]

More groups rotated into the Parachute School. Corporal (Cpl.) Turner typed up the lists as they came down from the Provisional Parachute Group HQ, always looking to see if his name had appeared. Meanwhile, he learned about sabotage and demolition, a course for which each trainee received a certificate of completion. Men continued transferring into the battalion; the strength of the 503rd was increased to 456 EM with an influx of volunteers from Camp Roberts, California. They, too, would begin Parachute Training and rotate into jump school.

In September, a group of fifty Officer Candidate School (OCS) volunteers had transferred from Camp Wolters to Ft. Benning for Parachute Training. Thirty-three more of these "ninety-day wonders" (so named for their three months of officer training) joined them in November. Up until now, the soldiers had had very little interaction with officers. The Drill and Parachute Instructors, mostly career "noncoms" (NCOs), were teacher, boss, mother, judge, and jury. Because the paratroopers were to be molded into an elite team, and the training began to involve larger units, the officers were actively involved. The officers of the 503rd took parachute training and jump school along with the enlisted men. They were not exempt from reproach by the instructors: "Give me fifty, SIR!"

Officers had been offered $100 for jump pay; the enlisted men agreed that $50 was probably not enough to induce them to jump out of airplanes. There was a marked pay differential as well: for a 2nd lieutenant, Airborne pay was $150. Dick Winters wrote that most of the officers with him in the Officer Prep Course (three weeks of lectures on intelligence-gathering, communications, and weapons with summaries of all aspects of the Army) came from ROTC with inadequate training. Turner said there was a perceptible difference in the bearing, preparation, decisiveness, and coolness under pressure in the officers from the United States Military Academy. "You could look at a West Pointer and see it. They didn't need to tell you."

While on a run, Turner noticed one of the company's young ninety-day wonders making a point of being in the lead. Turner, having run track in high school, figured he'd give him a run for his money. The two sprinted ahead of the company, taking turns as the front-runner. They came to a deep cut with a stream at the bottom. Together they jumped the cut. "I kept going," he smirked. "The lieutenant went in the drink."

One day Cpl. Turner passed a lieutenant who was in street clothes, returning from a weekend pass. Though Tom recognized him, he did not salute since the officer was not in uniform. The lieutenant had him busted back to private for the seeming infraction. Tom subsequently spoke to the battalion First Sergeant, who flatly told him he was not the first or last to have "committed a misdemeanor." He mentioned the incident in a letter to his future father-in-law, the Reverend Dockter, who thought the officer needed "a good change in personality" before a bullet "meant for another camp may put out his light." Shifting gears, he suggested Tom consider that perhaps something had been on that officer's mind, "perhaps some mistake or failure he had made himself, for which this was some kind of compensation."[11] Tom let it go. He never had another run-in with an officer.

Radios and newsreels announced good news. The British Eighth Army relieved Tobruk as Operation "Crusader" pushed Field Marshal Erwin Rommel's Afrika Korps back across Libya. The Panzer divisions in Russia, recently bogged down in the autumn mud, were now completely stalled in early winter snow and below-zero cold within view of the spires and onion domes of the Kremlin. Their fuel was coagulating and their soldiers, still in summer uniforms, were stripping Russian casualties for winter clothing. Field Marshal Georgy Zhukov, reassured by Japan's movements in Indochina to the south that he wouldn't be attacked in the east, unleashed his legions from Siberia onto the German armies freezing to the west. On the sixth of December, the *Wehrmacht* generals defied Hitler by drawing back for the first time in the war and digging in.

Most sensational yet were the next day's news broadcasts and headlines: Pearl Harbor. All leaves were cancelled. Units that had finished training some time ago got orders to be on the alert for further orders. Training units were rescheduled as a flurry of enlistments around the country doubled the size of the Army and camps sprang up to house and train them. At Fort Benning, groups in the 503rd and 504th that had been ready for Jump School were put on hold as planes were reassigned—Group #8 of the 503rd had been jump certified in November; Group #9 would not be until February. As Christmas 1941 approached, the Japanese Army overran Manila and advanced on Singapore and Hong Kong. President Roosevelt had already extended the draft service period to eighteen months, and now he added "for the duration of the war plus six months." Clearly, Turner figured, there would be no wedding next year.

The paratroopers began their final phase, Combined Arms Training. *The Infantry Manual on Attack* became the new Bible. Now the focus was on platoon, company, and battalion-strength maneuvers. In two- or three-day weapons cross-training exercises, each man became proficient should he need to fill in on a weapon crew. Each man and his friends now had to rely on their own and each other's wits, functioning as a cohesive unit to complete field exercises or fight mock battles with other battalions. For some exercises they were ferried across the Chattahoochee River into the Alabama swamps. For others they fought alongside tanks and artillery. The jump-certified men made a practice jump every month, sometimes as part of a field exercise, to maintain their jump status.

There was a surprise ten-day leave for New Year's. Everyone thought it might be the last one before they were sent off to war. Tom took the all-night bus home to Albany, where he saw his family for the first time since he'd finished boot camp. Betty was proud to be seen with her tall man in uniform with his shiny boots. They went to the movies and heard her dad's sermon at church. They took photos in front of the manse and in the park down the street.

Too soon, it was back to Georgia. Tom sent Betty a Western-Union telegram when he was back at the fort: "ARRIVED IN COLUMBUS...NASTY WEATHER IN NYC...SNOW AS FAR AS WASHINGTON...." At the time, General George Patton was also at Fort Benning. He had just taken command of the 2nd Armored Division, which had been formed there in 1940, before it shipped out for England and eventually Africa. As a lieutenant, Patton had been the first to use motor vehicles in an Army operation when Black Jack Pershing sent him after Pancho Villa. Ever since, he had been the major advocate for mechanized warfare. He would return to his native Southern California within a month to set up the Desert Training Center in the Mojave Desert before rejoining his beloved tankers in Morocco as head of the Western Task Force for Operation "Torch."[12]

Ben Guthrie noted that Patton's tankers "stole the paratroopers' proud jump boots," leading to countless arguments and fights. Turner said they saw the flamboyant Patton sporting a bright green jacket (and, according to the eponymous movie, a gold football helmet) which he tried to get the Army to adopt as the tankers' uniform. He failed in his efforts but would forever be remembered by the paratroopers. Tom grinned, "We called him the Green Hornet."

Some changes came in around New Year's. The newly qualified paratroopers and those further along in training moved into the older, but homier, brick barracks. New helmets ("brain buckets") replaced the old flat "soup bowls" for better protection. The paratroopers even got an upgraded model with a more secure chin strap and liner which would keep them from blowing off in the prop blast or being knocked off by the billowing parachute. The Army had been replacing the bolt-action Springfield with the semi-automatic M1 Garand rifle, which used the same .30-06-cal. bullet. The airborne battalions experimented with the .30-cal. M1 carbine—shorter, lighter, and easier to manipulate (and later with a folding metal stock) amongst all the parachute paraphernalia. Experientially, however, most preferred the standard M1 rifle with its larger caliber and heavier charge. A future platoon leader, William Calhoun, wrote in a letter after the war, "Most of us disliked the carbine and felt like it was too light in its hitting power." It would eventually be prescribed by the *Table of Operations and Equipment* (TO&E), mostly in lieu of the M1911 Colt pistol for rear-echelon troops and officers but issued to many paratroopers anyway.

Turner noticed one of the men on the firing range one day had a bloody nose. The man was shooting left-handed. The bolt-action Springfield had given him no trouble, but for some reason—improper grip, poor cheek placement on the stock, whatever the man's error—the Garand's recoil was jolting his thumb up into his nose. Tom, a lefty himself, tried to show him how to correct his sighting and shooting positions, to no avail. He spent the rest of the day teaching the man how to shoot right-handed. Somehow, abandoning the old habits and adopting the new posture solved the problem.

Throughout January and February 1942, the 503rd read reports and watched newsreels from Europe and the Pacific. The Japanese Empire had begun its own *blitzkrieg* and now had forces in New Guinea poised to strike Australia. Three German battlewagons, *Scharnhorst, Gneisenau,* and *Prinz Eugen* managed to evade the Royal Air Force and Navy in a daring "Channel dash" from Brest to Wilhelmshaven. Rommel, resupplied while the British air and navy base in Malta was briefly neutralized, began a new offensive in the Sahara.

Company B of the 503rd had been sent to Salt Lake City in mid-January. A *New York Times* clipping in Betty's scrapbook for the first of February reported that "the first para-ski troops, of the 503rd Parachute Battalion," were training in the Wasatch Mountains. The others hoped they would soon be joining the nearly two million men ready to deploy. On the last day of February, Col. Lee sent a letter of exhortation to the officers and men of the Provisional Parachute Group:

> We are now at war. Today we are faced with the task of building up a well-trained parachute force which, when called upon for the inevitable test of its ability as a fighting unit in combat with the enemy, will efficiently and relentlessly carry out its mission to its complete success.
>
> To this end we must devote all our time and energy.... The dividends will be paid on the battlefield.... When the crucial moment comes and the commands "Hook Up" and "Stand to Door" are given...victory then will be inevitable.[13]

---

1 Several authors (who may or may not have been observers) claim this jump was made from a B-18 bomber, and early experimentation with parachuting certainly did involve bombers. However, a C-33 transport could have been mistakenly identified as a B-18 "Bolo" bomber, since both were in use at the time and were variants of the Douglas DC-2. A post in Corregidor.org by former paratroopers states all the PTP's jumps were made from C-33s.

2 Nucleus of key personnel, typically a few officers, staff, and trained, reliable soldiers.

3 The 501ˢᵗ was the only parachute battalion that was never concurrently termed "Infantry."

4 It is noteworthy that at this point, the US Army had only one trained airborne battalion. The Germans, meanwhile, employed an entire *fliegerkorps* (airborne corps) on Crete: a parachute division, an air-landing division, and a glider regiment.

5 The terms "created," "activated," and "formed" are often used rather interchangeably. In reality, a unit is first "constituted," i.e., authorized by the War Department on paper and added to the US Army rolls; then "activated," or "created," by changing the unit from inactive to active status, usually with a cadre of troops and equipment; and finally, "formed"—filled by transferring in soldiers from IRTCs or other units or by consolidating two or more units.

6 The Army ran out of transport planes as well as airborne cadres. Although Gen. Lynch got the rest of the planes he had asked for, production and availability of planes always lagged behind the burgeoning demands of the airborne program. The first qualifying jumps for the 504ᵗʰ PIB were scheduled for December 1941. With the US entry into the war, all available planes were pressed into duty overseas, and none become available again until January 26, 1942. The whole battalion made their final jumps that day, thus becoming the only battalion to get their wings in entirety on the same day!

7 Unfortunately, my grandmother talked my mother into burning his letters.

8 Yarborough, who would soon be the Airborne advisor to General Mark Clark for Operation "Torch," eventually designed a herringbone twill two-piece suit with slanted side pockets that a trooper could access while in his parachute harness, and with oversized cargo pants pockets in front which, together with a musette bag strapped to the leg, essentially replaced an infantryman's backpack. Turner, in photos around camps, seemed to have preferred the one-piece jumpsuit.

9 Later incorporated into the western portion of F. D. Roosevelt State Park, so named for the President, who often came to nearby Warm Springs for polio therapy.

10 Both of the future Hall of Famers would spend the 1943-1945 seasons in the Army. MacArthur quoted Keeler's motto, "Hit 'em where they ain't," when describing his leapfrogging strategy.

11 Letter from Albert W. Dockter, Pastor, to Thomas Turner, Oct. 4, 1941.

12 After the war, Patton's family would commission a stained-glass window, depicting St. George slaying the dragon, for its church in San Gabriel, California. In a lower corner of the window, General George Patton appears in the turret of his tank near the dragon's foot. There has been speculation about which George the family implied should have the sainthood.

13 Historical and Pictorial Review of the Parachute Battalions. Fort Benning, 1942.

Chapter 4

FORT BRAGG
Birth of the 503rd Regiment

Months before the U.S. entry into the war, the 501st Parachute Battalion had been dispatched to the Panama Canal Zone in response to unrest spurred by Axis activity in South America and the consequent threat to the Canal Zone. The first parachute unit to be assigned foreign duty, the 501st trained volunteers from other units in the Canal Zone for their still-depleted companies, practiced jungle warfare, and took part in the first airborne training exercise that included bombers as well as transport planes. Officers flew over Central American capitals to check out possible landing sites should action become necessary.

During Army maneuvers in Delaware, Cpt. George Kenney of the Army Air Corps had air-landed an infantry platoon behind the "enemy" lines in a wargame. Old school generals, not knowing what to make of it claimed "Foul!" but that innovative event and Germany's air-landing of troops on Crete provided the impetus, within days of the activation of the 504th PIB in the fall of 1941, for an air-landing program at Fort Benning which would culminate in the formation of American glider units. Fort Benning became overcrowded with the additional battalions and armored units, so in March 1942, the Provisional Parachute Group was moved to Fort Bragg, not too many miles from Dunn, North Carolina, where "Bill" Lee had grown up—and not without his recommendation. It was renamed the Airborne Command in April, and he was awarded his first star. The Parachute School, however, remained at Ft. Benning. Airborne battalions would be formed and jump trained there before being shipped to Ft. Bragg for tactical training and testing.

The War Department, no longer bound by peacetime restrictions since Pearl Harbor, ordered the formation of full airborne regiments. The Army quickly activated the 503rd Parachute Infantry Regiment (PIR)[1] by transferring the 503rd and 504th Battalions to Fort Bragg along with Gen. Lee's headquarters and re-designating them as the 1st (Companies A, B, and C) and 2nd (Companies D, E, and F) Battalions, respectively, of this, the Army's first parachute *regiment*. The fighting strength of the new regiment and its two battalions was 101 commissioned officers, four warrant officers, and 1205 enlisted men. Disney Studio artists designed a regimental emblem: a wildcat wearing a flier's cap and suspended from a parachute, fangs bared and claws spread.[2]

Bud Miley was promoted to lieutenant colonel and recalled stateside to be the 503rd regimental commander. Maj. Kenneth Kinsler (U of Kansas ROTC), one of the first 29th Regiment volunteers, took over the 501st Battalion in Panama. Miley was CO of the 503rd PIR only briefly: he was promoted again, to brigadier, and transferred to the 82nd "All American" Infantry Division, whose most famous alumnus was WWI hero Alvin York. Miley would be assisting his new CO, Maj. Gen. Matthew Ridgway

(West Point '17), to convert the 82nd into the United States' first *Airborne* division. Miley's place in the 503rd was taken by Lt. Col. Robert Sink, who was promoted from battalion to regimental command. Maj. James Gavin (West Point '29), previously an instructor at West Point before heading up the G-3 (Operations and Training) Section for Lee's Provisional Parachute Group, was appointed Sink's XO.

Just before Tom Turner's battalion left Fort Benning, he was approached about staying on as a rifle range instructor. Unlike the assignment the Army had planned for him at Camp Wolters, this offer was tempting. He'd be outside with the men instead of stooped over his typewriter and bottles of ink. He was several years older than most of the men, and he was looked up to by many as a big brother or favorite uncle. He was a fine marksman, having spent many a deer season in the Adirondacks and Catskills Mountains. As company clerk, he was familiar with everyone who'd come in. The instructors had seen him helping the men who struggled with their weapons. He certainly was more suited to teaching them how to shoot than bossing them around. Perhaps because the memory of being busted (although he had plenty of company) still irked him, but more likely because he had trained for so long with his friends, was about to be part of something unique in Army annals, and didn't want to be left behind, he turned down the offer for a recommendation.

When the 503rd and 504th Battalions arrived at Fort Bragg to form the new regiment, Lt. Col. Sink moved Turner into Service (Quartermaster and Supply) Company, where he would continue as company clerk in its HQ section. Turner's circle of friends grew along with the ranks. Andy Amaty, a born raconteur, had been a stevedore downriver from Turner in Brooklyn. Oliver "Pat"

Patterson and Al Runyon were West Coast California boys. Verdery "Johnny" Grooms, from Fayetteville, North Carolina, was nearly in his own backyard.

Corporal Max W. Phillips had recently joined the airborne by way of the 31st Division. Born Maximillian Philippi Wermerskirschen (or so he always claimed) in Minnesota, Max had been a college boy and a tuba player in the band. Tom and Max would develop the closest of wartime relationships, eventually settling within twenty miles of each other.

With wedding plans on the back burner but 400 miles closer to each other, Tom and Betty corresponded daily and got together whenever the Army made it possible. She took another train trip, this time to see Tom's "new digs." After doing some sight-seeing on Saturday, March 21, they attended Sunday morning service at the First Presbyterian Church in Raleigh. In a letter to her he included an article that had a quip from an Army post: "The only bright spots in most headquarters clerks' lives are on the seats of their GI pants." On May 18, she received a telegram from Fayetteville: "BIRTHDAY GREETINGS WITH ALL MY LOVE TOM." It was the day before her birthday.

More parachute regiments were raised in rapid succession, just as the parachute battalions had been created the year before. The Army activated the 504th PIR on May Day, the 502nd PIR on July 1 (with a cadre from its like-numbered 502nd Parachute Battalion), and the 505th on July 6, all at Ft. Benning. Only two weeks later, on the twentieth, the 506th PIR was activated at just-opened Camp Toccoa, Georgia while the 507th was being activated at Ft. Benning. The Army activated the 501st PIR at Camp Toccoa in November. These and most of the other regiments to follow would wind up in the five airborne divisions activated during the war. A few, like the 503rd, would remain independent, to be attached to divisions as needed for spearheads or reserves.

Lee's purpose for the Airborne Command went beyond organizing and training paratroopers; it was also to allocate transport planes and gliders from the Army Air Corps as needed, coordinate joint training with the Air Corps, and determine procedures for airborne operations. Up to this point, there had been no formation protocols for airborne units, common doctrine for the parachute training centers, plans for ground and air coordination, or standards for essential combat equipment. In May 1942, Lee put out FM 31-30, the first Army Airborne field manual: *Tactics and Technique of Air-Borne Troops*. It outlined individual and unit parachute training, typical missions, and tactical objectives. It detailed the organizational structure and listed necessary equipment for parachute units. Finally, it covered the role of support aviation (bombers and fighters) and the delivery of supplies.

Within days of Lee's move, the Army Air Corps had formed the Troop Carrier Command (TCC) at Stout Field, outside Indianapolis. TCC was to deal strictly with movement of troops by air, starting with training of transport and glider pilots, and thereby played an integral part in the success or failure of every airborne operation. By June TCC was training the first glider pilots.

Late in May, the 2nd Battalion of the 503rd PIR (the original 504th Battalion) was ordered to Glasgow, Scotland. They boarded *Queen Mary* (whose sister ship, *Queen Elizabeth*, was currently transporting Australians home from the Middle East) on June 6. The battalion would be re-designated as the 2nd Battalion of the 509th PIR (2/509) in Scotland and put under the command of Lt. Col. Edson Raff (West Point '33), formerly the battalion's XO at

Ft. Benning. On November 7, 1942, Raff's battalion would fly 1500 miles from England (half of it over Spain) and jump into North Africa at the forefront of Operation Torch. Thus, they were to be the first US Airborne unit to jump into combat and would eventually see more action than any other airborne unit in the war.

The Army adopted a "triangular" command structure[3] and added third battalions to its regiments. Just as the 2nd Battalion was leaving for Great Britain, the 3rd Battalion of the 503rd (3/503) was created with a cadre from the 1st Battalion (1/503) and formed by transferring what was left of the old 502nd Battalion, still in Ft. Benning, to Ft. Bragg. The day before 2/503 set sail for Scotland, its XO, Maj. John Tolson, III (West Point '37), was transferred to command 3/503 (Companies G, H, and I).

With the 3rd Battalion came a unique character, Karl H. Landes. Karl grew up in the Carpathian Mountain region of Hungary. Among his acquaintances were the Gabor sisters who would later become famous in Hollywood. His father had been a wealthy landowner; he had shortened the family name from "Landesmann." Determined not to rely on his father's fortune, Karl earned three doctorates at the University of Berlin, prompting an offer from the Merck Corporation (the world's oldest pharmaceutical company) in Germany before he'd even finished his studies. He transferred to Merck's New York facility and took it upon himself to become a United States citizen. By 1929, he had started his own company, which grew despite the Depression. In 1940, correctly surmising both his native and adopted countries would be drawn into another world war, he joined the Army. He was assigned to Edgewood Arsenal, a chemical weapons development site in Maryland. The Army sent him to Fort Benning to give lectures on chemical warfare to Army officers and government officials. Intrigued by what he saw going on at Ft. Benning, he volunteered for, and was soon transferred to, the Provisional Parachute Group.

When Karl's new Army superiors found out about his extensive education and expertise, they urged him to go to OCS. "What's that?" he asked.

"Well, it's thirteen weeks' study on tactics, troop leadership, and logistics planning. Then they make you an officer."

"Look," Landes reasoned. "I have three doctorates. I speak seven languages fluently, if you don't count English (he never could lose the German accent). I have been in every capital city in Europe. I've taught *you* chemical warfare. What are you going to teach *me* in thirteen weeks that I don't already know?"

"Probably nothing," they confessed. But that's what you have to do to become an officer."

"OK, then I'll just stay an enlisted man." With that exchange, "Doc" Landes became, I suspect, the most highly educated foot soldier in the history of the United States Army.

Colonel Sink had moved on to command the 506th, so Lt. Col. Kinsler returned from Panama to head up the 503rd PIR. Maj. George Jones (West Point '35), who proudly (though with his tongue in his cheek) claimed to have been the thirty-first trooper in the PTP, moved up to command the first and last of the old Provisional Parachute Group's battalions, the 501st, in Panama. They were testing, as were the stateside regiments, different types of parachutes and planes. The Army settled on the T-5 parachute with a twenty-eight-foot diameter circular canopy and retained what would be the workhorse for Allied transport, the C-47 "Skytrain." The Marines' version was the R4D. The RAF designated the same plane the "Dakota." The men nicknamed them

"Gooney Birds," supposedly for their semblance to albatrosses which stubbornly and noisily resisted being evicted from their nests to make room for landing strips on Midway.[4]

The airborne units in Panama, Forts Bragg and Benning, and Camp Toccoa also experimented with night drops. Ben Guthrie recalled that 503rd troopers claiming to be on night maneuvers or jumps would have dress uniforms under their jump suits, which they ditched before heading into Fayetteville for a night out. Still, they impressed no less than the President. When Roosevelt saw their exhibition jump at Fort Jackson,[5] he scheduled 1/503 to march in the upcoming Memorial Day Parade in Washington. According to a *New York Times* article in Betty's scrapbook, for another field maneuver at Ft. Jackson on June 24, involving thousands of troops, hundreds of tanks, artillery, and live ammo, King George, Prime Minister Churchill, General Marshall, and Secretary Stimson were in attendance. Shrouded in secrecy as "the guest," Churchill, while "clamping on a cigar and working the breech block of a 75-mm gun," predicted British and Americans would "march into oppressed countries, not as invaders but as liberators." Later, as General Lee's six hundred paratroopers "put on a jumping demonstration," the Prime Minister "held a 'walkie-talkie'... listened with closed eyes and heard that strange battle cry of the parachutists—'Geronimo!' as they jumped into the fray."[6]

Apparently, the nearby populace, eighty years after the Civil War, still resented Yankee soldiers in their territory. Turner, having regained his corporal's stripes, and a couple other Service Company men were sent on an errand. They sat three abreast in the cab of a GMC "deuce and a half" (2½-ton truck) with a canvas top. Going down a hill, they got behind a hay truck taking its time. Tom moved into the oncoming lane to pass. "As I pulled up alongside that hay truck, the farmer grinned over at me and sped up. I dropped back. So did the farmer. Then I saw a Mack truck come around the corner up ahead towards us. I double-clutched and floored it, and we pulled ahead of that farmer and got in front of him just before that Mack truck went by. My hair was standing up," he recalled. "I said, 'Are you guys OK?' and one of them said, 'Yeah, but my [rear end] just opened up and bit a chunk out of this seat!'"

Johnny Grooms, the local boy, invited Tom to dinner at his folks' farm on a weekend. Of this excursion, Turner said, "Johnny and I borrowed a motorcycle. He didn't live very far off the base, but on the way, some nut in a car forced us off the road. We went through a six-foot hedge alongside the road, and an old house with a long porch all along the front was right behind it. We were spitting out leaves and the handlebar was rattling along the balusters like a snare drum!" Tom managed to get the bike back on the road. "It's a wonder," he reflected, "that we all got back to the fort and weren't in jail or a morgue!"

While the 503rd was being filled out in June, a twenty-four-page magazine called *Yank, The Army Weekly*, was launched. The brainchild of a WWI staffer for *Stars and Stripes*, but unlike its predecessor, *Yank* was a chronicle written by GIs to be read by GIs.[7] *Yank* included front line battle accounts and photos from every theater of the war, questions (mostly for airing beefs) and answers, cartoons (one was the advent of "GI Joe," by Dave Breger, and would evolve into comic books and toys), and problem solving (military or personal). It was shipped everywhere there were soldiers and cost them a nickel. Eventually it got so popular that two and a quarter million a week were printed at presses around the world. Most of the pages were common to all theaters;

the rest were from local fronts. Its most popular single page featured a Hollywood starlet. These studio publicity photos became the famous "pin-up girls" displayed on barracks and bunker walls, footlocker lids, and bomber noses. The issue for the first week of July portrayed Jane Russell in the first of her league-leading four appearances in *Yank*.

Later that month, as Tom sifted through and straightened the stack of requisitions, invoices, and personnel orders on his desk, one paper caused him to do a double take. "Cpl. Thomas E. Turner" was listed in the group of men ordered back to Fort Benning for Parachute School in July. At last, the order he had long awaited and nearly given up hope for had come across his desk! He put the paper on top of the stack. As he excitedly typed the quintuple copies on his Corona 3 for distribution, he shook his head and wondered, how could one of the first guys in the outfit be one of the last to get his turn? The answer, he reasoned, could only be attributed to Army Intelligence and logic embodied in the soldiers' ages-old motto, "Hurry up and wait!" The earliest groups had gotten their wings in October last year. On June 25, nearly ten months later, Tom was cabling Betty on the eve of an anticipated weekend together, "CANCEL YOUR RESERVATIONS. CIRCUMSTANCES WHICH WILL KEEP ME BUSY HAVE ARISEN NOTHING TO WORRY ABOUT THOUGH...." She worried about what that meant. A week later he packed his duffle bag and pitched it up into a deuce and a half for the ride back to Columbus. "See you in a few weeks!" he told the other HQ staffers. They retorted, "Hey, Turner, is that a promise or a threat?"

Back to the Frying Pan, which was exactly as Tom remembered it in July—hot and muggy. Back into the tar paper barracks and lumpy beds. The group did the requisite ground school climbing, jumping, twisting, and tumbling. They wrestled with their chutes and conquered the Lulu. They made their day and night Coney Island tower jumps. They packed and repacked their chutes. They never walked. Stage D was quickly upon them.

Early on day one, Tom and the others in his group talked excitedly in front of the checkered buildings at the edge of Lawson Field, in their jumpsuits, upgraded M1 combat helmets (which had also replaced the leather ones), and parachute harnesses, champing at the bit to go while trying to ignore the butterflies in their bellies. Only a handful had ever even been in an airplane. C-47s were lined up on the runway. Jumpers were assigned twenty to a plane, climbed in after their jumpmasters, and took off. Flying over the base, the Chattahoochee River, and the surrounding countryside at 100 miles per hour was exhilarating.

Ten minutes from Lawson Field, the pilot in each plane flipped a switch that turned on a red light on a panel by the door— the ready signal. The jumpmaster started shouting instructions over the noise of the engines: "Get ready!" The men fastened their helmets and unbuckled their seatbelts. "Stand up!" Everyone in the first stick stood up. "Hook up!" Each man of the stick hooked his "static line" to the anchor cable, which ran down the length of the cabin overhead. When he jumped, the fifteen-foot static line would pull the parachute out of its pack. "Check equipment!" Every man made sure his own buckles and belts were secure and then checked the man behind him. The jumpmaster checked the first man. "Sound off for equipment check!" They counted down from the end of the stick: "Ten OK! Nine OK!... Two OK! One OK!"

By now they were all jittery between excitement and anxiety. Ralph Leyva, in a letter written to me years after the war, summed up the feelings and thoughts ("if they were honest," he added) of the men about to make their first jump—"[darn] scared and thinking, oh, my God, what am I doing up here?" When the plane approached the edge of the drop zone (DZ), the pilot switched the light to green—the signal to go. The jumpmaster knelt by the door, checked each man's hookup as he got into position, and corrected his form before hollering "Go!" and slapping him on the back of the leg (or the rump) to exit the plane (hence these individual jumps were termed "tapouts"). Then he called the next man forward to "stand in the door" and repeated the process.

One man in Turner's stick had bragged he'd be the first one out of the plane and the first one on the ground. When he stepped up to the door, he looked down and suddenly paled (which is why you were supposed to look at the horizon). He promptly sat down in the doorway. Usually, a man who balked was pulled out of the door, made to watch everyone else exit, returned to the barracks, and gone before nightfall. In combat, this would be at best a court-martial offense; immediate shooting by an officer was warranted. Turner, next in line, looked down at him, then over at the jumpmaster, who raised an eyebrow and shrugged. "I planted a size eleven in the middle of his back and out he went," Dad snickered. "I followed him out."

Why a cactus patch at the edge of Lawson Field had never been cleared is unknown, but it provided maneuvering practice to be missed, and literally a pain in the butt if not. As they'd done dozens of times from the platforms and towers in their PLFs, the men hit toes first, knees bent, tumbled onto their sides, sprang up, and manhandled their chutes to collapse and get out of them. Of his own first landing, Sergeant (Sgt.) Danny Hayes said in a *Times* article, "lying on my back, I couldn't help but say, 'Thank God.'" Then they gathered up their equipment and headed for busses beside the field to take them back to the packing sheds. The planes circled around until all the jumpers had tumbled out and then returned to Lawson Field to pick up the next lift (planeloads of jumpers).

Each day the jumps got lower, still never as low as they would one day jump in combat. On the final qualifying jump, after equipment check and sound off, when the jumpmaster yelled, "Go!" the entire stick did the "shuffle step" (each man's feet and body right behind the other's) until each man pivoted into the opening and stepped out into the wild blue a fraction of a second ahead of the next. Turner grinned when he told me, "We were taught to count: 'One, one thousand, two, one thousand, three, one thousand.' If your chute hadn't opened by then, you had to pull the ripcord on your emergency chute. [The yelling also relieved head pressure as their bodies dropped.] Boy, I heard a lot of different stuff—usually a stream of four-letter words—but I never heard anybody counting!" Once the canopies blossomed and the jumpers breathed with relief, the fun began. "We would have races by yanking on our risers to spill our chutes and see who could land first."

After assembling on Lawson Field, Tom and the other jumpers were accredited as *bonafide* paratroopers. There was a ceremony in which they received the coveted Parachute Badges and were allowed—like college grads throwing their mortar boards —to "blouse your boots!" Not to mention finally qualifying for that fifty-dollar "jump pay" bonus every payday. When the group returned to Ft. Bragg, Lt. Col. Kinsler issued each man a certificate, dated July 28, with an etching of the Parachute Badge below the United States Army heading verifying that the bearer had "completed the prescribed course in parachute packing, ground training, and jumping from a plane while in flight" and was—*finally*—"a qualified Parachutist."

The 503rd were granted furloughs the first week of August and took what would turn out to be their last trips home for the next three years. Tom had worn his itchy wool OD uniform on his previous leave. This time, he was in cotton khakis for his last photos stateside. Betty's favorite picture forever remained one of him leaning on a railing next to a lamp post in the park across the street from West End Presbyterian.

Tom stalled but finally showed Betty and their parents his winged Parachute Badge. They were surprised—Betty was "downright upset"—to see the wings. Now the cryptic telegram made sense. He had told nobody that his original transfer to Ft. Benning or the postponed leave had been for parachute training. "I was afraid someone would talk me out of it," was his excuse. (Another 503rd trooper, when told by his CO that his wife had written a letter requesting he be transferred out of "that suicide outfit," gave her an ultimatum: airborne or divorce. She chose the former. He did make it home.) Certainly the blue parachute patch on Tom's cap and the Corcoran boots had made his intentions obvious. Perhaps Betty envisioned him spending the duration of the war on the rifle range at Benning or hunkered over a desk at Bragg, but he had already passed up two opportunities to stay in the States. Betty resigned herself to the fact that Tom was determined to "go with the guys." He gave his qualification certificate to her for the scrapbook. Never having graduated from high school, he wrote on the back, "This is my diploma." Her pride overcame her fears. A week later the Albany *Knickerbocker News* reported that "Corp. Thomas E. Turner...Qualifies as Chutist." He cabled her when he got back on base on August 10: "ARRIVED

TWELVE THIRTY EVERYTHING OK." He and the 503rd resumed their tactical training. Cpl. Turner could now happily jump instead of trudge into the maneuvers and mock battles.

Just days before, on the seventh, the US 1st Marine Division had landed on Guadalcanal[8] to start their trek through the Solomon Islands, in the first US offensive of the war. Ironically, Rommel's *final* offensive—to gain the Suez Canal—was stymied at El Alamein by British General Claude Auchinleck. Panzers diverted by Hitler from their resurgent summer thrust for the Caucasian oil fields began to assault Stalingrad, a target with little value other than the *Führer's* personal obsession with obliterating the Soviet dictator's name. The 82nd and 101st Infantry Divisions officially became "Airborne" ("The 101st," Gen. Lee would prophesy to his men at the time, "has no history, but it has a rendezvous with destiny.") Company A of the 503rd took a train to California, where they practice jumped near the Route 66 town of Needles as part of desert maneuvers along with Patton's armor and other units.

Fort Bragg, besides being a tactical training center, was a staging base for units deploying to the European Theater of Operations (ETO). In October 1942, the 1st and 3rd Battalions of the 503rd got orders to prepare to ship out. The men expected to go to England and join the 2nd Battalion, which was not yet part of the 509th. Turner had written to his mother for addresses of distant relatives in England and Scotland whom he might have a chance to look up when he got there. Since some of the 1st Battalion had ski-trained in Utah, they thought perhaps they'd wind up in Scandinavia. Meanwhile, Col. Kinsler left Ft. Bragg to complete the regiment's arrangements.

Company A of the 504th PIR (which was now part of the 82nd Airborne Division) was detached to the 503rd just before the latter departed from Ft. Bragg. Gen. Ridgway, in an unheard-of move, gave the 503rd "the best rifle company in the division." They marched into the Fayetteville station the afternoon of October 10, 1942, and the train left after sundown. The paratroopers awoke to see farmlands and mountains surrounding them but the sunrise behind them. Obviously, the train was not bound for New York. Unbeknownst to them, Kinsler had already flown to California and on to Australia. The ski-training had been a ruse. It worked: Hitler sent troops to Norway that would be sorely needed elsewhere.

John "Jack" Tolson had been a captain and company CO in the 504th Battalion, then a major in the cadre for the 503rd PIR. Now Lieutenant Colonel and Regimental XO, he commanded the troop train to Pittsburg, California, forty miles northeast of San Francisco, at the mouth of the Sacramento River. At every stop, men hung out of the windows with handfuls of money to get townspeople to buy them cigarettes, snacks, or beer. Some of the citizens delivered; others disappeared with the doughboys' dough. Arnie Williams, who joined the 503rd later as a replacement, grinned and chuckled as he told of his similar week-long cross-country railroad trip, "You'd have thought you were in a cartoon. It seemed as if that train was breathing. It was pregnant with GIs. Every time it stopped you could see it deflate—it would spew out the guys to buy booze or sandwiches or flirt with girls. The whistle would blow, and the cars would swell up as they sucked us all back in again when the train left the station." Guthrie saw officers trying to maintain order but as often as not turning a blind eye in return for a half-pint. As the days wore on, enthusiasm waned, but vistas of the Rocky Mountains and American West that most of the men had only seen in silent Tom Mix or William Hart movies as kids and more recent "B" Westerns opened up to more than one

Depression-weary trooper the thought that this might be the place to raise a family after the war. (There would indeed come to be a large number of western US Army associations and reunions.)

Camp Stoneman, sprawling out from the intersection of Railroad Avenue and California Avenue (now the California Delta Highway) in Pittsburg, was the major west-coast staging center for the Pacific Theater of Operations (PTO). Although the downtown area hasn't changed much, there is only a memorial there now in a city park with a Sherman tank, photo-banners of camp activities and troop trains, and plaques for a few resident units. Between 20,000 and 38,000 GIs were billeted there at a time in its two-story barracks, and the millionth one would go through just days before the Japanese surrender. Roll calls were held twice a day; missing a troop movement was a court martial offense. Final overseas preparations were made: equipment, clothing, and security checks; ammo distribution and final range practice for weapon sighting; first aid classes and inoculations for tropical diseases. Turner recollected, "We walked through a gauntlet of medics on both sides, sticking us in both arms simultaneously. I'm sure they were using blunt needles. As I walked away the last one hollered, 'Hey, come back here!' The needle was broken off in my arm."

There were upsides: the barracks were the most comfortable any foot soldier had been in, the food was excellent, there were movies in the camp's three theaters, and, if you were lucky, you might see a USO show at the outdoor amphitheater in the week or two you were there. The 503rd was only there for four busy days. Even with eight PXs, there were long lines at the phone booths. Troopers called their girlfriends, wives, or mothers, to say they were fine but not where they were. Lastly came instruction about life belts, lifeboats, and abandoning ship. Japanese subs lurked along the coast. The soldiers bought GI insurance, filed last wills, and wrote letters home.

Usually, the Army ferried soldiers from Camp Stoneman to the Embarcadero piers, about a three- or four-hour ride. Not for the 503rd—a night march ensued on October 19. Silence was enforced, the soldiers' loads heavy with weapons, full gear and two barracks bags apiece. No one seems to know exactly where *SS Poelau Laut* was docked—perhaps Port Chicago on Suisan Bay, a brisk three-hour hike even without baggage—but even on this chilly Frisco night the troopers were soaked with sweat by the time they boarded. The old ship was one of a handful of East Indian freighters that had eluded the Japanese and had been converted to a troop carrier by cramming the holds full of pipe-frame bunk beds, four and five tiers high, with mattresses little more than two by six canvas rectangles laced to the pipes. By dawn of the twentieth, it had passed under the Golden Gate Bridge. As they steamed by San Quentin, some troopers joked that they might rather be there than on the ship: free room and board, no shooting, and you knew when you'd get out. The freighter followed the California coast south for twelve days, arriving at Balboa, on the Pacific side of the Panama Canal Zone, on November 1.

The men of the 501st Battalion, most of whom had been in Panama over a year, came aboard, leaving Company C behind at Fort Kobbe. That day many of the longest-serving paratroopers became members of the 503rd. Nine of them were from the original PTP, including Aubrey Eberhardt, the first to holler "Geronimo!" Company C would continue to monitor the area and train other arriving units before being absorbed itself into the 551st PIB.[9] Company A of the 504th and Companies A, B, and HHQ from the 501st were amalgamated into the 2nd Battalion (Companies D, E, F, and HHQ, respectively) of the 503ʳᵈ, thus replacing Raff's battalion. The 503ʳᵈ Parachute Infantry Regiment—formed piecemeal from the four original battalions—was now complete, and after all the months of training, anxious to get into the war.

1 The 503ʳᵈ PIR was constituted on Feb. 24, 1942. The 1ˢᵗ and 2ⁿᵈ Battalions were activated with cadres from the 503ʳᵈ and 504ᵗʰ Battalions on March 2. The regiment was formed when the rest of the soldiers from the 503ʳᵈ and 504ᵗʰ PIBs were transferred in and "consolidated," or merged, with the cadres in the 1ˢᵗ and 2ⁿᵈ Battalions of the 503ʳᵈ Regiment on March 14, 1942. Once the regiment was formed, the old 503ʳᵈ and 504ᵗʰ PIBs were deactivated (off the Army rolls).

2 The design came as a response to a letter from Lt. James Hite while he was still in the 501ˢᵗ PB. By the time Disney answered, he was in the 503ʳᵈ PIR. He followed up with more correspondence. Disney sent him the drawing and a contract: it was to be used strictly for military purposes and not business enterprises. Never officially sanctioned by the Army, it nevertheless appeared on uniform patches and on the sign hanging outside 503ʳᵈ Headquarters at Forts Benning and Bragg. Hite rose through the ranks as the Airborne Command gathered steam and new units were formed. Eventually he attained the rank of lieutenant colonel as a battalion commander in the 515ᵗʰ but was killed in a training accident.

3 Three squads in a platoon; three platoons in a company; three companies in a battalion. Brigades were largely scrapped so that divisions were formed with three regiments. Units could thus tactically be deployed with a left wing, right wing, and reserve.

4 This versatile plane had double doors which were removed for parachute jumps but with use of a ramp could be loaded with three or four tons of supplies; a jeep, a howitzer, or an anti-tank gun and a gun crew of eight or nine men; fifteen men and bundles for a mortar and machine gun; four motorcycles, four bicycles, and a dozen men; or twenty riflemen and their equipment. Later it was found that eighteen wounded men on litters could be evacuated. Over 10,000 C-

47s were produced during the war.

5 At the time, Ft. Jackson was the world's largest post. Turner's great-grandson would eventually have boot camp at "Relaxin' Jackson."

6 The origin of the "Geronimo!" cry is generally attributed to Private Aubrey Eberhardt of the PTP, who bet his platoon mates the night before their first jump that not only would he not be too scared to jump but in fact he'd call out the name of the famous chief they'd just seen in a movie. Appropriately enough, the 501st PIR (although not formed from the 501st PB) adopted "Geronimo!" as their motto.

7 Although the original creator, Egbert White, and editor, Hartzell Spence, were officers, they were soon reassigned. Afterwards, the editor was Master Sergeant Joe McCarthy, a former sportswriter (not the baseball manager). One officer, Maj. Franklin Forsberg, remained as business manager but had nothing to do with reporting or writing.

8 The 1st Marine Parachute Battalion saw combat on Gavatu in the Guadalcanal Campaign three months before the 509th did in Africa but had landed amphibiously. The Marine paratroopers were used mostly as Rangers or conventional infantry and were disbanded early in 1944.

9 The 551st PIB was soon alerted to make a jump in the Caribbean onto Martinique, which housed German U-boat pens and Vichy French warships. Martinique turned Free French just before the operation, so the 551st was instead sent to Europe, along with the 550th, which had in the meantime been re-designated as a Glider Infantry Battalion. They participated in the invasion of Southern France and the Battle of the Bulge, taking huge losses before being consolidated with other units.

Chapter 5

GORDONVALE
Deployment

S Poelau Laut, built in Amsterdam in 1929, registered in Java, and crewed by Indonesians, was 494 feet long and 61 feet abeam, and powered by a single 8-cylinder engine for a top speed of fifteen knots. She would cruise at twelve. On board were 1939 officers and men, not far off from the 1958 authorized for a full airborne regiment by the War Department. Lt. Col. George Jones, originally from Memphis, commander of the 501st in Panama, outranked Tolson and so took over the troops on the ship. Knowing the voyage would be long and their attention spans short, he instigated a regimen of on-board physical training, equipment cleaning and inspection, military procedures review, and Japanese tactics lessons. Having once overseen MPs at Ft. Kobbe, he was a strict disciplinarian. He confined several officers to quarters for being drunk. He would later say the best way to get men to toe the mark was to issue orders, ensure everyone understood the orders, then find a captain not enforcing the orders and have him court-martialed. It did not take long for Jones to pick up a new moniker, "The Warden."

Besides Jones's schedule, shipboard duties were inevitable: deck swabbing, kitchen police, and the ship's version of latrine duty. The latrine was a trough with sea water running through it, and a cover with holes in it for fifteen men at a time to sit on, reminiscent of an old outhouse but the width of the stern. With constant seasickness on board, there was plenty to clean up. Tom Turner scoffed and shook his head when he remembered, "It was anything but music to my ears the day I heard 'Turner, Bassetti, and Drosey report to the fantail' in the daily announcements." As with all GIs in every theater of the war, and despite the Warden's efforts, pranks and puerile behaviors occurred. "You'd light a paper in the latrine," Tom continued, "drop it in a hole, and it'd float down the trough. Then the guys would jump and holler as their fannies got singed!"

Soon after dusk, when the Dutch Captain Van der Meer would announce, "Lights oudt, no more schmokin' on der deck," poker and craps games would break out below decks. Guitars, harmonicas, and horns appeared, and the troopers sang swing-era hits, especially those having to do with drinking, like *Little Brown Jug* and *Beer Barrel Polka*. The singing usually devolved into the songs they'd learned at Ft. Benning poking fun at the tragic consequences of parachuting. The chorus of *Blood on the Risers*, sung to *Battle Hymn of the Republic*, ended with "Gory, gory, what a [heck] of a way to die/ he ain't gonna jump no more!" *Beautiful Streamer* was a parody of the 100-year-old Stephen Foster lullaby, *Beautiful Dreamer*, recently made popular again by Bing Crosby. Someone even wrote *The 503d Song*, which prophetically proclaimed, "From the islands of the Philippines to the shores of Germany/ You will hear our battle cry/ as we float down from the sky." In quieter moments, after the racket was squelched (submarine sonar could pick up the revelry), the men wrote letters and read well-circulated dog-eared books and magazines.

Not only had areas of the hold been turned into cramped, sweaty, putrid bunkhouses, the tropical heat soon made them intolerable. Tom Turner, Max Phillips, Bill Ryle, and Ollie Patterson, seeking relief from the oppressive smell and heat, decided to seek out roomier and more breathable space. By sneaking past bulkheads through off-limits areas, they found themselves inside a spacious, less gamey hold. As they settled in, it occurred to one of the group, "Geez, Tom, we're in the prow of the ship. What if we get torpedoed?"

"Well," he replied, lighting his pipe, "I guess I'll stand up and sing *Nearer My God to Thee*."[1]

On another expedition, they came upon a cage full of banana stalks suspended from the ceiling. They fashioned a lasso by buckling several GI belts together. When passed through the bars of the cage and held by a man on either end, it could be flipped jump-rope fashion up behind a stalk. They pulled stalk after stalk to the bars of the cage and divested them of bananas. "When we were done," my father told me, eyes twinkling, "there was nothing left but the empty stalks swinging from the ceiling!"

The officers complained about the shortage of fruit, so the men were barred from the holds after the banana caper. So now the group, looking for relief elsewhere, decided to sleep in a lifeboat. Max Phillips said of the boats, "They were ridiculous, maybe enough space for half the men on board, and in a storm there would be no chance for survival anyway, but they provided a well-ventilated bedroom, and you couldn't roll off the deck!" After a few nights (they had unknowingly used the captain's launch), their friends from below wanted to know, "Where the [heck] do you guys go every night?"

Al Viera soon found out that "the chow lines were a never-ending thing. Guys would eat and get right back in line and sit and wait for the next meal." He soon stumbled upon a solution. Many men were not shaving, even though shaving was included in the general orders. Al and his buddy, Edward Puctor, were among those who thought they'd get away with it. "A sergeant stopped between our bunks and wanted our names. I told him mine was 'Philip Morris' (a cigarette company). It was the first name I could think of. As he started to write on his pad, a cry came from a few bunks away, 'Is that you, Viera?' It was Top Sgt. Albert Baldwin. He said, 'You're on KP!'

"It turned out to be a blessing. When taking out the kitchen trash, we were taking out chickens, hams, and roast beef underneath the lettuce leaves. One day we carried a large tray of roast beef with a few loaves of bread to where the troopers bunked and Ed yelled, 'Chow!' The pan never got set down. There was a stampede. The pan was empty in less than a second! After a couple weeks, Sgt. Baldwin ran into us and asked if we were still on KP. We said, 'Yes,' and he said he'd take us off. We begged him to keep us on and told him why. We stayed on for the rest of the trip!"[2]

The ship crossed the Equator on November 5 and closed on Polynesia. By walking a plank blindfolded and falling off into an impromptu pool—an inverted hatch cover full of sea water—the troopers earned certificates, deeming them "worthy to be numbered as one of our Trusty Shellbacks," and signed (of course) by Davy Jones and King Neptune. Two days later, while they chugged on towards the South Sea Islands, their comrades in the old 2/503 (unaware that they were now 2/509) were flying across

71

Spain to make their historic jump at Oran in Algeria.³ Next morning, French planes strafed Patton's Western Task Force of infantry and armor as they splashed ashore at Casablanca, and French ships traded broadsides with Allied ships at Algiers, before Eisenhower convinced the Vichy commander, Admiral Darlan, to end resistance. Within two weeks, Field Marshal Georgy Zhukov's Operation "Uranus" would not only relieve Stalingrad but also overrun the Romanians on the thinly held flanks of the German Sixth Army and encircle a quarter million Germans and their allies. Churchill's new commander in Egypt, Bernard Montgomery, would break through Rommel's defenses and begin to drive him back towards the American, British, and Free French forces advancing from the Western Sahara. The Third Reich's high tide was beginning to ebb.

In the meantime, a hurricane-force Pacific storm hit *Poelau Laut* so hard that the crashing of the sixty-foot waves and the pitching of the ship churned the stomachs of even the most sea-worthy of the men. "Most of us had never been on a boat bigger than a rowboat or a ferry, certainly not on the high seas," one veteran (whose name I inexcusably lost) wrote me. "We couldn't stand it down below so we came up for air. But then guys were hanging over the sides and throwing up everywhere. Every step you took you were slipping in puke or getting rocked by a wave. Kind of funny to watch, all those guys with their legs kicking every which way like a bunch of drunks, but not if you got in the middle of it."

Viera mused, "I wasn't feeling too bad, but I had to go to the toilet. When I got to the latrine, it was packed with guys. Literally, there wasn't an empty seat in the house! Guys were filling the sinks with upchuck and the floors were slipperier than ice. It made you sick just to go in there, and with the ship rocking, all I could think about was to get me out of there!"

In calmer water, one of the feared Japanese subs pursued *Poelau Laut*. The ship's only armaments for self-defense were a single eight-inch gun on both the bow and stern, and pom-pom anti-aircraft guns on the sides, all ineffective against subs. Barely out of torpedo range, the ship was unable to call for help because of radio silence. Captain Van der Meer fired up smoke pots and circled within his own smoke screen for a while to thwart the sub from locking on target before resuming his zigzag course. As they approached Tahiti, a PBY "Catalina" (Navy patrol bomber and anti-submarine aircraft) flew over the freighter and let go a machine gun burst across the bow. The crew ran up the American and Dutch flags in a hurry. The sub peeled off to avoid the hunter and seek other prey.

On November 21, the 503rd crossed the International Date Line and suddenly it was tomorrow! A couple days later they caught sight of New Zealand. As if tropic squalls and prowling subs hadn't caused enough distraction from without, close quarters living inevitably provided the regiment its first battle within: a lice infestation broke out on board *Poelau Laut*. Tom chortled as he told my brother and me, "We rechristened that banana boat 'The Polluted Louse.'"

On the twenty-fifth, they were finally within hailing distance of Australia but were told there was no room to dock at Brisbane (and the men wouldn't have been allowed off the boat anyway until the infestation was under control). The old grain freighter continued on and stopped briefly at Townsville, Queensland, Australia, on December 1, 1942. The Japanese had been bombing the northern coast of Australia since February, particularly Darwin's port and airfields, to prevent the Allies from interfering with their upcoming attacks on Java and Timor. They had also raided as far as Broome in West Australia and Townsville, here in the east, where the American Fifth Air Force was based. To avoid the risk of losing the entire regiment, *Poelau Laut* was ordered to a safer, less-targeted harbor. The next day, a month to the day after leaving Panama, the Polluted Louse docked at Cairns in Queensland, Australia, at 1645. The 503rd had sailed nearly 13,000 miles in forty-two days at sea.

Colonel Kinsler was there to greet them and take over command. The rest of the day, deuce and a halfs relayed troops fourteen miles south to Gordonvale. Several local women's organizations treated the new American visitors to "crumpets and tea," watermelon, and hamburgers—which the Australians were making for the first time. They sat at picnic tables underneath "trestles and tops set up from the Gordonvale Hotel to the corner newsagency." So began a pleasant relationship between the American Army and the little town they would call home for the next eight months.

The 503rd spent their first night in Australia in pup tents, erected while it rained, beneath eucalyptus trees. The designated area for the 503rd encampment was a mile and a half southwest of Gordonvale along the Gillies Highway. Every day started, as usual, with calisthenics. Then the men went to work unloading the ship. Supplies were piled at first under tarps on the Gordonvale Square until storage buildings could be built. The troopers slept on cots in sixteen-foot-square tents with pyramidal roofs and wooden floors. Each tent held a squad (up to a dozen men). They built "corduroy" walkways out of tree trunks between company sectors, and drainage ditches for the upcoming monsoon rains. Companies were spread out to avoid mass destruction in the event of air raids by Japanese squadrons from New Guinea or Rabaul.

On December 11, Turner finally got a chance to send his fiancée a telegram to assure her he hadn't been sunk or blown up: "AM QUITE OK HOPE YOU ARE FINE LETTER FOLLOWING TOM." She still didn't know where Tom was; the address was coded beyond the Army Post Office (APO) in San Francisco. Her scrapbook was full of stories of troops in England and Africa. When she got the telegram, she was snipping out a *New York Times* article with the heading, "Somewhere in Algeria." There was a photo of Col. Raff receiving the Legion of Honor award from Free French General Edoard Welvert. Raff would also earn a Silver Star and, before the year was out, publish one of the first books of WWII, about the exploits of 2/503 (509th) in Africa. Betty would buy a First Edition. Another headline gave Betty a pretty good bet what Tom would be up to: "Allied Offensive Looms in Pacific."

Gordonvale, described by troopers as a Wild West-looking town, with Victorian buildings and dirt streets, was transformed. The Army requisitioned the Gordonvale and Commercial Hotels as hospitals. The Service Company rigging crew was released for regular duty by hiring and training two dozen Australian women to pack parachutes in a converted shed (said to be the first air-conditioned building in Gordonvale) near the Central Hotel. This hotel housed the Red Cross Canteen, where there would be dances for the GIs and chaperoned ladies. The troopers resented paying for food and drinks here, knowing their hometown folks had been donating all along, but they were certainly not going to turn down the opportunity to relax, imbibe, and dance with the girls.

North Queensland has a climate much like the US Pacific

Northwest. There is plenty of rain on the ocean side of the coastal mountains, but the interior is arid. There was abundant space for practice jumps on sugarcane fields and long hikes back to camp. Sometimes these were rewarded by barbeques, including beer (usually warm) from the brewery in Cairns, courtesy of company slush funds.

It was summer in the Southern Hemisphere. The ten- to twenty-five-mile "rat races," which had contributed to the men's conditioning in the States but were particularly grueling here, were discontinued. Long marches in full gear persisted, often several days long and requiring camping in the jungles beyond the cane fields. Christmas dinner for the 503rd was an insipid turkey dinner. Sometimes ice cream, a welcome treat in the tropics, accompanied supper. Each man was issued a ticket to make sure he got his scoop. Those who didn't want ice cream would trade their tickets to those who did for money, cigarettes, or favors. With an extra ticket a guy could go back through the ice cream line again. Turner, who preferred his pipe anyway, gladly traded away cigarettes for tickets.

Back in Albany, the New Year was being ushered in with a midnight showing of *Yankee Doodle Dandy* with James Cagney at the Strand. Richard Greene was starring in *Flying Fortress* at the Ritz. Mickey Rooney and Ava Gardner, married less than a year, were splitting up. Headlines on the seventh reported the temperature had risen all the way to 7° from the previous day's high of -4°. In Gordonvale, it was 90°. The humidity along the coast, where it rained two out of every three days, made it feel well over 100.

Troopers with weekend or holiday passes took the slow train they came to call the "Toonerville Trolley" (from an early twentieth-century cartoon strip) to Cairns, where there were night clubs, theaters, pubs, and lawn bowling clubs. On one excursion, some of them took a tram to the beach. Turner wondered why some of the "dumb clucks" were running out into the water with their army boots on. He and those who followed barefoot found out why: the midpoint of The Great Barrier Reef is just offshore from Cairns. Several men had to come home early and report to sick bay with the soles of their feet shredded. On another beach trip, they swam with and rode on dolphins which had come inside the reef.

Cairns was also home to a large naval base. George Clay noted that, "When we got to Cairns, there was nobody [that is, men] there; all the Australian troops were in the Middle East. Of course, we were all young guys on that base, all doing the same thing: looking for women, going out with guys' girlfriends and wives. So they put out the word when they came back to Australia: don't let a Yank show his face in Cairns, especially on Saturday night. So we carried our brass knuckle knives into town."[4]

The quest for alcohol was, likewise, perpetual. The troopers happily built a PX which sold the Cairns beer. The 503rd found out bootleg spirits could be procured in after-hours pubs and at some local vendors which offered "backdoor cocktail service" in Gordonvale and other nearby towns. There were even stashes in the regimental supply buildings. When they left the States, each company had its own crates of parachutes, all numbered. A company sergeant had to keep track of the crates. Clay was one of the sergeants. "Guys would ask me to put booze in those boxes. I had to sweat not getting caught when the officers came searching. They were usually looking for evidence to court-martial someone."

Colonel Kinsler would eventually order a prison compound built including a "sweat box" to discourage excessive drinking.

The men dubbed the compound the "Barbed Wire Hotel." Turner took it upon himself to be the "safety guy"—the forerunner of the "designated driver." Doc Landes confirmed this: "I remember your dad wasn't much of a drinker. He always made sure the rest of us got back to the camp."

There were other paratrooper pastimes in the towns, typically bar brawls. These often started with quarrels between the Australian Home Guards (local militia) and the Diggers (regular infantry). Other fights were with sugarcane cutters, who were deemed necessary civilian workers by the government but considered shirkers by the soldiers. Sometimes it was a Yank wooing a Digger's Sheila. Whatever the cause, the effect was that the paratroopers couldn't resist joining in.

The area surrounding Gordonvale was largely planted with sugarcane. There was a cane processing plant with a railroad spur for shipping cane in and sugar out. Thus, the town, and particularly the pubs, always had an ample population of cane cutters. One night the Aussies were slinging insults at each other, and in typical fashion a fight erupted. The Americans, seeing that the cane cutters outnumbered the soldiers, decided to even the odds. Turner remembered, "There were guys punching it out everywhere, breaking bottles and furniture. I knew the MPs would show up and I said to myself, 'I gotta find Max and get us oughta here.' So I started looking for him. I pulled guys off of dog piles, looked under tables, dodged punches, threw a couple, but no Max. Finally, I saw him. There he was up on the bandstand beating the bass drum." Max's version, when asked about the brouhaha years later was, "Beating the bass drum? [Heck], I was *wearing* the bass drum."

Indeed, the MPs arrived, cleared the place out, lined the

soldiers up on one side of the street and the cane cutters on the other side. Tom continued, "I thought the MPs were going to let us settle it in the street, so I started to roll up my sleeves. A huge Aussie, a head taller than me, leaned over and said, 'Give 'em [heck], Yank.' I was glad he was going to be on my side." It was not to be. Army trucks drove up, the MPs herded the paratroopers in, and off they went back to the camp. Ringleaders wound up in the Barbed Wire Hotel and were docked pay (as were some Aussies) to help pay for damages. The next weekend in town, another big Aussie, one of the cane cutters' foremen, passed a group of GIs and said, "Good fight, Yanks. Buy you a beer?"

Like many regiments, the 503rd picked up pets and mascots, sometimes to be used as jumping partners. One battalion of the 505th, while training at Fort Benning, had fitted a boxer named Max with his own parachute and claimed he loved jumping from the planes. A German shepherd named Geronimo jumped with the 507th in Nebraska with an audience of several thousand residents looking on. Each dog had a shirt with sergeant's stripes.[5] Smaller animals like cats and birds were strapped to jumpers' chests or legs. Ben Guthrie said they once managed to shove a donkey out the door of a C-47 before it destroyed the plane. He did not mention how much of a kickback the pilot got for allowing the near disaster.

Now they went after strange new animals. Photos were taken of Turner and others holding koala bears.[6] One day, Tom remembered, some troopers who were civilian cowboys lassoed a kangaroo and put it in a stockyard with a high fence. The kangaroo began hopping around the perimeter to pick up speed, jumped the fence, and headed in Turner's direction. "Catch him!" someone yelled. "You catch him!" he yelled back as he dove out its way.

Some animals they kept as far away from as possible. Snakes seemed a mile long and hid anywhere. Men never put on boots or opened a bag without checking first. They marched past anthills two feet high whose architects, Bull Ants, were up to an inch and a half long and could reduce an animal carcass to a skeleton in a few days. Birds had strange calls; kookaburras sounded like they were laughing. What the Americans thought were coyotes howling at night turned out to be dingoes.

Intense jungle warfare training began in the rainforests, directed by Australian officers and noncoms. There were both day and night practice drops, and tactical problems that required several days' hiking. The paratroopers got used to marching and stumbling through mud, rocks, vine- and fern-covered trails, and slimy creeks in driving rain and blazing sun. The risks of the hazard pay began to show. A private drowned on maneuvers in February. Swimming was not a paratrooper qualification, but it probably didn't matter: he was swept away when he lost his grasp on a rope across a swollen river after a monsoon. Then, on a night jump, several men heard a trooper calling for help and found his parachute at the edge of a lake. They pulled on the silk and the suspension lines. When they got him to shore, he too had drowned. What they couldn't see was that the lines had drifted under a fallen tree trunk, and their tugging had pulled him under. Another trooper was electrocuted upon landing in power lines beside the highway.

A luckier trooper landed in a grove of tall eucalyptus trees on a night jump. Each man carried a thirty-foot length of rope to get down out of trees, but in the darkness, he could not tell how far up he was. He too started calling for help. It turned out he could have cut the lines with his switchblade and easily dropped to the ground, for a few minutes later another trooper walked up to him, just a few feet below, and said, "What's all the fuss about?"

One battalion officer had a disagreeable temperament and a visage to match. Tom said his men called him "the Gargoyle." He decided the battalion should have a run through the cane fields and out into the jungle-covered hills and back to camp. The summer heat was waning but still brutal. As the men straggled back into their tents and plopped down onto their cots, one said, "I wonder if the [expletive] Gargoyle made it." Immediately the tent flap opened, the officer stuck his head inside, and he growled, "Yeah, the [expletive] Gargoyle made it!"

General MacArthur turned sixty-three on January 26. Betty's scrapbook article noted that "Last year MacArthur observed his birthday anniversary on bombwracked Corregidor...in Manila Bay." This year he had the enemy on the run, and today he was awarding a Distinguished Service Cross to Brig. Gen. Hanford MacNider for "extraordinary heroism in New Guinea." He was just one of sixteen officers cited by the General for courage, leadership, and inspiration. A week later, on the first of February, the *Knickerbocker News* ran a photo of FDR and Churchill meeting in Casablanca. On the same page, Judy Garland, George Murphy, and Gene Kelly were noted to be starring in *For Me and My Gal* at the Madison Theater in Albany. Abbott and Costello were in *Who Done It?* at the Delaware. The second show in the double bill there featured young William Holden in *Meet the Stewarts*. The next day, Field Marshal Friedrich Paulus notified Hitler, after *Der Führer* had refused to let him fight through to an escape corridor, that his 91,000 isolated Germans had held out "to the last man and the last round" and were surrendering to the Russians at Stalingrad. Only 5000 of them would ever make it home. Another three-quarters of a million Axis troops had already been casualties or been taken prisoner during the five months' battle. The Reds had lost over a million men. No one ever knew how many civilians had been killed.

Tom Turner, on the other side of the world, could commiserate with the cartoon character "Sad Sack" in an issue of *Yank* the same month. The hapless, big-eared, big-nosed GI was the creation of Staff Sergeant (S/Sgt.) George Baker, a Disney cartoonist in civilian life. Sad Sack was forever out of luck: he'd dig a foxhole and then, come an air raid, find it already full of men; turn the wrong way during drill and get poked by a bayonet; discover a dry bed in a deserted house on a rainy night just in time for an officer to show up; do an exceptional job only to see someone else get the credit. Sad Sack never got a PFC's stripe. In fact, the only promotion he ever got—for doing such a good job on latrine duty—was over "to the officers' side." In the current issue, Sad Sack was digging a foxhole and neglected to salute a lieutenant. The lieutenant, while bawling out Sad Sack, in turn missed saluting a passing captain, and so on until a colonel miffed a brigadier. All fingers pointed down the line to you-know-who.

By March 1943, the Japanese had evacuated the last of their men, 20,000 of whom had been killed by combat or disease, from Guadalcanal to reinforce New Guinea. The US Marines had suffered 15,000 casualties of their own but had stopped Japan's expansion. Major General Orde Wingate's Chindits were raiding Japanese garrisons in Burma. Patton's tanks beat Rommel's for the first time at El Guettar in Tunisia. With prodding from some of his pals, Turner applied for OCS. Two of his former officers, Cpt. Benjamin Bache of Company G, and Cpt. Francis Donovan, the Headquarters Adjutant, had known him since his appointment as personnel clerk at Fort Benning. They recognized him to be "proficient, sober, hard-working, and trustworthy, with lengthy administrative experience," but undoubtedly his unfinished education stood in his way. Despite their "unreservedly" and "unqualifiedly" recommendations, he was turned down. Like Doc Landes, he would remain a non-com. A friend of George Clay's, having made the first cut, began OCS in Cairns. "He got kicked out of OCS for drinking," George said. "They busted him and sent him back down into the ranks."

The 503rd made five practice jumps in May at nearby Green Field. The fall heat was tolerable; the rains were abating. Mother's Day found many troopers having communion at St. Michael's Church, followed by a "Communion Breakfast" in the park. Parachutes had been packed in the same park before the packing shed was ready. Protestant Chaplain Probert Herb visited local shut-ins and thanked the townsfolk for their kindness to the Americans. The Afrika Korps, surrounded by Allied armies in Tunisia, surrendered the same week.

On June 25, Gen. MacArthur and the Australian Commander-in-Chief, Gen. Sir Thomas Blamey, were on hand for an exhibition jump at Green Field following their visit to a Higgins Boat (Landing Craft) assembly plant in Cairns. Another tragedy marred the review. Pvt. Donald Wilson was the victim of a "streamer"—the subject of the song they had learned at Ft. Benning—a parachute that got tangled in its lines (or perhaps with the emergency chute) and failed to open. MacArthur ordered that he be awarded a Purple Heart, the regiment's first. Later reviews and inspections were attended by Lord Mountbatten of the British Royal Navy and American Generals Krueger and Eichelberger from Sixth Army,[7] getting their first glimpses of the American airborne in training.

A month later, Patton's tankers fought alongside the 509th Parachute Battalion, whose boots they'd delightedly pilfered in Georgia, to liberate Palermo and Messina. The airborne assaults in Sicily and in mainland Italy were poorly planned, air transport pilots inadequately trained, and parachute regiments randomly scattered. The results were disappointing strategically. Only the confusion sown behind German lines was positive. The Germans had had a similarly unsatisfactory experience on Crete. The German victory had been overshadowed by its cost in men and equipment.[8]

Secretary Stimson and Lt. Gen. Lesley McNair, commander of Army Ground Forces, recommended that in the future, airborne units should be kept at regimental size or less and be used much like commando units. 82nd Division's Generals Ridgway and Maxwell Taylor (West Point '22) apparently agreed. Eisenhower's conclusion for Marshall was that the logistics for airborne divisions would be too hard to control. He consequently advised relegating smaller airborne units to smaller tasks, and nearly killed the Airborne program.

Paratrooper Colonels James Gavin of the 505th and Rueben Tucker (West Point '35) of the 504th, however, maintained that with B-17 protection, intense transport crew training, and marked DZs, airborne divisions would be effective. Ridgway did note that the Germans had gotten a lot of troops onto Crete in a short time and felt that concentrated airborne operations would eventually become feasible. Former PTP leader Lt. Col. William Ryder wrote of the Italian operations, "The prescribed missions were not successful, but the employment of parachute troops was most successful." He was convinced that their aggression was a deciding factor in the subsequent landings. Furthermore, Maj. Gen. Joseph

Swing (West Point '15, Army football player and future CO of the 11th Airborne Division) recommended that instead of being dropped as individual regiments, paratroopers should be dropped *en masse,* to deliver, as Napoleon would say, *un coup de main.* Obviously, piecemeal drops were worthless.

General MacArthur, seeing both sides of the debate from afar, felt better training and planning all around would pay off and decided to prove it. He envisioned airborne troops being used for in-and-out operations and not subjected to drawn-out frontline work as had been the case after the previous drops.

For the past year, MacArthur's first order of business for the slowly growing armies in Australia[9] had been to expel the Japanese from New Guinea, both to remove the threat to Australia and to use it as a springboard towards the Philippines and Indonesia. He was determined to use the paratroopers in his upcoming Operation "Postern," designed as a joint American-Australian venture to relieve pressure on, and develop a more suitable base of operations further from, Australia.

Under the guise of moving out to join the 32nd Division for a training exercise, the regiment tore down and packed up the camp. They were transported by battalions—the 2nd on the sixteenth of August by air-landing, the 1st and 3rd (arriving on the twentieth) aboard *TSMV Duntroon*[10]—525 miles from Cairns to Port Moresby, on the southeastern coast of Papua Territory, New Guinea. There is still a marker at the site of the camp, and there are two plaques in Gordonvale which commemorate the time the paratroopers were there. One of them, placed by the townspeople, calls each member of the 503rd "One of us." The other, provided by the 503rd Association after the war for the people of Gordonvale, thanks them for making the area a pleasant home. Australia was the only place my dad said he'd ever been that he wanted to go back to.

1 Reportedly played by the ship's orchestra as the Titanic sank.

2 Letter from Al Viera to Jim Turner, Sept. 9, 1986.

3 Oddly, for a while, the 503rd had two 2nd Battalions—one in Europe, one in the Pacific. The one sent to Scotland was attached to the British 1st Airborne Division and was already in North Africa, as 2/503, when its paperwork denoting it as 2/509 (as of November '42) caught up to it. They had just sent their first casualty reports to 503rd HQ in Australia! The battalion was fighting the Germans in Italy when it was determined there would be no 509th Regiment, and 2/509 simply became the 509th PIB.

4 Taped interview, 503rd Association Annual Corregidor Day Dinner, Feb. 21, 1987.

5 Army dogs were used to deliver medicine and messages and to stand guard duty in off-limits areas. Some of them indeed parachuted.

6 Unfortunately, the photos were loaned out at a reunion and subsequently lost.

7 Krueger and Eichelberger, as well as George Marshall, had been posted together along with MacArthur as lieutenants at Fort Leavenworth, Kansas, in the early 1900s.

8 Crete (May 1941) is considered "the graveyard of the German airborne," despite their capturing the island. Whole companies were killed upon landing. Five thousand of 13,000 paratroopers were lost, as were half of their 350 transport planes. When 2/509 (formerly 2/503) flew into Africa on November 8, 1942, some off-course pilots dropped their sticks in Morocco. Others, out of gas, made desert landings. Some were shot down by the Vichy French. Raff's closest company was mis-dropped thirty-five miles from its destination. His troops took weeks to regroup. For Operation "Husky," July 10-12, 1943, Col. Gavin's 505th

flew from Malta to Sicily. Only twelve percent were dropped near their targets and even those were scattered. They did what they could: cut phone lines and ambushed patrols. Even so, according to Field Marshal Albert Kesselring, the paratroopers impeded the advance of the Hermann Göring Division. German parachute commander Karl Student said more specifically that the American Airborne kept Göring's Division from counterattacking the beach. Patton said they bought him forty-eight hours for his offensive. However, when Patton ordered Rueben Tucker's 504th in on the eleventh, they took hits from US Army and Navy anti-aircraft guns resulting in twenty-three C-47s shot down and well over 300 friendly-fire deaths. Gen. Joe Swing, tasked by Eisenhower to report on the airborne problems, reported that the bottom line was that cooperation with the 52nd Troop Carrier Wing was deficient. Furthermore, the "Swing Board" recommended that all branches—Army, Navy, and Air Corps—be made aware of and be expected to support any impending air assault. *Training Circular 113*, outlining and demanding full knowledge by and cooperation between the services for all airborne operations, soon followed.

9 Sixth Army had been activated in January 1943 but consisted only of the 32nd and 41st Army Divisions (comprising I Corps) and the 1st Marine Division. Since it was not a full-sized army, it was referred to as "the Alamo Force" (perhaps because its CO, Gen. Krueger, had gotten his first star in Texas, or maybe because they were expected to hold off the invading hordes against all odds) and was commanded directly by MacArthur. Its reduced staff at that time was headquartered in Brisbane and was strictly administrative. MacArthur gave the orders; Krueger made them happen. Once the 24th Infantry and 1st Cavalry Divisions arrived in Australia late in the year to fill out Sixth Army, Krueger's HQ moved with them to New Guinea, where he assumed command. Australia had four combat divisions, also under MacArthur's control, and four reserve divisions garrisoning the continent.

10 Twin Screw Motor Vessel *Duntroon* was a converted Australian passenger liner. Built to carry 373 passengers, it was loaded with several times that many soldiers. It had the distinction of sinking *two* Allied warships: an Australian minesweeper (the Royal Australian Navy's first loss of WWII) and an American destroyer. *Duntroon* cut both in half amidships while blacked out on night

moves. Thirty sailors were lost. The captain was exonerated in both cases. The 503rd had an uneventful voyage.

Chapter 6

NADZAB

First Blood and the Aussies

N ew Guinea, second only to Greenland in land mass, is an island the size of Texas but shaped, some say, like a turkey with its head pointing west. At the time of the war, the southeast quarter of New Guinea was known as Papua Territory. The northeast quarter was New Guinea Territory. Both were administered by Australia, and after the war merged into Papua New Guinea. The Netherlands controlled, and still do, the western half as part of the East Indies. Upon launching their Pacific campaign in January 1942, the Japanese Empire had captured New Britain, to the northeast of New Guinea in the Bismarck Archipelago, and had built up a formidable naval, air, staging, and supply depot at Rabaul. From there, naval and air forces had interfered with Allied communications, troop movements, and supply lines between the United States, Australia, and New Guinea. To shield Rabaul, the Japanese had occupied the Solomon Islands to the southeast and northern New Guinea to the southwest. Next, they had planned to take Port Moresby, the colonial capital of Papua Territory, as a base of operations against

Australia, a mere 300 miles away.

The Japanese Eighth Area Army (similar to a US Army Group) was commanded by General Hitoshi Imamura and based at Rabaul for the defense of the Solomons and New Guinea. In March of 1942, Imamura had landed his Eighteenth Army at Lae, 200 miles due north of Port Moresby but separated from it by the Owen-Stanley Mountain Range—jagged, steep, moss-covered, up to 13,000 feet high, and running the length of the island. The invaders had quickly spread out from Lae in all directions along the coastal plain and its coconut plantations, spilling into Dutch New Guinea to the west and fortifying Buna and Gona villages, halfway to Milne Bay at the eastern tip of New Guinea. The few nearby Australian and Papuan battalions gave ground stubbornly.

General MacArthur recognized Imamura's intent and determined to hold Port Moresby at all costs. In May, an IJN invasion fleet headed that way was intercepted in the Coral Sea. Each navy lost a carrier (*Lexington* for the USN and *Shoho* for the IJN), and the Japanese sank more ships than the Americans but failed to reach Port Moresby. Another setback for the Empire came in August, when 2000 Japanese soldiers landed at Milne Bay but were driven back into the sea by the Australian 5th and 7th Divisions. Finally, the Australians stopped another enemy attack, launched from the west, just short of Milne Bay. Then, reinforced by their own 6th Division and the US 32nd Division, they pursued the retreating Japanese towards Buna.

The only remaining option for the Japanese to get to Port Moresby was to try overland through the 6000-foot-high Kokoda Pass. Eleven thousand Imperial soldiers struggled along the narrow muddy mountain trail against the Australian-Papuan Kokoda contingent to get within twenty miles of Port Moresby. Extended supply lines and debilitating sickness checked them. Detached brigades from the 6th and 7th Divisions[1] posted at Moresby counterattacked, pushed the Japanese back over the mountains, and ended the threat while establishing their own forward bases along the Kokoda Trail.

The Japanese air force, however, never let up on Port Moresby. Planes from New Britain raided it over seventy times. Radar was ineffective for the Australians. They resorted to "Coastwatchers," men dropped into the hills on the islands with no more than a rifle and a radio. They were sporadically re-supplied by subs, to which they communicated Japanese air, sea, and land movements. These men, in turn, were guided through the jungles and warned of Japanese patrols by the local natives.

By November 1942, Eighteenth Army (about the size of an American corps), under Lt. Gen. Hatazo Adachi, had given up on Moresby but was still holding onto its Buna-Gona stronghold near the head of the Kokoda Trail. Early in the war, the Australian Prime Minister, John Curtin, had considered conceding the northern two-thirds of Australia to the Japanese and defending the more populous south, but MacArthur had persuaded him that static defense was a losing strategy. Now, he exhorted, after the Kokoda victory, was the time to go on the offensive with the veteran Australian divisions and the few green Americans at hand. But the Aussies were exhausted after battling through the mountains and defending Port Moresby and Milne Bay. The US 32nd, mostly National Guardsmen with as little as five weeks' BIT and about as much jungle training, had already suffered from heat exhaustion, hunger, malaria, waterlogged clothing, and failed equipment just getting to the battle zone. The Allied advance up the coast lagged.

The enemy could neither be outmaneuvered on land due to

swamps, nor bypassed by sea because there weren't enough transports, and the Navy was unwilling to release warships into the uncharted reef-filled waters without air cover. Air cover in turn was limited, because airbases could only be moved up after an area was under control, and no carriers were available (even though MacArthur had begged Washington as had PM Curtin with London). Reduced to the nineteenth-century linear brand of warfare that had failed so miserably in WWI, MacArthur ordered I Corps commander, Lt. Gen. Robert Eichelberger (West Point '09), to take direct control of the 32nd against the well-entrenched, camouflaged, experienced enemy and "to take Buna, or not to come back alive." Having once been given the same ultimatum in WWI, MacArthur had always made it a point to personally reconnoiter his front and look for weak spots, but apparently he did not this time and consequently underestimated the enemy. Staggering losses forced Eichelberger[2] to abandon repeated frontal assaults against their superb defenses in favor of "surround and harass" tactics. It took longer, till January after the 41st Division arrived to throw in its weight, but cost fewer casualties. As it was, they exceeded those on Guadalcanal by 2000 dead and 1200 wounded. MacArthur, estimating he had at best ten percent of the overseas Army and Air Force, and even less of the Navy, would come to embrace the isolation strategy. "The paucity of resources at my command," he reminisced, "made me adopt this method of campaign."

Despite the deficiencies in ground, air, and sea forces, Operation "Cartwheel," the Allies' plan to regain the Solomon Islands and New Guinea, was already rolling. The operation was designed to close in on Rabaul with parallel advances by MacArthur's South West Pacific Area (SWPA) Sixth Army and

Admiral John "Bull" Halsey's South Pacific (SOPAC) Third Fleet. The understrength Sixth Army—the "Alamo Force"—and Sir Thomas Blamey's Australian "New Guinea Force" continued to hem in the Japanese Eighteenth Army along the New Guinea coast while Marine Raiders and Army infantry landed on New Georgia in the central Solomons.

Beginning with the Guadalcanal invasion the previous August, the Americans had been repelling repeated IJN attempts to dislodge them from the Solomons with Japanese reinforcements and supplies brought via Rabaul by the "Tokyo Express." The navies clashed several times in the surrounding seas, particularly in the New Georgia Sound between Guadalcanal and Florida (now Nggela) Islands, which because of the number of ships sunk— nearly five dozen, including the first two Japanese battleships scored by the Allies—is known to history as "Iron-bottom Sound." Fully a year later, on a night patrol in early August 1943, PT-109 was rammed and sliced in half by an IJN destroyer near New Georgia. The young skipper, Lieutenant Junior Grade John Kennedy, would be decorated as a war hero for saving his crew (Aussie coastwatchers and island natives helped rescue them) and would later be elected President.

In the middle of it all, in April, the IJN had suffered an irreplaceable loss when Admiral Yamamoto, on a visit to various island bases to boost morale and to commend his pilots (not knowing their reports of Allied losses had been greatly exaggerated), had his itinerary decoded. P-38 "Lightnings" shot him down shortly after he took off from Bougainville. Always dubious as to the wisdom of attacking Pearl Harbor in the first place, he once said, "Should hostilities break out between Japan and the United States...we would have to march into Washington and sign the treaty in the White House." He was one of the few who realized that no amount of territory taken, even all the way from San Diego to Seattle, would force America to come to terms.

Although the Japanese had abandoned Guadalcanal, fighting in the Solomons would continue for the duration of the war. While the battles raged on in New Guinea and the islands, US Bomber Command began blasting oil refineries in Ploesti, Romania. Patton was rebuked and relieved of command for slapping two soldiers in Italy, one so hard that his helmet flew off. Americans and Canadians took back the Aleutian Islands. In foxholes and tents everywhere, dog faces stared at Ava Gardner wearing a two-piece swimsuit in *Yank*.

The newly disembarked 503rd PIR assembled on the outskirts of rain drenched Port Moresby on August 22, 1943, the second anniversary of the 503rd Battalion's activation. It was a typical parachute regiment for early WWII. Colonel Kinsler's XO was Lt. Col. Jones. The regimental staff headed several sections. S-1 (Executive) was responsible for administrative orders, troop movements, and battalion and company liaison. S-2 (Intelligence) oversaw reconnaissance, security, and interpreters. S-3 (Plans and Training) took care of communications and various assignments for combat. S-4 (Supply) handled food, ammunition, clothing, other essential supplies, transportation, and mail.[3] There were demolition and MP platoons. Each of these sections employed from half a dozen to fifty men depending on the scope of their assignments. These sections were all contained within Regimental HHQ, or "Regimental Headquarters" (RHQ), totaling fourteen officers and 117 EM. An additional sixty-some surgeons, aides, and medics staffed the regimental medical section. Some stayed within the Regimental Headquarters area. Others were delegated to the battalions to man command post and forward position aid stations.

Service Company had its own commander and staff who were overseen by the S-4 officer. Its Quartermaster section collected, loaded, unloaded, and dispersed supplies throughout the regiment, and re-supplied the companies during combat. Service Company provided a supply sergeant to each rifle company. The parachute maintenance platoon had riggers, packers, and repairmen. Mechanics, drivers, and vehicles were all part of the transportation platoon.[4] The chaplains were in Service Company. This was a large company, with as many as 200 officers and EM in the standard infantry regiments, where there were more men to supply and vehicles to transport them. As the war progressed, Service Company of the 503rd was lucky to have a hundred.

The three battalions were organized alike and numbered 530 officers and men apiece, each commanded by a major or lieutenant colonel. Each had its own Headquarters Company, a scaled-down version of RHQ, with admin, clerical, and comm sections. Each battalion had its own cooks, medics, and a surgeon. The "weapons" section was comprised of a "light" machine gun platoon consisting of four squads, each with a pair of .30-cal. M1919A4 Browning machine guns, as well as a mortar platoon with four 81-mm mortars (with a range of 3200 yards). These could be attached to the rifle companies as needed. Each battalion HHQ was filled out with eleven officers and 138 EM.

A battalion's firepower derived from its three rifle companies. A full rifle company had eight officers and 119 men[5] amongst an HQ section (CO, XO, three sergeants, three radiomen, three messengers, and five riflemen) and three platoons. Each platoon command post (CP) contained two lieutenants—one for each of two planes required to drop a platoon—a "platoon" staff sergeant, a "radio and code" corporal, a radio operator, a runner or two, and a medic (assigned from Regimental or Battalion HHQ). Two of a platoon's three squads were rifle squads of a dozen men each, led by a sergeant and assisted by a corporal. The third was a mortar squad with half a dozen men crewing a 60-mm mortar (with a range of 2000 yards). Each rifle squad carried a .30-cal. machine gun. The platoon CP kept two extras. Most of the riflemen carried M1 Garands; some had M1903 Springfields. Officers and support personnel carried M1A1 carbines; assistant squad leaders (usually corporals—who also did double duty as demolition men) had .45-cal. M1928A1 Thompson sub-machine guns, of which gangsters had been fond in the Roaring '20s.

Everyone carried the M1911A1 Colt .45-cal. pistol, a trench knife with brass knuckles grip (found to be useful in barfights as well as melees), a machete, a switchblade pocketknife (usually used for cutting away parachute lines), and as many hand grenades for which he could find room. Combined with helmet and liner, several days' rations, ammunition belts and/or bandoliers, change of underwear, first aid kit, leather gloves, mosquito netting, entrenching tool, canteen and mess kit, cans of foot powder, bug repellant and matches, a thirty-foot rope, a waterproof poncho, a pup tent side, perhaps a mortar or machine gun barrel (or in Turner's case, a Remington 5T Portable Typewriter strapped to his leg), a paratrooper bailed out of a Gooney Bird with at least eighty —and at times 100—pounds of equipment.

From Port Moresby, deuce and a halfs (also called "6 by 6s" for their three-axle drive capability) trucked the troops to Rigo Valley, at the foot of the Owen-Stanley Mountains. The nearby 5th Fighter Command HQ had just moved up from Cairns. The 503rd spent a week reviewing Japanese battle tactics and practicing their own in the steamy jungles surrounding Rigo Valley.

Kinsler's men got their first glimpse of what war in the South Pacific was going to entail. They soon found out New Guinea has the densest jungles on the planet, with ungodly climate, terrain, and pestilence to boot. For starters, one Australian summarized the seasons: "Summer—rains every day. Winter—rains all day." In short, the rain was never-ending. As another Australian saw it, "There was a carpet of swamp ooze…and the perpetual stench of vegetable decay." Trails were stinking rivers of mud broken up by slimy roots. Fungi and mold covered everything. George Clay recalled, "Even the water was full of fungus." He added, "In the tropics it was always hot. We were never NOT sweating. The flies were terrible." Another American claimed, "flies and mosquitoes regarded us as nothing but walking blood banks." Bug bites festered from continual scratching. The waving away of flying bugs became known as the "New Guinea salute." Besides the ubiquitous bugs, there were pythons in the trees and crocodiles in the water. MacArthur described the terrain, weather, and disease as "unrelenting," with "an unchanging cocoon of tropical heat." New Guinea, he said, would prove to be "as tough and tenacious an enemy as the Japanese."

Almost immediately, the better part of the regiment came down with "the GIs" (dysentery). George remarked, "In Port Moresby, everybody had dysentery—and I mean EVERYBODY!" Some men got tired of dropping their pants, so they cut out the backsides like BVDs. The 2nd Battalion leader, Maj. John Haltom, was among the sick, already suffering with malaria. To replace him, Kinsler had Jones once again take charge of his boys in the 2nd Battalion and moved Lt. Col. Joe Lawrie—another "mustang" officer, sporting an Errol Flynn mustache—up to XO. Lt. Col. John Britten took over 1st Battalion from Lawrie. Jack Tolson remained with the 3rd Battalion.

After Buna and Gona finally fell in January 1943, the American 41st and Australian 5th Divisions had taken over the push towards the Huon Gulf. They pressed against Salamaua, forcing Gen. Adachi to draw reinforcements from the Lae vicinity to the north, where the Markham River flows into the gulf, and from Finschhafen, farther around the gulf at the tip of the Huon Peninsula. Adachi had at his immediate disposal the 51st Division, three additional regiments, and a battalion of Imperial Marines, all under Maj. Gen. Ryoichi Shoge[6] and headquartered at Lae.

MacArthur viewed the situation at Lae as a perfect opportunity to display the proper use of vertical envelopment. He imagined dropping a battalion near Lae to cut the Japanese pipeline to and line of retreat from Salamaua. He alerted Col. Kinsler to prepare one battalion for such an action. Australian 7th Division's Maj. Gen. "Bloody George" (for his favorite adjective) Vasey, to whom the 503rd would be attached once they were on the ground, thought the whole regiment should be used.[7] MacArthur concurred and began planning with Brig. Gen. Ennis Whitehead, a WWI aviator and Deputy Commander of US Fifth Army Air Force. MacArthur ordered practice flights over the DZs for flight crews and told Kinsler to ready the regiment, not just a battalion.

Kinsler jumped at Vasey's idea to get his entire regiment into action. He made a recon flight around Lae on the thirtieth. A 3-D sand table mockup of the area for the paratroopers' action, constructed by Sixth Army's G-2 Intel section from maps and photos, appeared in the S-3 Ops tent. Platoons were brought in singly to study the terrain and learn their objectives. Actual names of hills, towns, and streams were replaced by letter and number codes (e.g., Village D-6, Hill 410) so that no details could be leaked. They went back into the jungles to rehearse their particular tasks. Equipment, weapon, and parachute checks began on September 1. Supply sergeants distributed food and water rations, ammunition, grenades, and first aid kits. On the third, Turner's thirtieth birthday, after typing up flight manifest lists for Service Company's planes and lending a hand to the supply sergeant, he spent the rest of the day much like the other men, drawing his rations, cleaning and sharpening his weapons, and laying out and packing his equipment. General MacArthur visited the camp; jumpmasters were assembled and told that if anyone refused to jump, to shoot them. George Clay wondered if he'd heard the order correctly. "We [jumpmasters] couldn't believe it." On the fourth, a Saturday, Father John Powers and Reverend Probert Herb held Communion Services. The paratroopers knew they were in for more than an exercise. The 503rd was going to be baptized through combat on Sunday.

At dawn, September 5, after *Reveille* at 0300, a bland breakfast of soggy pancakes, and a bumpy truck ride at 0430, the 1700 fittest men of the 503rd clanked across the perforated metal plates of Port Moresby's Ward and Jackson Dromes (airstrips). Many of them had to fall out and dig a hole along the way for yet another pit stop. Seventy-nine C-47 Skytrains of the 317th Troop Carrier Group (TCG), under Lt. Col. John Lackey, from Col. Paul Prentiss's 54th Troop Carrier Wing (TCW) were lined up. The General was there again, walking the line, talking to platoons as they gathered near their planes, sharing a cigarette here and there, joking, calming their jitters.

Several days previously, Col. Lackey's planes had made a

practice drop, in formation, at the prescribed altitude of 500 feet, thirty miles west of Port Moresby—with dummies strapped into parachutes. The practice run had come off without a hitch. Now, after strapping themselves into the parachutes laid out next to the planes, the real paratroopers climbed in with their eighty pounds of equipment per man. A dozen more C-47s were filled with supplies. Another five transports held thirty-some Australians and a couple 25-pound artillery pieces from the 2nd Battalion of the 4th Field (Artillery) Regiment, who were to follow in two hours. The Aussies, who volunteered for this mission, had received a one-week crash course in jumping and landing techniques but only one practice jump from a plane! Those injured in the practice jump were replaced by others who had none. The artillerists had broken down the guns, crated and bundled all the parts and ammo, and attached the bundles to the planes to be dropped, also by parachute, when they jumped.

Rain and fog delayed takeoff for three hours. Finally at 0825 the first plane was in the air. Within fifteen minutes all the C-47s were flying northeast parallel to the mountains. They flew in a "V of Vs" formation: nine planes forming an inverted "V" with a three-plane triangle at the vertex and each end. An air flotilla from eight airfields joined the Gooney Birds. Six squadrons of B-25 "Mitchell" bombers from Fifth Air Force (Maj. Gen. George Kenney—the same aviator who had surprised his wargame adversaries a couple years ago with the unorthodox air-landing in their rear) led the way. Half a dozen A-20 "Havoc" bombers immediately preceded the troop carriers. More than 100 fighters flew above and beside the bombers and transports. Generals Kenney, Vasey, and MacArthur were in B-17 "Flying Fortresses" high above the mix of 302 planes.

"There were so many planes," George Clay remembered. "One almost hit us and would have knocked us out of the sky. The pilot had to dive, and when he did, we all hit the ceiling. I almost went out the door—I was jumpmaster so I was right next to it. One of my friends got wounded right there. He didn't have his helmet on, hit his head, cut his arm...but he still wanted to go. So we patched him up. He got his Purple Heart before the jump."

The air armada crossed the Owen-Stanley range, followed the Watut River out of the mountains, and banked east at the Markham River. Its valley, some 250 miles northeast of Port Moresby, sprawled out before them between jungle-covered hills on its way to the Huon Gulf. Cold when they took off, the air was suddenly hot and balmy. Between the heat, anxiety, uncomfortableness, weight of equipment, unsettled breakfasts, and sporadic turbulence, many troopers got airsick. "Honey buckets" were passed around. The resultant stench got to others. MacArthur's plane lost an engine, and the pilot suggested they go back. How would that look, the General wanted to know, to these men who were about to make their first combat jump? The pilot stayed with the formation.

Up ahead of the C-47s, the B-25s were bombing the drop zones near the objective of the 503rd, the abandoned Nadzab Drome (where Amelia Earhart's Electra had last been seen just over six years ago), on the north bank twenty-five miles west of Lae. The A-20s, trailing the Mitchells and flying wingtip to wingtip, laid down a smokescreen over the DZs. The transports split into three columns, one for each battalion's DZ, and dropped down to 500 feet. Then they assumed the drop formation they had practiced: groups of six, thirty seconds apart, staggered back and upwards from left to right, so that every jumper would be below and could not get hung up in a following plane. At a quarter to ten, the pilots called out, "Get ready!" Cigarettes were crushed out, helmets buckled, and equipment checked. At nine after, the red lights came on. The familiar "Stand up! Hook up! Sound off!" rang out. "Stand in the door!" Each stick waddled toward the door at the rear of the plane. At 1022, the lights turned green, jumpmasters kicked out equipment bundles and yelled "Go!" Tolson, in the lead plane, was the first jumper in the PTO. The sticks did their quick shuffles and exits. Within four and a half minutes, the transports were empty, static lines plastered against the fuselages behind the doors by the prop wash, and on their way back to Port Moresby.

General Kenney saw General MacArthur "jumping up and down like a kid" in his Flying Fortress. MacArthur later recalled that "One plane after another poured out its stream of dropping men over the target field. Everything went like clockwork." This, the first parachute jump—and the only drop of an entire regiment —in the Pacific, was also the first completely successful airborne operation of WWII for either side, "the most perfect example of training and discipline" he'd ever seen. To his wife he would write, "It was a honey." Unfortunately, two troopers were victims of streamers and one fell from a tall palm tree at the edge of a DZ. Thirty-three more were injured falling onto abandoned vehicles, chunks of concrete, or splintered tree stumps around the airstrip.

George Clay, last out of his plane, got caught high in a tree. He successfully let himself down by tying his rope onto his harness while dangling from the parachute shrouds, then loosening the straps that held him in. Within fifty feet he came across one of his ammo carriers "cussing out someone in another tree. It was another ammo carrier, afraid to come out of the tree. We finally coaxed him down by reminding him he was an excellent target up there."

The 503rd pulled their rifles and Tommy guns out of "fiddle cases" (actually, padded canvas pouches) which had been strapped to their harnesses, put them together, and went to work on their assigned tasks. Britten's 1st Battalion had jumped directly onto the airstrip and began clearing it so Australian engineers could repair it and prepare for their 7th Division to come in. Jones's 2nd Battalion spread out to cover the western and northern flanks for protection against counterattack. Tolson's 3rd Battalion followed the Markham about three miles southeast, in the direction of Lae, and occupied the town of Gabmatzung, the site of a German Lutheran mission. Just as in rehearsal, patrols cleared the perimeter and platoons dug in to defend the airstrip. Not long after, the Australian cannoneers came down. It took them till the next day to find all the pieces to assemble their guns. Turner, Phillips, and their friends were kept busy as Service Company collected and stockpiled over fifteen tons of supplies dropped by C-47s and B-17s over the next two days.

Until now, paratroopers around "Gnat's Ass" had faced few of the Japanese Eighteenth Army soldiers who were supposed to be guarding the airfield but plenty of tropical heat and kunai grass—thick, razor-edged, and higher than the men's heads. Men who landed in it singly sliced through to each other with machetes to form small groups on the way to their assembly points. Two companies started shooting blindly through it at each other and wounded two men before Kinsler found out and put a stop to it. The engineers tried to burn it off the runways with flamethrowers and started a brush fire which burned up several hundred empty parachutes.

Sergeant Clay gathered his squad and started out. "That kunai grass was as high as this room. We had to take turns. A couple guys would chop for a while, then fall back, and someone else took over. We hadn't gotten more than another fifty feet before we came to a clearing. The Japanese had been there. There was a mortar there and a little cooking fire. We probably scared the [heck] out of them. They must have decided 'It's a SNAFU'[8] and were long gone!"

Doc Landes, with 3rd Battalion HHQ, was cutting his way through the grass with his machete and waded into another clearing. A young Japanese soldier emerged from the kunai grass on the other side. "We stared at each other a moment, then pulled our triggers. His gun went 'click.' Mine went 'bang.' I spent the next couple of hours throwing up. I had never killed a man. I knew he was the enemy, but I couldn't get past the thought of taking a human life."

The Americans got over their queasiness as they began to realize the kind of enemy with which they were dealing. I had asked my father, when I was eleven or twelve, how he could bring himself to shoot another man. "When you saw your buddies who'd been taken prisoner and tied to trees..." he started. His usually quiet voice steadily rose as he graphically but succinctly described how the helpless men had been tortured to death and their bodies mutilated. Finally, his voice cracked (one of only a couple times I remember it happening) and his watery eyes stared far off. After a pause he lowered his voice again. "It got easier." Not only were the reports they'd gotten of the barbaric Bataan Death March confirmed, but the Japanese had even resorted to cannibalism since the Navy had blockaded their supply lines. Inside the haversacks of dead Japanese were cooked strips of thigh meat and severed fingers.

The day before the jump, the recently arrived Australian 9th

Division (Maj. Gen. George Wooten) had boarded Higgins boats[9] at Milne Bay, sailed past Buna and Gona, crossed the gulf, and landed between Lae and Finschhafen on the peninsula. It was Australia's first amphibious landing since Gallipoli. Despite being immediately attacked by Japanese ground units and "Betty" bombers (several transports were hit with nearly sixty casualties), the Australians advanced towards Lae. The 7th Division, under Gen. Vasey, was to advance from the west once they were air-landed at the Nadzab Drome. Wooten and Vasey had a bet on who would be the first into Lae: twenty cases of whiskey.

An Australian pioneer (engineer) company and a Papuan infantry company had trekked sixty miles in a week from Tsili-Tsili, one of the forward Allied bases along the Kokoda Trail, south of Nadzab yet unknown to the enemy. The pioneers had taken boats down the Watut River on the way but had lost three boatloads of supplies and a man in rapids. Then they got several hundred native packers to help them through swamps and over mountains. They were able to watch the whole air show from beside the Watut before crossing the Markham and linking up with the paratroopers in the late afternoon. The pioneers worked all night and by morning had the 1500-foot runway ready for the arrival of a company of the US 871st Airborne Engineer Battalion. The 871st immediately pitched in with bulldozers brought in by C-47s. By sunset on the sixth, the 7th Division already had units of its 25th Brigade landing at Nadzab.[10] Within ten days, to accommodate the rest of Vasey's division, the Allied engineers built two parallel 6000-foot runways, comprised of perforated steel sheets, like those at Port Moresby, which would keep planes from sinking in the mud. The entire division was on the ground by the tenth, followed by another 420 planeloads of supplies and Aussies. Nadzab would become the main Allied airbase in New Guinea for the rest of the war.

General Blamey, upon landing with the 7th Division, set out after Vasey towards Lae and had Tolson's 3rd Battalion advance with them to cover the flank and rear. The 25th Brigade, with 3/503 alongside, soon reached the jungle-covered Finisterre Mountains north of Lae, where they battled the retreating Japanese 51st Division, which their general, Hidemitsu Nakano, had pulled out of Salamaua and Lae as the 9th Australian Division closed in from the east. Never expecting an attack from Nadzab, the 51st was effectively cut in half and trying to avoid encirclement. Deprived of a route of retreat through the Markham Valley, the Japanese attempted to slip through the jungle between Allied patrols, regroup in the mountains, and get out through the next valley.

A few paratroopers, in their first shootout, panicked at the sound of a Japanese knee mortar (actually, a small grenade launcher with a base plate), running haphazardly and crowding together. Tolson calmly but sternly called men by name and told them, "At ease, men." They settled down, and their two years or more of training kicked in. Frank Boginski, now the First Sergeant of 3rd Battalion HHQ, killed a Japanese hiding in a riverbed. The latter was a medical officer whose decorated doctor's bag full of instruments was put to use by the 3rd Battalion's surgeon. Clay's machine gun crew joined the action. "I saw my first friend get killed. Whitaker was his name. Then, I was given orders to set up my machine gun quick and cover the river. All of a sudden, my helmet got knocked off; I didn't have it hooked. It was that sniper up in a tree shooting at us that was the first Japanese soldier I saw. We shot the whole top of that tree off trying to get him. I went down by the water to check and saw another Japanese going in. At that time I had a carbine, so I emptied the whole clip—bang, bang, bang, bang—into his butt. And he kept going...."

Living on K-rations[11] up till now, the paratroopers got to partake of the Australians' corned "bully" beef and tea. As more of the Australian 7th Division arrived and marched toward Lae, they sang songs which the 503rd had learned in the Gordonvale and Cairns pubs. *It's a Long Way to Tipperary* and *Bless 'em All* were hold-overs from WWI. In the chorus of the latter, "Bless 'em all, bless 'em all, the long and the short and the tall," the Aussies substituted a four-letter word for "bless" which means pretty much the opposite. The verses of *Colonel Bogey's March* (later the theme song for the movie *Bridge on the River Kwai)*, when sung instead of whistled, described defects in the male anatomies of Nazi leaders. The Aussies' favorite, of course, was their future national anthem, *Waltzing Matilda*. Tom Turner accompanied the singing and regimental bands, when he was in the vicinity, on his harmonica from home or an ocarina he'd bought in Cairns.

Not all the troopers were delighted by the Aussies. One had decided to make his foxhole comfier. He dug it six feet wide, reinforced the walls, and added a floor so he could stretch out and stay dry when he slept. While he was out on patrol, an Australian company, marching by, thought it must be a "slit trench" (latrine). He came back to find his abode reeking and completely ruined.

On the thirteenth, the US 41st and Australian 5th Divisions took Salamaua.[12] The Japanese previously thought it was the Allies' objective but had been forced to thin the defense to reinforce Lae, MacArthur's true goal. On the fifteenth, the last of the air-landed Australian battalions began to relieve the paratroopers from their positions around "Gnat's Ass." When the two Australian pincers captured Lae on the sixteenth—Vasey won the bet by a couple hours because Wooten got stuck crossing a swollen river—the 3rd Battalion began pulling back to Nadzab. Company I had a final skirmish that lasted more than two hours before it could disengage. RHQ and the 1st and 2nd Battalions flew back to Port Moresby from their newly acquired airfield on the seventeenth. The 3rd Battalion followed on the nineteenth. Thirty-five hundred of the 10,000 Japanese around Lae had been killed or fatally wounded. Another 600 died of sickness or exhaustion during the retreat into the mountains. The cost to the 503rd was eight killed and twelve wounded, mostly in the 3rd Battalion, besides the jump casualties and twenty-six more on the sick list. The Salamaua-Lae operation in its entirety had cost the Japanese nearly 12,000 casualties, the Australians 1800, and the Americans close to 500.

The 503rd had passed its trial by fire. After-action reports for Operation Postern noted that the attack on Salamaua had been a successful diversion from the actual objective, Lae; the Air Corps had exhibited air superiority; accurate drops had achieved complete surprise; and within two hours of jumping, the paratroopers had achieved their objectives. MacArthur sent a unit commendation to Kinsler dated September 18 via courier:

NOW THAT THE FALL OF LAE IS AN ACCOMPLISHED FACT I WISH TO MAKE OF RECORD THE SPLENDID AND IMPORTANT PART TAKEN BY FIVE NOUGHT THREE PARACHUTE INFANTRY REGIMENT UNDER YOUR ABLE LEADERSHIP OFFICERS AND MEN EXHIBITED THE HIGHEST ORDER OF COMBAT EFFICIENCY STOP PLEASE EXPRESS TO ALL RANKS MY GRATIFICATION AND DEEP PRIDE

Since the awarding of small stars for combat jumps to be worn on the jump wings had not yet been authorized, Col. Kinsler had Combat Mission Certificates printed for each soldier. The October 15 issue of *Yank* ran a two-page spread of photos of the 503rd jumping into the smoke screen over Markham Valley "to block the escape of 20,000 Japanese who were faced by the Australian forces to the east." When Betty Dockter saw a copy of one of the photos in the newspaper alongside an article headed "Australians Set to Swoop on Airdrome," it was her first inkling that Tom had left Australia.

The lessons learned by the success at Nadzab coupled with the shortcomings in North Africa and Sicily refocused the Army's view of airborne operations. The "Swing Board" recommended, and the Army formed, additional TCGs as well as the 11th and 17th Airborne Divisions. It could now be assumed the threat of being dropped anywhere in large numbers would cause the enemy to disperse over a larger area. Airborne units were to be used for limited missions, not as regular line troops. They should be used for critical assaults, not "frittered away" as support troops. General Swing further recommended that the TCGs should be rehearsing between drops, not running supply. His final point, which MacArthur had proven, was the crucial need for joint planning and training.

To test the new operational doctrine, Gen. Marshall ordered a large-scale airborne maneuver: Swing's 11th Airborne Division was to capture the Knollwood Airport in North Carolina from Miley's 17th. The "Knollwood Maneuvers," in December 1943, convinced the brass that Gen. Swing's suggestions were sound and Operation Postern was no fluke. Division-sized drops would prove to be an important strategy on D-Day and later in the ETO. As Col.

Jones succinctly put it: "The [Nadzab] jump saved the Airborne effort."

As the Army revised and honed its Airborne operating and training manuals, Turner got his most undesirable job as Personnel Clerk. Officers he knew had him write condolence letters to the families of some of the fallen soldiers to accompany "The Army regrets...." telegrams. Doc explained why. "Your dad knew all those guys. He would always write something about their character —how funny or well-liked the guy was—or how his actions saved others' lives. It was always better than anything the officers could have written (even though the CO signed it), and something the families could hold on to." Tom felt lucky to be able to write to his own family that he was okay.

Now combat veterans, the 503rd could proclaim themselves, as had the Alamo Force and Diggers in homage to their brothers in North Africa, "Swamp Rats." For the next couple months the paratroopers resumed jungle training around muddy, infested, suffocating Port Moresby, welcomed their injured and sick friends who returned, and trained 350 incoming replacements for those who didn't (a cadre had returned to Gordonvale from Nadzab earlier to initiate them). Twenty-one-year-old Pvt. Arnold Williams and 2nd Lt. John Lindgren were two of the replacements. They had been in Camp Stoneman, fresh off the "cartoon" train from Fort Bragg and still awaiting further orders, when the jump at Nadzab was announced. "We knew then," Williams said, "that we would be replacements for the 503rd."

The regiment reorganized its battalion firepower. By adding newcomers to each company, an extra rifle squad was added to each platoon. This gave each platoon three squads of up to a dozen riflemen. Only one of the three squads would now have a light machine gun. The other two each had an M1918A2 "BAR" (Browning Automatic Rifle[13]) man as a more mobile machine gunner. One man in each squad carried the M1903 Springfield with a grenade launcher attachment (there were no bazookas until 1944). The extra machine guns, 60-mm mortars, and more new men were added to the battalion weapons sections, which now had three platoons of four .30-cal. machine guns and three platoons of 60-mm mortars (typically one platoon of each per company) as well as the 81-mm mortars. The centralization allowed the company commanders to request extra firepower from battalion HQ, or the battalion CO to amass firepower against strong points or to strengthen defensive weak spots.

In between jungle training forays, while they awaited their next combat alert, the troopers battled jungle rot, malaria, typhus, dysentery—throughout the war in the PTO, five men would be out sick for every man wounded in battle—and boredom. It didn't take long to get back to business as usual. George Clay and two buddies went to see a movie at the Fifth Air Force base. On the way back to the airborne camp, coming through woods, they smelled something cooking. "It was the mortar team with a stew pot. But that was just to cover up what they had cooking deeper in the woods—a still made of spare parts. So we ran and got our mess kits and came back and got some too."

The initiative in the war had shifted. The German battleship *Tirpitz* was crippled in a Norwegian fjord, and *Scharnhorst*—trying to intercept a Murmansk convoy—was sunk in the last engagement between battleships in the Atlantic. The RAF started bombing industrial towns on the Rhine, whose citizens now learned to endure what Londoners had already. Thanks to long-range aircraft and radar, the Allies had been able to sink as many

U-boats as had torpedoed Allied ships. The Russians, after stopping the last German offensive on the Eastern Front at Kursk, recaptured Kharkov and Smolensk. Italy surrendered. The papers announced that this would at long last release ships from the Mediterranean to the Pacific and the Atlantic. Italy's King Emmanuel had Mussolini arrested and turned over to the Allies. Almost as important (enough so to make the front page), crooner Frank Sinatra paid Tommy Dorsey $50,000 to buy out his contract, which would have given Dorsey and Sinatra's manager forty percent of his earnings over the next ten years as he went solo.

In October, Lt. Gen. Walter Krueger, now overall commander of SWPA's Sixth Army, sent his Inspector General (IG) to the 503rd camp. The IG interviewed several NCOs, other EM, and officers over several days. There were rumors throughout the camp that Col. Kinsler was perhaps going to be relieved, having lost the confidence of some of his staff and troops. Nicknamed "Eggshells" for having his ankles wrapped before each jump, Kinsler appeared more concerned with his own safety than the men's. It was felt by some that the training accidents in Australia could have and should have been avoided. Kinsler was also said to have kept his own CP well behind the Aussies' at Nadzab. The IG debriefed Col. Kinsler and left on the twenty-second. Kinsler had the XO and the battalion commanders to his HQ tent that night for a rare cocktail hour. After they left, he went into a nearby gravel pit and committed suicide.

When Lawrie found out the next morning, he notified Jones, the senior officer. General Krueger summoned Jones to his HQ on Goodenough Island, just north of Milne Bay and recently recaptured as well. Krueger, Prussian born, had emigrated to America when he was a small boy. He'd enlisted as a private in the

Spanish-American War. At the beginning of WWI, Krueger had been offered a post in the German army. He turned it down since he had his family and career in the United States, and by 1936 he had advanced to brigadier general. MacArthur had personally picked him to run Sixth Army. Krueger pointed out to Jones that he had been in the Army longer than Jones had been alive, and that future performance would dictate whether Jones would be promoted or relieved. Jones laconically remarked later, "To the point, eh?" The Warden now had full charge. He kept the regiment as sharp and healthy as possible for anticipated action.

The 503rd restructured its command while the Marines landed on Bougainville and Choiseul (including their 2nd Parachute Battalion, again amphibiously) at the western end of the Solomon chain. Now within striking distance of Rabaul, Gen. MacArthur launched an attack aimed at it. On December 22, the First Marine Division, having conquered and held Guadalcanal, landed at Cape Gloucester, the western tip of New Britain. The original plans called for the 503rd to capture nearby airfields, but Gen. Kenney told MacArthur that to get enough transport planes into New Guinea Territory, he'd have to move bombers back to Port Moresby and thereby lose their support. Even then he'd have to drop the paratroopers by companies at a time: contrary to Gen. Swing's recommendation, planes were already tied up flying supply. The drop the regiment had been preparing for was cancelled, but the Marines took the airfields anyway and contained Rabaul. Kenney's bombers destroyed Rabaul's sea and air power, effectively isolating its 100,000 defenders and all but taking it out of the war. Though never directly attacked, Rabaul was to be slowly strangled. It was one of those strongholds that MacArthur elected to let "wither on the vine."

In November, Kiev had been liberated. RAF bombers had finally reached Berlin. Churchill and FDR had met with Chiang Kai-Shek in Cairo and with Stalin in Tehran to discuss strategies. They appointed Dwight Eisenhower Supreme Allied Commander in Europe just before Christmas. A week later, US soldiers in Port Moresby found themselves paying an astonishing £20 for a bottle of whiskey for New Year's.

By now the 503rd was well-versed in the Army dictum, "Hurry up and wait!" In January 1944, Col. Jones requested of Gen. Krueger that the 503rd either be given an assignment or R and R in Australia. Gen. Krueger granted the latter; the 503rd left Port Moresby on January 25 aboard a British liner and the Liberty Ship, *John Carroll*.[14]

While the paratroopers sailed back to Australia dreaming about thick steaks, Cairns beer, and friendly young ladies, the Allies in Italy mistakenly assumed the Germans had garrisoned the historical abbey at Monte Cassino. They demolished it; the Germans took the cue and fortified themselves in the ruins. Admiral Nimitz attacked the Marshall Islands, even while the Marines were still slugging it out in Bougainville and New Britain. Generals Vasey and Wooten advanced up the Markham Valley and into the Huon Peninsula, scattering the last of the Japanese in Papua. The Australians and Japanese would continue to fight in New Guinea until the war ended. The 503rd would be back.

---

1 These two divisions and the 9th, originally trained for desert combat and sent to the Sahara, had been pulled out of the Mediterranean when the Japanese invaded New Guinea (the entire 8th Division had been destroyed or surrendered in Malaya). The 6th had had a hand in forcing the Italians out of Egypt and back into Libya before being sent to Greece. The 7th and 9th had held Tobruk until

Rommel gave up and moved on, leaving the siege to the Italians. (Tobruk only fell in June of 1942 on Rommel's second surge into Egypt after the Aussies were gone.) Later, the 7th had moved to Lebanon from where they put down a pro-Nazi coup attempt in Syria amid savage fighting with Vichy French. At El Alamein, the 9th had been dubbed "Monty's Secret Weapon" against the Afrika Korps. Having suffered heavy casualties, all three divisions returned to Australia. They were refitted, converted to jungle divisions, and sent to New Guinea. They were, in fact, the only Allied divisions to fight against all three Axis Powers.

2 Near the end of WWI, Eichelberger had been posted in Vladivostok to help a Czech army revive the Eastern front after the Bolshevik revolution. While there, he also worked with a large Japanese force which took over the East China Railway. Consequently, he had a better awareness than most of the Japanese military discipline and fighting skills.

3 S-designations (staff) were for brigade and smaller commands. Division and corps used G-designations (general). The latter had higher-ranking officers in similarly numbered positions: G-1: Personnel (and liaison between HQ and units); G-2: Intelligence (including cartography); G-3: Operations (plans and training); G-4: Logistics (materials, transport, medical); G-5: Planning (including military and civil impact); G-6: Communications. The higher organizations had additional sections: G-7: Training and Combat Engineers; G-8: Finance; G-9: Legal (Civil/Public Affairs).

4 When fully arrived—requiring a subsequent amphibious landing—the motor pool contained a sedan, thirteen jeeps, two ambulances, eight ¾-ton trucks, sixteen 2½-ton trucks, and fourteen 1-ton trailers.

5 These are the "authorized" numbers on the TO&E. Inevitable casualties and omnipresent tropical disease often resulted in much lower numbers in the field, especially in a protracted operation. Later, when the 503rd centralized its mortar platoons in the battalion HHQs and added an extra rifle squad to each company, a rifle company would top out at 137 enlisted men. On Corregidor, a half dozen companies came within ten men of this max. Most had quite a few less. Richard Winters said the 506th platoons (average for the ETO) had three rifle squads

AND a mortar squad each. Whether these mortar squads were organic to the platoon or the battalion, he did not specify. John Lindgren eventually referred to his mortar platoon as "the fourth platoon" of his company. So, even when the mortar squads became organic to the battalion, they were apparently still generally assigned to companies. Clearly, regiments reorganized their firepower as necessary to suit the environment and tactics.

6 Although a major outranks a lieutenant, a lieutenant general outranks a major general.

7 Airborne units came under various command control during an operation. They were under orders of the Theater or Army commander while on base, the Air Corps or Navy commander during transport, and finally the local ground force commander upon arrival.

8 Situation Normal: All [Fouled] Up.

9 Plywood, flat-bottomed boat which carried a platoon of men or a jeep and a squad. The front dropped down to become a ramp.

10 Originally, the Australian 7th Division was to be delivered by gliders. It would have been the only Pacific operation to employ gliders for troops. Vasey decided against it, due to the risk of crash-landings, so they came in on C-47s instead.

11 K-Rations had been tested in the California desert by troops on maneuvers. One "ration" contained three small packages (3" x 2" x 2") per day, marked for breakfast, dinner, and supper (not necessarily eaten in that order). A small round tin contained a few spoonfuls of meat, ham and eggs, spam, cereal, or pea soup. Wax paper or cellophane packs held biscuits, chewing gum, a chocolate bar, powdered coffee, cocoa, or fruit drink, a four-pack of Chesterfield cigarettes, or toilet paper. Supposedly providing 2800 kcals a day, men often threw away unpalatable portions, thus reducing the already minimal caloric intake. Deficient in calories, vitamins, and bulk, they were intended for no more than five days in a row. Troops on extended patrols or whose supply was slow went for weeks on K-Rations. Some of Merrill's and Wingate's men in Burma subsisted for as long

as five months on them and suffered severe weight loss. Some later threw up just at the sight of the packages.

12 This ended a grueling string of seventy-six consecutive days of combat for the 41st. Some of the men were wearing captured Japanese naval uniforms; their own had been torn to tatters in the jungle.

13 Turner said this powerful weapon seemed to have a stronger forward kick reloading than backward ejecting spent shells. The resultant recoil effect, he noted, was that "You felt like it was trying to drag you out of your foxhole!"

14 Cargo capacity 10,000 tons (e.g., 400,000 cases of supplies or 400 tanks). Crew of ninety Merchant Marine and Navy sailors. 900 soldiers could be reasonably accommodated on deck or between holds, though as many as 1500 were embarked at times. 2700 Liberty Ships were built during the war. 200 were lost. Many were sold after the war to other countries and shipping companies (thus Aristotle Onassis began his fleet). Others were repurposed—freight, storage, research ships, radar-picket duty, even a power plant in the Panama Canal Zone. Two hulls currently support floating docks in Portland, OR. Many were mothballed in Astoria, OR and Tarrytown, NY and eventually scrapped. Only two are operational today: *SS John W Brown* in Baltimore, and *SS Jeremiah O'Brien*, in San Francisco. Both are museum ships that occasionally put out to sea. Others, non-operational but still extant are: *Mary Cassatt*, used for storage in Vladivostok, and *Arthur M Huddell*, a maritime museum in Piraeus Harbor, Greece. The last one built, *Albert M Boe*, renamed the *Star of Kodiak*, is used by Trident Seafoods Canning as its HQ in Alaska.

Turner on his horse. Camp Wolters, Texas. March, 1941

Training squad, DI, staff. (Note WWI Leggings.)
Camp Wolters, Texas. 1941
Turner standing, second from the left.

Deep in the heart of Texas. 1941

The poster that started the journey. June, 1941

Jump Tower. Fort Benning, Georgia. 1941

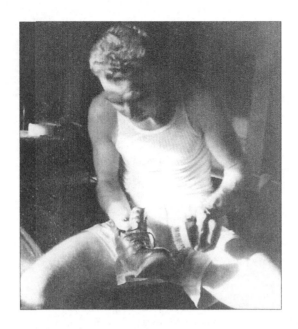

Shining his boots. Fort Benning. 1941

Tom and Betty. Albany, NY. January, 1942

Jump practice. Ft. Benning. July, 1942

United States Army
HEADQUARTERS 503D PARACHUTE INFANTRY
FORT BRAGG, NORTH CAROLINA

This is to Certify That:

Corporal THOMAS E. TURNER, 32043861, Service Company, 503d Parachute Infantry

has satisfactorily completed the prescribed course in Parachute Packing, Ground Training, and Jumping from a plane in flight. He is, therefore, entitled to be rated from this date, July 28, 1942 **, as a qualified Parachutist.**

KENNETH H. KINSLER,
Lt. Col., 503d Parachute Infantry,
Commanding.

Turner's "Diploma." Fort Bragg, NC. July, 1942

Tom's drawings sent to Betty from Ft. Benning. March, 1942

Last Furlough. Albany. August, 1942

Training maneuvers at Fort Bragg. Top: Sticks emplaning on
C-47s (75mm howitzers on loading ramp in nearest plane).
Insert: Attacking enemy foxhole.
Bottom: Rapid assembly after practice jump.
From Betty's scrapbook. September, 1942

The "Polluted Louse." November, 1942

Domain of 🜨 Neptunus Rex

To ALL SAILORS wherever ye may be
And to all Mermaids, Sea Serpents, Whales, Sharks and other Living
Things of the Sea, GREETINGS: Know Ye that on this Certain day
of Nov. 1942, in Lat. 00-00, Long. 361' W., there appeared within
our Royal Domain the U. S. A. T. 01 bound Southward for the Equator
and beyond. Be it REMEMBERED said Vessel, Officers and Crew
have been inspected and passed upon by Ourself and Royal Staff; and
Be It KNOWN by all Ye Sailors, Marines and Landlubbers who may
be honored by his presence that:—

Corp. Thomas E. Turner 32043861

having been found worthy to be numbered as One of our Trusty
Shellbacks, has been gathered to our Fold and initiated into the Solemn
Mysteries of the Ancient Order of the Deep. By virtue of the Power
invested in Me, I hereby Command All of My Subjects to show him
due honor and respect whenever he may enter our Realm.
Disobey this Order under penalty of Our Royal Displeasure.
Given under our hand and Seal this Certain day of Nov. 1942.

Davy Jones   NEPTUNUS REX
Royal Scribe.   Ruler of the Raging Main.

Soldiers' certificate (instead of sailors' tattoo) for crossing the
Equator. November, 1942

Original 503rd Wild Cat uniform patch by Disney.

Australian, Dutch Money (Invasion, Prewar)

Service Company HQ Section. Tom second from left front.
Max Phillips second from right front.
Cairns, Queensland, Australia. 1943

Central Hotel/Red Cross Canteen. Gordonvale, Queensland,
Australia. 1943

Tom, Bill Ryle, and unknown Aussie.
Cairns, Queensland, Australia. 1943

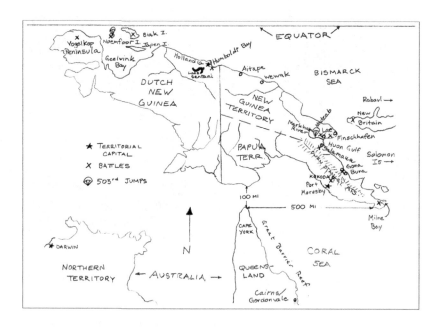

Northern Australia/New Guinea.

Chapter 7

HOLLANDIA
Netherlands New Guinea

The 503rd landed at Cairns on January 27, 1944, but so many men had malaria that the Army decided not to send them back to Gordonvale, which did not have adequate facilities for treatment but did have an aboriginal population that would be decimated if infected. The troops were rerouted to Brisbane and arrived there on February 2. Those who were not hospitalized settled into Camp Cable, twenty-eight miles from Brisbane. The US 32nd Division had trained for jungle warfare there alongside the Australian divisions before joining them in New Guinea. Originally called Camp Tamborine, it was renamed for Sgt. Gerald Cable, the first (and remarkably, only) casualty of the 32nd when they were torpedoed on the way there.

Surrounded by tropical forest, the 503rd sharpened their jungle combat skills at the Australian Jungle Warfare School at Canungra (now part of a national park). Their training involved forced marches, land navigation, more climate acclimation (as if it were possible), and amphibious exercises. They made their practice jumps—one on the Brisbane Golf Course to the ire of local duffers—and indoctrinated the newcomers who had joined them here or in New Guinea. Malarial fevers and jungle rot subsided, although many men would suffer from either or both for years. Col. Jones, good to his word, gave the men two-week leaves and weekend passes to Brisbane and the nearby towns. Hospital rolls decreased and regimental morale improved. Harold Templeman, a civilian from Iowa, was jump trained here by the 503rd and joined it as its Red Cross Field Director. He would be an integral part of the regiment from here on out as he set up canteens for each camp.

The Yanks also perfected Australian lingo used by their teachers. A "drongo," in actuality a tropical bird, was also slang for an idiot. A "scunger" loafed around, usually by the mess area hoping to scrounge some "tucker" (food). "Digger" came from their fathers' trench-digging at Gallipoli. A "bonzer little dame" was good looking. A "prawn" was not. "Blue" was a redhead. "Cobbers" were lifelong buddies, "Abos" were the local natives, and "doovers" were thingamajigs. The real deal was "fair dinkum," and "going troppo" was craziness brought on by the tropical heat.

The "bully beef" the Aussies had shared with the Americans was tinned corned beef. The name may have come from the French word *bouilli* (boiled) or the picture of a bull's head on Hereford tins. According to a small twenty-page paperback book of poems, *Memories of Moresby,* written and illustrated by an anonymous Aussie and picked up by Turner along the way, Bully Beef was leftovers from when "our Dads once fed upon it in the '14-'18 brawl."

Always on the lookout for another mascot, Service Company adopted a mongrel dog that hung around the camp. They named him Ripper. He had great fun accompanying them on hikes and runs, going from tent to tent looking for food scraps, or chasing the men into town. After a while the novelty wore off and Ripper became a nuisance. Putting him outside the camp was of no use. He just snuck back in. "One day," Tom Turner said, "we came back from a run, and we had to fight Ripper just to get a drink from the water tank and food out of our pockets. 'That's it,' I told the guys. 'I'll get rid of him.'" Tom procured a jeep from the motor pool, got Ripper in, and drove the jeep a few miles up into jungle-covered hills along a dirt track. "I let the dog go, turned around, and gunned it back down the hill. When I got back to camp, there was Ripper wagging his tail to greet me."

Half a world away, the 509th PIB, now commanded by Miley's old cohort Yarborough (Raff having moved into the 82nd Airborne Division), was at last being pulled out of the Anzio perimeter. With help from the Navy's big guns, they had fended off a massive German counterattack from the Gustav Line on Leap Year Day, saving VI Corps from collapse and thereby earning a Presidential Unit Citation. The 509th at that point had barely enough men left to fill one company. The 504th PIR, with an equally high casualty rate, accompanied them back to England to recoup and refit. The Marines had concurrently disbanded the 1st Marine Parachute Regiment, reasoning that they had only been used for amphibious assault and as regular infantry. It seemed inefficient and costly to expose the "Elite of the Elite" to prolonged battles and the consequent disproportionate casualties. The Army paratroopers at Anzio had good reason to agree with the assessment. The Marine paratroopers were reassigned to bolster diminished units. The Army's readied themselves for D-Day.

Early in April, the Allies bombed Budapest and Bucharest. Charles DeGaulle, who had led a French remnant in North Africa, was elevated to command of all Free French Forces. World renowned aviator Charles Lindbergh arrived on Guadalcanal. The Navy had "unofficially" (neither the President nor the Secretary of the Navy knew) sent him to the PTO as a civilian tech advisor to correct problems with the "bent-winged bird," the F4U "Corsair." He then flew a P-38 "Lightning" for the first time with the 5th Fighter Command, now based at Nadzab. He reckoned that P-38s could add 400 miles to their range and keep up with bombers by reducing RPMs, setting a leaner fuel mixture, and increasing manifold pressure. To prove his theory, he flew with sorties as far as Geelvink Bay in Dutch New Guinea, over 800 miles from Nadzab. Although never authorized as a military pilot, and probably the only one called "Mister" rather than "Sir," as an "observer" he once found himself caught up in a dogfight and shot down a Mitzubishi 51 "Sonia" that had outmaneuvered a pack of Lightnings. He flew straight at it, let go a machine gun burst, and pulled up just as the Sonia, spewing smoke, rolled over. In another dogfight he escaped from a Zero on his tail with a last-second high-speed turn.[1]

The 503rd received orders to move out. After tearing down and packing up the camp, they left Australia for the last time, from Brisbane, on April 8. A rock monument marks the old entrance to Camp Cable with a plaque inscribed: "U.S.A. Camp Cable. They passed this way. 1942-1944." The ship[2] stopped at Cairns on the ninth to take on supplies. On the fourteenth, the 188 officers and 2400 EM in the 503rd arrived at Milne Bay, New Guinea Territory. They debarked on the sixteenth at Oro Bay, 200 miles further up the coast. After their 2000-mile cruise, they got their first ride on "ducks" (DUKWs[3]) to get to their campsite farther around Cape Sudest in the Buna-Gona-Dobodura area, from where the joint advance on Lae had started. It was now completely in Allied hands; the 1st Cavalry Division had just left the camp. The 503rd was to be in Sixth Army's reserve for the next impending operation.

Now that the Bismarck Islands, and Rabaul in particular, were neutralized, MacArthur planned to get into Netherlands New Guinea. Operation "Reckless," the next stage of Cartwheel, involved another two-pronged attack. Eichelberger's I Corps, comprised of the veteran 41st and 32nd Divisions and untried 24th Division (although two of its regiments had been stationed on Oahu and had suffered casualties in the Pearl Harbor attack), set sail from Finschhafen and Goodenough Island on American and Australian ships of Task Force 77. This was part of Vice Admiral (V.Adm.) Thomas Kinkaid's Seventh Fleet, which, like Fifth Air Force and Sixth Army, MacArthur directly controlled. Kinkaid was headed for Hollandia, a large Japanese supply and staging base in Humboldt Bay, a few miles west of the border between Australian and Dutch New Guinea. West of Hollandia (now known as Jayapura) is a short coastal range, the Cyclops Mountains, with Tanahmerah Bay at the opposite end. At the inland base of the mountains is Lake Sentani and between them at the time lay three airdromes and the Japanese Second Army (Gen. Fusataro Teshima) headquarters. Kenney's bombers had begun blasting the beaches and airfields around Humboldt Bay on March 30 from their new bases at Nadzab 500 miles away. They destroyed 400 enemy planes on the ground or in the air. The USN's Fast Carrier Task Force 58 (V.Adm. Marc Mitscher) sank or scattered Japanese supply ships and troop transports, and took out another 150 planes on nearby islands. Never again would the Japanese air force pose a threat in New Guinea. Task Force (TF) 77 bypassed the Japanese

Eighteenth Army, still holed up in the Finisterre Mountains and their strong point at Wewak, and landed 30,000 men at dawn of April 22 in the bays on either end of the Cyclops Mountains. The amphibious assault surprised the garrison of 10,000 or so in and around Hollandia such that they disappeared into the interior. A simultaneous landing at Aitape between Wewak and Hollandia by 20,000 more of Eichelberger's GIs stymied a counterattack from the east.

Upon arriving in Dobadura, the 503rd was alerted to jump onto and hold the three airfields, but the infantry captured them by the twenty-sixth, so quickly that Royal Australian Air Force (RAAF) engineers were already working on them, and the drops were cancelled. The paratroopers "hurried up and waited" in the Dobodura mud for another month before being air-lifted to the rebuilt Cyclops Drome on the morning of May 30. They flew over their previous objective, the Nadzab Drome, on the way. The 503rd moved into Hollekang Camp, southeast of Hollandia on Humboldt Bay, and put up their tent city. The Army had started to furlough some of the longest-serving men back to the States. By mid-May, the ranks of the 503rd were depleted by the first rotation of fifteen officers and a little over a hundred men.

The rest waited for furloughs (which for most never came) and guarded supply dumps, Gen. Krueger's HQ, and the airfields as the engineers worked on them. They patrolled the hills, streams, and swamps around Hollandia. The dense jungles made lugging mortars, machine guns, and ammo difficult. Shooting machine guns directly through the jungle and mortars indirectly through the thick treetops was nearly impossible. Despite the handicaps, the patrols went as far as 150 miles back into New Guinea Territory to keep Adachi's Eighteenth Army bottled up between Lae and

Hollandia and to deny a linkup with Teshima. Most of the Japanese that they came across were starved and diseased and put up little resistance.

The weather was familiar to the patrolling Nadzab vets—hot, humid, and rainy. Along with the kunai grass were swamps full of crocodiles and mosquitoes, the latter guaranteeing almost everyone suffered from malaria or dengue fever. Ever-present lice added typhus. According to Andy Amaty, "You couldn't do anything to get away from the bugs." Turner concurred: "They were in your eyes, your ears, your nose, your mouth. If you tried to eat a ration or a bite out of a mess kit, they were in it before you could get to it." Some men tried eating underneath ponchos. Nothing worked.

Of the rain, Turner said, "It would be pouring rain one minute, and the sun out blazing the next. Either way you were up to the tops of your boots in mud." Foxholes filled with water as fast as they were dug. Tommy guns and rifles got jammed with mud. Turner wrote home to his fiancée, "This war is 10% enemy and 90% elements." It is amazing that Betty received that much information, given that all correspondence since leaving Ft. Bragg had been censored. Each letter was stamped "Censored" in a lower corner and signed by an officer. Any pertinent information which the enemy could use if captured had been snipped out. Betty once noted that "Tom's letters looked like doilies by the time I got them."

In between patrols, Turner had been typing up the daily morning—or "moaning"—announcements for the camp, as he had previously in Australia and Port Moresby. He passed them on to Doc Landes, who would then read them over the PA system. Doc added with a grin and a twinkle in his eye, "I always tried to inject a little humor by telling a story...eh, not always clean...here and there." Ingrid Bergman made her first of two appearances in *Yank*. Sad Sack was in trouble yet again. A captain chastised him for not saluting while he dug his foxhole. Then, after saluting a never-ending parade of lieutenants, he got bawled out by the sergeant for not finishing the hole.

One day Tom got new orders from RHQ: he was reassigned from company clerk to "armorer" and traded his portable Remington for a .45-cal. Thompson. He would now make sure every man was armed to the teeth and every weapon had a stockpile of ammo. His general knowledge of firearms extending back to the black powder cap-and-ball era came in handy as he stripped, cleaned, and un-jammed anything that could be used in combat by the battalion. If he couldn't refurbish it, he replaced it. Somehow, he managed to find and finagle a deal for a Colt .45 "Peacemaker" revolver, which he would eventually use in battle and bring home.

Operation Reckless turned out to be a low-intensity way to break in the replacements, who had quickly learned another axiom: Army life was "months of boredom interrupted by moments of terror." In their month of patrolling, the 503rd miraculously had only one man wounded in action, and twenty down with tropical fevers. They had killed fifty-six Japanese and captured twelve (eleven of whom turned out to be slave laborers from Formosa). I Corps losses were 150 killed and 1050 wounded. Japan had lost over 3300 killed and 600 captured. Thousands more fled to the west. Hollandia and Humboldt Bay were denied to the Japanese for supplying and reinforcing New Guinea and instead provided a major naval and air base for the Allies. Fifth Air Force moved up again, from Port Moresby. MacArthur reminisced that "The

Hollandia invasion initiated a marked change in the tempo of my advance westward.... I was now determined to reach the Philippines before December."

1 Lindbergh was shunned at the beginning of the war by the government, and FDR in particular, for his anti-interventionist stance (he had been the spokesman for the isolationist America First Committee) and some racially charged remarks. He had resigned his Air Corps Reserve commission after a Presidential rebuke. By 1944 they had all changed their tunes. Although FDR had refused to reinstate him even after Pearl Harbor, Lindbergh had test-flown every combat plane available. He would spend the next few months with the 475th Fighter Group, which had escorted the 503rd to Nadzab and would continue to do so in campaigns yet to come.

2 Some said a Dutch liner, the SS *Van der Lijn,* others said the US transport *Sea Cat.* Maybe both.

3 General Motors nomenclature: D—1942; U—Utility; K—All-wheel drive; W —Dual rear axles. Built with a steel hull on a 6 by 6 chassis, this amphibious vehicle carried twenty-five men and could go fifty mph on land and five and a half knots in water. Some had a mounted .50-cal. machine gun.

Chapter 8

NOEMFOOR
The 3000 Thieves

The General pushed Krueger's Alamo Force relentlessly to the west. Even before Reckless was finished Operation "Horlicks" began. MacArthur saw Biak Island in Geelvink Bay, 325 miles to the northwest of Hollandia and with three more airfields, as the next steppingstone to the Philippines. Also from Biak, he proposed to eliminate the enemy on the Vogelkop (Bird's Head) Peninsula at the western end of New Guinea. On May 27, just days after the Allies broke out of the Anzio beachhead, and while GIs all over the United Kingdom were betting on what date Ike would give the "go" for D-Day, two regiments of the 41st Division which had been pulled out of Hollandia landed on Biak. The first tank battle of the PTO occurred when Japanese *Ha-Go* ("third model") tanks counterattacked the beachhead and Sherman M4 tanks rushed ashore to destroy them.

Except for the brief foray of the Ha-Gos, this garrison remained well dug-in and tenacious. The island's commander, Col. Naoyuki Kuzume, had deduced that beach defense was useless and had withdrawn his 11,000 men inland. Here the attack bogged down, requiring the flushing out of "coral catacombs"—reinforced positions built around interconnected caves, a system at which Japanese defenders would become more adept. The reserve regiment of the 41st Division was called into Biak, and the division's CO, still unable to advance, was relieved. Eichelberger took over, like he had at Buna. It was rumored that the 503rd would jump in as well, to break the stalemate. They prepared as usual: checked chutes, drew rations and ammo, cleaned their weapons, studied the sand table model, and practiced their objectives.

The 503rd stood down when the first of Biak's airfields was finally captured on June 7. Later the same day, Allied forces in northern Europe moved inland from the Normandy beaches and, in southern Europe, marched through Rome. Within a week, Betty would find amid all the D-Day articles one from United Press, an interview with paratrooper Chaplain Raymond Hall. Laconically describing the battle for Carentan, which involved the 101st Airborne (having already lost, as had the 82nd, 1200 men on D-Day), Hall said, "It's [heck] down there; I know because I've been with those kids...." Stretcher bearers confirmed that "the Parson" stayed in the front lines, holding arms and legs together and injecting morphine as the medics and doctors worked on wounded men.

Other headlines halfway through June said that the US Fifth Fleet[1] (V.Adm. Raymond Spruance), having recaptured the Solomon, Gilbert, and Marshall Islands, had its own D-Day by landing three divisions in Saipan. In response, the IJN launched Operation *A-Go* to stop the invasion of the Mariana Islands. The Japanese Mobile Fleet (V.Adm. Jizaburo Ozawa) had five battleships and nine carriers with 450 planes aboard, but was mismatched. Admiral Spruance had seven battleships, fifteen flattops, and twice the number of Ozawa's destroyers and planes. Ozawa was counting on 300 island-based planes as well, but preliminary bombing had destroyed most of them. Furthermore, few of Japan's remaining pilots had adequate training and experience, so the results of dogfights around the fleets were the opposite of those on Luzon. American pilots and AA crews shot down all but fifty of the enemy planes while losing only 130 of their own—and eighty of those had run out of gas returning from an evening scramble and had to ditch in the water or crash on the decks. It was so one-sided that the fliers would dub the Battle of the Philippine Sea "The Marianas Turkey Shoot." Thus deprived of protection, three of Ozawa's carriers were sunk before he withdrew.

Meanwhile, Gen. Eichelberger found out the reason for the standoff: he radioed Gen. Krueger that supplies and reinforcements were coming to Biak nightly from the Vogelkop Peninsula via Noemfoor Island, seventy-five miles to his west. MacArthur agreed with Krueger that Noemfoor must be taken, and they planned Operation "Table Tennis." A task force, codenamed "Cyclone," was comprised of the 158th "Regimental Combat Team" (RCT)—like the 503rd, an independent unit attached where necessary. A combat team had its firepower augmented by attaching more units to the infantry: in this case, an artillery battalion, a tank platoon, two anti-aircraft battalions, and several engineer companies. Australian and American aviation engineer battalions and even forty civilian Dutch administrators were included. An Engineer Boat and Shore (landing craft) regiment would carry them to the beaches. The 503rd and the 34th IR, recently detached from the 24th Division to reinforce the 41st on

Biak, formed Cyclone's reserve. This gave the Cyclone Task Force commander, Brig. Gen. Edwin Patrick, 8000 combat troops and 5500 service troops.

Noemfoor looks like a catcher's mitt, similar to Michigan, with the thumb (the Broe Peninsula) on the right. It is fourteen miles long and eleven wide. It has sandy beaches on the north end, and flat terrain from there to the midsection where it becomes hilly, as high as 650 feet, with cliffs along the southern coast. Coral reefs surround the island. Except for the beaches, it is covered in jungle, with mangrove swamps at several inlets. A few thousand natives, some of them cannibals, lived in jungle villages near the coast at the time.

The Japanese Army had occupied Noemfoor in December 1943. They brought in 3000 Formosan and Indonesian[2] slave laborers to build airdromes. Kornasoren Drome was near the north central coast, Kamiri the northwest, and Namber the southwest. The latter two were nearly completed. The Dutch had done nothing to develop the island, and advance Alamo scouts confirmed there were few roads larger than foot trails. G-2 (Division HQ's Intelligence Section) estimated 3200 defenders from the Japanese 36th Division, largely the 219th Regiment, and some from the 222nd who got stuck on the way to Biak.

As early as April, Fifth Air Force, flying out of Nadzab (and accompanied by Lindbergh), had begun preliminary bombardment. By June 20, when Biak was finally secured and its airfields patched up,[3] the RAAF No. 10 Operational Group and five attached US Army Air Force (USAAF) fighter and bombardment groups stepped up the pace, eventually dropping a total of 800 tons of explosives and napalm on Noemfoor. Colonel Jones received orders to put the paratroopers on alert June 28. A shortage of landing craft and the assumption that Noemfoor's airfields would not be ready for air-landing (full of craters and wrecks) meant the 503rd would be jumping if they were needed at all. The regiment moved to a temporary camp on the Ebeli Plantation, close to the Hollandia Drome. They strung up jungle hammocks covered with tarps in a cocoa grove for napping between patrols and preparations.

Two battalions of the 158th (Col. J.P. Herndon) traveled a day and two nights in forty LCMs[4] from VII Amphibious Force (Rear Admiral Daniel Barbey) escorted by American and Australian warships from TF 74 and TF 75. Twenty-one destroyers, cruisers, and rocket launching LCIs[5] opened up on the approach reefs and landing beaches for an hour before the assault on July 2. When they stopped, a last run of bombers went in, just before the LCMs came through the reefs at 0800.

The landings were unopposed. The beachfront defenders were dead or stunned. Only an hour later did mortars behind the ridges finally start to zero in on the Cyclone Task Force, but they were quickly silenced by naval fire, and by then the invaders already controlled the Kamiri Drome. A prisoner said that 3000 reinforcements had arrived recently. This led Gen. Patrick to believe he would have a tough time holding Kamiri while trying to capture the other airfields, so he radioed Gen. Krueger to request the 503rd. There were only thirty-eight C-47s available, enough to drop just one battalion. All the others were flying supply for the Air Force. Krueger immediately radioed Jones to get a battalion ready to go in each of the next three days.

The Warden had left nothing to chance. He had ordered 2200 new parachutes. They'd been delivered from Gordonvale on July 1. Equipment had been checked and replaced by Service

Company where necessary. G-2 had sand table models built of Noemfoor, and Jones held briefing sessions with maps, photos, and lectures. He and the battalion commanders flew recon flights over the drop zone at Kamiri. He had the C-47 pilots practice their "V of V" flights, which they had not flown since Nadzab, with jumpmasters aboard. After they landed, he had the doors removed, the doorways taped (some troops—my father included—had previously sliced their hands on the rough metal edges), and thirty-eight trucks numbered with chalk. Each man was assigned to a truck and its like-numbered plane to facilitate loading up.

As the camp methodically scrambled to get ready, the S-2 section looked for interpreters from amongst the Japanese-Americans. George Kojima, like many other Nisei, had enlisted in the Army to get out of the Relocation Camps. He was a machine gunner in Second Battalion's weapons section. The S-2 officer called him in. Their short conversation went something like:

S2: "Kojima?"

GK: "Yes, sir."

S2: "You're Japanese?"

GK: "Yes, sir."

S2: "Do you speak Japanese?"

GK: "No, sir."

S2: "Do you understand Japanese?"

GK: "No, sir."

S2: "Kojima, you're the dumbest [Japanese] I know. Get out of here!"

GK: "Yes, sir." [6]

Koshi "Andy" Ando, a Nisei who was able to answer all the questions in the affirmative, got the interpreter's job.

At 0500 on July 3, the numbered trucks carrying Col.

145

Jones, 1ˢᵗ Battalion (Maj. Cameron Knox) and parts of RHQ and Service Companies arrived at the Cyclops Field beside Lake Sentani. The men examined their parachutes, strapped them on, and pushed and pulled each other into the planes at 0605. The transports were in the air by 0630, and after grouping over Humboldt Bay and being surrounded by their escort, the "Vs of Vs" headed for Kamiri Drome on Noemfoor. Only then did a message come from Gen. Patrick to Hollandia (although he'd been aware of the jump since the previous day) that because of equipment and vehicles still on the runway, the planes should come in single file. They had been ordered to assume a double file for the drop. Also, the pilots in the lead planes had neglected to compensate for the island's altitude, so that the jumps were about to be made from 175 feet—the lowest parachute jump ever recorded—instead of the planned 300 feet. Even planes close behind in the stair step formation were well below 300 feet. In the event of a streamer, a man would hit the ground before his backup chute could deploy.[7] Col. Jones thought they looked too low but brushed it off as an optical illusion.

The first men went out the doors at 1005. Their chutes were barely open before they started crash landing on what one diarist described as "no field at all but a pocked coral strip strewn with wrecked Japanese equipment, blasted stumps, and US trucks and Alligators [tractors] of the initial landing force." Many of those who missed the mud-covered coral runway banged into those obstacles at the edges of the drop zone.

Consequently, seventy-two of the 739 men in the first drop had injuries, including Jones's radioman and half the men in his plane. Maj. Knox broke a foot. So did Captains Donovan and Rambo. The two captains propped their legs up and attended to what duties they could at RHQ. The major required evacuation, along with thirty others whose injuries were so severe as to preclude them from future jumps. Col. Jones hit his head on the rock-hard runway. The layer of mud and his helmet saved him from a crushed skull. Even at that he had a headache for a week. He never reported it.

George Clay barely missed becoming an early casualty. He jumped holding his machine gun, avoided the obstacles, but came down into a water-filled bomb crater. "The weight of my machine gun and extra ammo would have drowned me," he recalled at a reunion, "except the wind grabbed my chute and pulled me out of that hole." Other men got hung up in tall palm trees beyond the DZ. Tom Turner missed the trees and trucks, but remembered that "the mud just about sucked the boots off my feet."

To get into action more quickly, most of the men had abandoned using the "fiddle cases," simply strapping their rifles and Tommy guns to their legs with cleaning patches in the muzzles to keep out the mud. Despite the injuries and close calls, 1st Battalion scrambled in the mire and muck, relieved 1/158, set up headquarters and supply areas, and secured the perimeter around Kamiri Drome before nightfall.

At 0950 on Independence Day, the 3rd Battalion (Maj. John Erickson) and the rest of HQ and Service Companies jumped. Altimeters had been recalibrated, Krueger had ordered Patrick to clear the runway, and the 54th TCW flew over in single file. There were fifty-six more injuries out of 685 jumpers anyway, some of these because of just-installed steel runway plates.

The regiment already had nearly ten percent casualties, with several company commanders and veteran noncoms out of action, without a fight! Jones called Patrick and asked that the 2nd

Battalion be flown into the Kamiri Drome as soon as it was serviceable. Gen. Krueger didn't want to wait for airfield construction and consequently ordered 2/503 to be flown from Cyclops Drome to Biak Island and then to be ferried to Noemfoor by LCIs. They would not arrive for another week. Had Patrick requested the 34th Regiment as backup in the first place, they could have been delivered overnight, since they were already formed up on the beaches of Biak. The 503rd would have been spared 128 jump casualties. Two more were killed on Biak when they zealously joined the 34th for a firefight against Japanese holdouts. Regardless, Gen. Krueger was impressed with Jones's preparation, promptness, and doggedness. Krueger approved his full colonel's eagle.

Later that day, 3/158 captured Kornasoren Drome. The RAAF 10th Operational Group started landing planes there. During the night, 1/158, which moved out after the 503rd relieved it, surrounded a large overgrown Japanese garden planted around a hill near the village of Kamiri. The Japanese 219th was entrenched there and offered resistance. Mortars and howitzers pulverized the hill and garden, yet the Japanese counterattacked on the fifth. Four hundred of the enemy were killed. The rest fled. Only a few individual Japanese planes tried to attack, with minimal results.

General Patrick found out from a prisoner that the Japanese had abandoned Namber Drome, so he had his 1st Battalion occupy it. On July 6, his 2nd Battalion landed in Roemboi Bay near Namber Drome and relieved the 1st. Simultaneously, a detachment of 2/503 landed on tiny Manim Island, three miles out in the bay, to install a radar tower. In a short skirmish to take out a pillbox, one paratrooper was wounded while eight Japanese were killed. On the same day, a squadron of RAAF P-40 "Warhawks" landed at

148

Kamiri Drome. Namber Field would soon be abandoned as too far gone to salvage, but Kornasoren would become home to squadrons of P-38 night-fighters and B-24 "Liberators" before the end of July. From there the bombers would begin attacking oil facilities on Borneo and the last of the Japanese positions in western New Guinea.

The two regiments began patrolling south and east from their perimeters around the airdromes. It became a game of chasing the Japanese, led by their colonel, Suesada Shimitzu, across the island. As on Biak, the defenders retreated into the hills and their prepared defenses. On July 10, Patrick decided that the 158th would clear the northern half of Noemfoor and the 503rd the southern half. The 158th, with all its inherent firepower—its tanks and artillery had already been landed by LSTs[8]—drew the lighter of the assignments. The 503rd was given only one battery of 155-mm howitzers, Battery A of the 147th Field Artillery Battalion, to augment its firepower and would come up against the most resistance in the worst terrain. The reason for Patrick's previous reassignment from General Staff back to field command was becoming apparent.

Back in New York, where dawn of the tenth would break fifteen hours later than it had in Dutch New Guinea, a headline in the Albany *Knickerbocker News* (later glued to a page in Betty's scrapbook) read: "Saipan's Fall Opens Road to Tokyo." Admiral Nimitz, the article went on to say, announced that the US now had a base within B-29 range of Japan and the Philippine Islands. Another article told of "robot bombs" (radio-controlled V1 "Vengeance" rockets) destroying the Guards Chapel at Wellington Barracks in London.

At midnight in Biak, while Americans read yesterday's

headlines, 2/503 (Lt. Col. John Britten) embarked on LCIs of VII Amphibious Force and landed in Roemboi Bay at 0930 of the eleventh. After contacting 2/158, they patrolled due east and, by the thirteenth, reached the village of Inasi on Broe Bay.

As the paratroopers spread out by squads along native paths and chopped through kunai grass and thick tangled jungle vines, they ran into pockets of Japanese troops who fought fanatically and refused to surrender. It took hours to carry paratroop casualties out of the jungle and hills. Supply to and communication with forward units was all but impossible: the SCR 536 walkie-talkie signals could not penetrate the jungle or hills and were basically useless without a clear line of sight. Col. Jones resorted to flying over in a Piper L-4 "Grasshopper" (the military variant of the "Cub" used as an artillery spotter plane) to keep track of his companies, and at times, to drop ammo, food, medical supplies, and even messages.

As night fell the troopers dug foxholes and set up machine guns with overlapping fields of fire while the jungle turned pitch black. Anything that moved before dawn was fired upon. Passwords involved "Ls"—"Silly Tilly" or "Eleanor Powell"—difficult for the Japanese to pronounce. One held his tongue, tried to ignore the stench of the rotting jungle and the unburied dead, gave endless New Guinea salutes to flies, and heard natives' dogs eating bodies, all the while waiting for his turn for a short, fitful sleep.

Turner was leading a Service Company patrol one day, bringing supplies forward, when his squad met a Japanese squad. Everyone dove off the trail and started shooting. What Japanese weren't killed melted back into the jungle. Turner counted heads and came up one short. Fearing the worst, he was about to send the men out to search when the missing trooper appeared. "Where the

[heck] were you?" snapped Turner.

"Geez, Tom," pleaded the younger man, "I had to take a leak!"

After a firefight on another day, a Japanese survivor bolted out of the bushes onto a trail in front of Turner and took off running. Turner's Tommy gun jammed, so he pulled the Peacemaker out of the cut-down holster he'd made and started after the man, shooting as he ran. Trying to reload on the run, he tripped on a root and dropped his handful of .45 shells. As he knelt to pick them up, he simultaneously cursed his misfortune and prayed the soldier would not turn around. The prayer was answered.

Machine gunner Kojima, the Nisei who had the brief S-2 interview before the battle, was covering one flank of a patrol advancing up ahead. He, like mortar crewmen and artillerymen, was a prime target for the enemy. A Japanese knee mortar round (grenade) landed and exploded at his feet. His legs went numb, so he hollered for a medic. Someone nearby called to him, "Hey, George, you get a homer?" The baseball jargon implied that one had an injury bad enough to warrant evacuation back to the States. His legs were indeed crippled, relegating George to a wheelchair for the rest of his life.

On the thirteenth, the 1st Battalion was attacked from a hill simply numbered "670" on the maps, five miles southeast of Kamiri Drome in the central western area. Cpt. John Rucker, whose C Company was already reduced by jump casualties and earlier skirmishes, thought from the volume of fire coming from rifles, machine guns, and mortars on the hill, that there must be 400 enemy soldiers up there. A POW taken later said it was more like 1200. Companies A and B came up into the line and the battalion entrenched around the north side of the hill. Battery B, which had replaced Battery A, helped the advance by taking out machine gun emplacements. It still took two days for Maj. Robert "Pug" Woods, who had taken over for the evacuated Knox, to battle to the top. The defenders had disappeared.

A week later, Shimitzu popped up again, this time near Inasi, where he cut off a platoon of D Company, 2nd Battalion. Sgt. Roy Eubanks's squad was dispatched to cut through to them. When they came under fire, he and a couple scouts (point men) crawled forward to within a few yards of the enemy, stood up, and opened fire. He charged the position firing a BAR but was knocked down and his weapon wrecked by return fire. Badly wounded, he got up and bludgeoned four more soldiers with the broken gunstock before he finally collapsed. Men said there were twenty bodies around Roy's. His action drew the attention away from the surrounded platoon long enough to allow them to return to the company. It also earned him a posthumous Congressional Medal of Honor, the first for the 503rd. Still, when this battle concluded, they found only forty-five dead Japanese. Shimitzu, like the Swamp Fox against the British, had run away to fight again.

The game of cat and mouse continued into August. On the tenth, Erickson's G Company came upon Shimitzu's men in another well-prepared position on "Hill 380", between Inasi and the southernmost village of Menoekweri. After a daylong firefight, a morning barrage from the howitzers and mortars, and a bombing run by B-25s from Kornasoren, the paratroopers charged up the hill. Just like last time, the Japanese were gone with a few casualties left behind. Company H pursued Shimitzu, but he had dug in again and repelled them. Company H retreated to Hill 380 and followed another barrage down the hill the morning of the thirteenth. Besides more Japanese casualties, Company H found three of their buddies who had been butchered.

The Japanese, as before under constant pressure from the US Army, Navy, and Air Corps, were suffering from lack of supply, and again turned to cannibalism. A captured surgeon admitted to Andy Ando, the S-2 interpreter, that he had shown his men how to carve the flesh. Gen. Patrick could not believe it until Col. Jones sent him photos, Japanese rucksacks, and even some of the bodies. The atrocities perpetrated upon the GIs captured by the Japanese did not abate either, to the point where it became nearly impossible to get the men to take prisoners. Andy Amaty, "not a big guy," had to turn his Thompson on his own squad comrades to convince them to leave prisoners alone long enough to be escorted back to HQ. Ando was questioning a POW who suddenly jumped him. With no nearby MPs to help in the two-man melee, Ando grappled with the prisoner and was forced to kill him.

Late in the afternoon of the fourteenth, 1st Battalion engaged Shimitzu for the last time near the southern coast. By nightfall of the seventeenth, they and the 3rd Battalion had the remnant of the 219th surrounded on three sides with their backs to the shore. The natives reported to Col. Jones that some Japanese were trying to escape in a boat from Menoekweri. Taking off from Namber Drome in an L-4, he eventually saw a hollowed-out canoe full of Japanese pretending to be fishermen. As the plane came towards them, they dove out of the boat. He sprayed bullets with his Thompson and dropped hand grenades on them. Navy PT boats picked up the last dozen for interrogation by the Cyclone Intel section. Presumably, Col. Jones was the only paratrooper to lead a naval attack in World War II. Thus ended organized resistance on Noemfoor.

Most of the men were "worn to a frazzle" and their water and food rations "slim" when they returned to their Kamiri tent camp on August 23. Company D continued to patrol around Namber Field, as did Company C at Menoekweri and Company I at Inasi. The three companies were relieved by 1/158 over the next few days and trickled back to Kamiri by the twenty-eighth. Gen. Krueger announced that Noemfoor was "secure" and Operation Table Tennis was officially over on the thirty-first.

The Cyclone Task Force had lost forty-five men, thirty-nine of them paratroopers. Of 113 wounded, seventy-two were paratroopers.[9] Besides the 128 jump injuries, 400 more were suffering from jungle maladies. Officers had Turner writing condolence letters to families again.

The paratroopers accounted for 1100 of the 1700 Japanese casualties and a third of the 250 prisoners. Only 500 of the 3000 slave laborers were still alive. About 300 of them were Formosans who had been pressed into service against the Americans and surrendered. Perhaps a dozen had been accidentally killed by the Americans, the rest by Japanese mistreatment. Survivors said their captors had executed many prisoners, after being put on quarter rations, for stealing food. Sick prisoners had been denied treatment until too late, or simply buried alive. The 3000 Japanese "reinforcements" had either come and gone quickly or been a figment of imagination. Col. Shimitzu was never found.

While the Cyclone Task Force had been busy trying to corral Shimitzu, Fifth Fleet had landed more troops in the Marianas on Guam, a thousand miles north of New Guinea and within 1500 miles of both Japan and the Philippines. It was the first American territory to be redeemed. Naval Construction Battalions (CBs—or "Seabees") were already building air bases, as on Saipan, for B-29 "Superfortresses" to carry the war towards Japan's home islands.

Having freely given the Americans information about the Japanese movements and concentrations on Noemfoor, the local natives began to hang around the camp's mosquito-net-covered pyramidal canvas tents. The GIs would barter with them. For a couple coins, a man would shinny up a palm tree like a lineman up a telephone pole, except bare-handed and barefoot, and drop down an armload of coconuts. The natives pedaled moonshine made of coconut sap fermented in hollowed-out bamboo tubes. Aptly named "tuber," according to Ben Jermolowicz of 1st Battalion HHQ, "It came with its own monstrous kick, hangover, and GIs."

Along with the legitimate Dutch currency, *guldens*, many of the men picked up "invasion money," Dutch bills engraved with *Japansche Regeering* (Government). They were, of course, worthless, but the troopers honored them, and they made good souvenirs. Turner got a picture with a couple of the native children. "We'd give kids our D-rations of chocolate," Turner recalled. Concocted to be an emergency ration, the "Logan Bar" (after the Quartermaster General who contracted Hershey for it) was purposely not very good, to discourage early consumption by sweet-toothed troops. Described as "little better than boiled potato" to begin with, it was hard, often requiring a knife to shave or cut, and had a wax-like coating to keep it from melting in the desert or tropics. "The children would make faces as they chewed that candy," Turner said, "so we'd pantomime spitting it out to show them it was OK, and we wouldn't be offended."

The 503rd had a couple of welcome additions as the battle progressed. Up to this point they had had to wait for air or naval support, or to borrow engineers and artillery from the other

155

divisions to which they were attached. The first augmentation was Company C of the 161st Airborne Engineer Battalion (AEB), with ten officers and 128 men in three platoons led by Cpt. James Byer. They brought along their own cooks, heavy equipment drivers, and medical detachment. Each of the three squads in a platoon had three flamethrowers and a bazooka (the first time the 503rd had seen them). Platoon CPs each maintained a couple light machine guns. These squads and weapons could be divvied up amongst the parachute rifle companies for added firepower and demolition work or operate as separate infantry units. The 161st was born in Colorado in August 1943. Company C was detached to Laurinburg-Maxton[10] Army Air Base, twenty-five miles south of Camp Mackall, North Carolina, for engineer training and Stage A of jump training. They got their wings at Ft. Benning and their Advanced Engineer Training at Camp Mackall.

The 161st left California in April 1944 and sailed to Sydney on a converted luxury liner. Fifteen hundred nurses and Women's Army Corps (WAC) volunteers were on separate decks, guarded (unfortunately for the men) by Marines. They experienced New Guinea's miserable weather at Milne Bay upon arrival in late May but set about building roads, warehouses, and supply dumps. Company C arrived on Noemfoor July 6, by boat, as reserves for the 503rd. They chopped down trees to enlarge the airfields and built service roads for them. They established camps for the regiments (who appreciated their drier, cleaner accommodations) and a water purification center from which all units could get their fresh water supply. Having already accompanied patrols, they were permanently attached to the 503rd in September.

The impact of attached artillery had been negligible. The Aussies with them at Nadzab had not even fired a shot, and the

American infantry had been stingy with its artillery. Now the 503rd got its own—the 462nd Parachute Field Artillery Battalion (PFAB). A Parachute Test Battery had originated in July 1942, at Ft. Benning, where it was found that the standard 105-mm howitzer could not be feasibly dropped in bundles, but the 75-mm "pack" howitzer (originally designed to be carried by pack mules) could. Its range was 9500 yards compared to the 105's 12,300, but at 1268 pounds it weighed only one-fourth as much. Most of it could be packed into six bundles or crates (called "coffin bombs"), strung together with web belts, and attached to the underbelly of a C-47. Three more bundles inside were to be kicked out the doors by the men just before they jumped. Batteries A, B, and C had six each of the pack howitzers—four for the line and two for replacement, a .50-cal. "heavy" machine gun section, and ninety-one men. Each howitzer was crewed by nine or ten men.

The two hundred men of Battery D protected the other three batteries. Battery D had two antitank (AT) platoons, each with two 37-mm antitank guns, and two antiaircraft (AA) platoons, each toting four .50-cal. machine guns with interchangeable tripods for ground support and AA mounts for aerial defense. Three machine gun platoons carried another dozen "fifty-cals" and some bazookas between them. All these weapons and their ammo were also secured in pouches, canisters, or coffin bombs under the planes (except the AT guns, which were delivered to a beachhead or air-landed). Once vehicles came ashore or were air-landed, each howitzer could be towed by a jeep, with a second jeep pulling an ammo trailer. More often than not, the men had to man-handle the guns along jungle paths and mountain passes. Besides their own admin, supply, mess, parachute maintenance, transportation, and medical sections, the HQ and Service Battery included a Fire

Direction Center in its S-3 Ops section. The 462nd even had two Stinson L-5 "Sentinel" spotter planes, their own pilots, and airplane mechanics.

The 462nd (Lt. Col. Donald Madigan) had been activated in June of 1943 at Camp Mackall, and most of these 600 men got their wings there. Some of the "Red Legs"—artillerymen had traditionally worn a red stripe on their trousers; now their caps had red piping—were from the original 112 men in the Parachute Test Battery. They left Camp Mackall on February 28, 1944, and Camp Stoneman on March 11 (and got the ferry ride to the wharf). They were at Camp Cable for three months beginning in early April. Besides training in jungle warfare and maintaining jump status, they practiced gunnery, especially direct fire as opposed to a howitzer's normal arched fire. Early July saw them on a Dutch ship which hugged the coast of New Guinea till arriving on Noemfoor August 7. Like the engineers, they wasted no time getting into action. In an early fire-support mission, Col. Madigan was severely wounded (by an exploding tree) while sighting and spotting and was evacuated home. Maj. Arlis Kline, the senior Fire Direction officer, took command. The 503rd was now designated, similarly to the 158th, a "Parachute Regimental Combat Team" (PRCT). Bennett Guthrie referred to the new team as "The Three Winds of Death."

As Table Tennis had played out, the Germans had launched more V1 rockets (which the Brits came to call "buzz bombs" or "doodle bugs") into London and their new Me262 jets against the RAF. Tokyo had been bombed for the first time since the Doolittle Raid, prompting Tojo to resign as Prime Minister. Colonel Claus von Stauffenberg's plot to assassinate Hitler went awry. On August 17, the *Albany Times-Union* had published a Signal Corps photo with the caption "Parachutes over the Coast of Southern France between Nice and Marseilles," as Operation "Dragoon," the invasion of the French Riviera, opened up. In the Normandy pocket, the "Yanks" began a "New Drive to Snare Nazis" while pushing on towards Paris. The governments of Belgium, Luxembourg, Netherlands, and France returned to the continent. The Chinese Minister of War, General Ho Ying-Chin, broadcast from Chungking that by his calculations Hitler would be beaten in two or three more months and Japan would surrender unconditionally within a year. Lucky Lindy went home, having extended the Navy fighters' range even before auxiliary tanks were added, flown forty missions, covered the landings at Hollandia, Biak, and Noemfoor, and scored a Japanese fighter to boot.

Though "organized resistance" had ended, the 158th continued to "mop up" (hunting for small, isolated remnants of the enemy) while the 503rd waited for a new job on Noemfoor. While they relaxed, they got to hear some of the Armed Forces Radio broadcasts of the only ever all-St. Louis World Series. After a season played mostly with youngsters and has-beens (most of the stars were in the military) the Browns won two of the first three games. But the Cardinals, who would not lose Stan "the Man" Musial to the ranks until the next season, and with slick-fielding shortstop Marty Marion behind the league's best pitching, racked up the last three in a row. The troops gambled their *guldens* and bought whiskey from the Aussie fliers.

Then the combat teams were graced by two visitors. The first, later in October, was Lt. Col. Robert Alexander, who was a qualified parachutist from the Corps of Engineers, Sixth Army. He brought an M1 Garand with six inches cut off the barrel by Army Ordnance. This made it about the length and weight of a carbine, yet still firing the bigger .30-06 slug and its heavier charge. He thought his version, the T-26, would be the paratroopers' answer for a lighter, more maneuverable weapon for jumping and jungle fighting. Col. Jones had a dozen platoon and squad leaders act as a test panel. Bill Calhoun, one of the platoon leaders, commented, "We all loved the little gun, but it had a defect which we all felt made it totally unsuitable. The muzzle blast was terrific. In the darker forest it was like a flash bulb going off. Even in sunlight it was obvious." The colonel left disappointed, questioning the reliability of the panel—who had just helped knock the Japanese Army out of New Guinea. He still managed to talk the Army's senior staff, including MacArthur, into producing a prototype of his cut-down T-26 for limited distribution. Calhoun concluded, "This is a prime example of how the troops are sometimes denied the best weapons. Some high-ranking officers in their infinite wisdom overrule subordinates' decisions."[11] Once again the 503rd elected to hold on to their regulation M1s. Alexander would return to the 503rd for subsequent campaigns, but his choice of weapon is not recorded.

The other visitor was the famous radio and movie star, Bob Hope, with his USO Show. Turner took pictures, but they disappeared along with the koala bear photos. Thankfully, Bob Weber of Service Company photographed too (from backstage, where he got Hope's "southern exposure") and sent copies to Turner. Hope and fellow comedian Jerry Colonna, who in a few years would be the voice of the March Hare in Disney's *Alice in Wonderland,* cracked jokes, did skits, and impersonated other celebrities.

Then out came what 10,000 soldiers, sailors, and airmen sitting on the ground for as far as the eye could see were waiting for ("We couldn't have cared less about Hope and Colonna," admitted one soldier). Patty Thomas, picked by Bob because she "looked like the girl next door," in a black leotard edged top and bottom in pink lace, bantered with Bob awhile and then tap-danced. Weber wrote on the back of a photo, "All she'd had to have done was stand there. What did I hear you say about WOLVES?" Hope then said what would become a mainstay in his USO shows, "Just wanted you guys to know what you're fighting for." (Indeed—the 462nd had hiked "eight or nine miles from the other end of the island.") When the hooting, whistling, and hollering stopped, there followed another movie and radio star, Frances Langford. She traded a few quips with Hope, mostly double entendres, and then sang to the troops. The favorite was her signature hit, *I'm in the Mood for Love.* (A Marine on another island was reputed to have called out, "You came to the right place, baby!") Weber's comment was, "Quite a treat to see an American girl as you can see by the expressions on the faces in the first few rows." Patty returned, this time in a short skirt, for a second round of dancing, applause, and wolf calls. Amid all of it, an MP security guard off in the jungle fringe accidentally fired a shot. Bob, the two combat teams, and Navy and Air Corps personnel ducked, looked wildly around, and collectively sighed. He told them, and swore afterwards, "I think that was a sniper trying to get me!"

Due to the number of incapacitating jump injuries and battle wounds of platoon and squad leaders (including 3rd Battalion commander Erickson, who, it was thought, wouldn't make it), Turner got a battlefield promotion to T-4 or "Tech Sergeant" (T/Sgt.), another stripe, $40 more a month, and a new title: Supply NCO. As such he was to "assist the regimental supply sergeant and battalion supply sergeant. Requisition, store, issue Quartermaster and Ordnance supplies and equipment to regular units. In charge of warehouse stock of supplies." To Turner, it sounded just like his old job at the Montgomery Ward stockroom in Albany. He groomed his month-old beard into a Vandyke with a mustache, both of which he parted in the middle. Guys with supply requisitions began asking for "the Beard."

Always short of rations, ammo, replacement parts, and above all, beer—the rear echelon troops and bigger units siphoned off most—the independent units learned to scrap. Tom recalled, "Max or Al [Runyon] or Walt [Hyudema] and I would get a jeep and trailer from the motor pool, put on regular infantry caps and coats, and go on a 'milk run.'" They would patrol the shoreline and airstrips where supplies were being unloaded and stacked. They "appropriated" any unattended crates and cases. Maybe a case of grapefruit, maybe a case of grenades, it didn't matter. Rarely questioned and usually suspected too late, they and other Service Company members supplemented the paratroopers' inventories with Navy and Air Corps goods. Whenever they were put to work unloading cargo ships, 503rd companies made sure a few extra cases of food, beer, or whiskey made it back to their camp. The Warden, knowing generals above him had already gotten first dibs, didn't interfere. He gladly accepted an occasional fifth for a kickback. The 503rd PRCT soon boasted a new identity along the Sixth Army supply pipeline: "Panama Jones and his 3000 Thieves."

On the thirtieth of July, Gen. MacArthur had begun the final phase of the New Guinea campaign. Sixth Army made one more amphibious landing, on the Vogelkop Peninsula, supported by RAAF Warhawks from Kamiri and USAAF Lightnings and Mitchells from Kornasoren. MacArthur's "three K's"—Krueger,

Kinkaid, and Kenney—moved rapidly again and cut off 18,000 Japanese on the south side of the peninsula. Operation Cartwheel was for all intents and purposes finished. The threat to Australia had been removed. Rabaul had been rendered harmless. Borneo and the Philippines were within reach.

The Americans would move on. The Australians would continue to mop up in New Guinea and the Solomons and invade Indonesia. The joint American-Australian efforts had retaken 1300 miles of the New Guinea coastline in twelve months and isolated 135,000 Japanese troops there while killing 127,000 more. A very small fraction of those had actually been killed in action. The vast majority succumbed to starvation and tropical diseases. By leapfrogging[12] with the same units over and over, MacArthur had been able to continue to advance despite the bulk of the USA's resources going to Europe. When Gen. Marshall wondered what would become of all those pockets MacArthur had bypassed, he answered "attrition will account for their final disposition...the actual time...is of little or no importance." He added, as an aide saw him stare at the sky in the direction of the Philippine Islands, "They are waiting for me there. It has been a long time."

---

1 Third and Fifth Fleet were basically the same fleet. Halsey (Third) and Spruance (Fifth) alternated command; one would go off to sea to relieve the other, who returned to Hawaii with his staff for operation planning. The fleet number changed at that time. The first digit of each task force was also its fleet number. An inadvertent benefit was that the enemy always thought there were more US ships in the Pacific than were actually available.

2 Twenty years later, Turner would work in an office in California with a Javanese who, as a young man, had been a slave laborer. Being forced by the Japanese to carry boulders on his shoulders had permanently injured his back.

3 The 41st Division, previously nicknamed "The Sunset Division" for its Northwest origins, was retitled "The Jungleers" after this operation, its costliest. The division lost 435 killed in action (KIA) and 2360 wounded in action (WIA) in securing the island. The Japanese lost over 6,000 KIA and 460 POWs. Those not captured or killed were "contained" by ongoing patrols. There were 360 additional POWs from Formosa, slave laborers who had been forced to fight the Americans.

4 Landing Craft, Mechanized. Each could hold sixty men or a light tank. Later models (1943 on) held 100 men or a medium (Sherman) tank. Armed with two . 50-cal. machine guns.

5 Landing Craft, Infantry. A small version of an LST, but larger than an LCM, it was designed to transport 200 men.

6 As related by George Kojima to my brother, Jonathan Turner.

7 By the time a trooper and his risers, suspension lines, and canopy cleared the plane, he was about fifty feet below the plane. It took at least another fifty feet for the canopy to expand fully. By then, about two and a half seconds since jumping, he would be falling at nearly eighty miles per hour. If the canopy took any longer, the man could be dropping upwards of 100 miles per hour when he got the opening jolt. Some men experienced a second drop and jolt as their risers unfurled. Jones was lucky that men weren't killed. The lead pilot who made the mistake was busted from lieutenant colonel to captain.

8 Landing Ship, Tank. The largest landing craft at 328 feet long and 50 feet wide. It had two decks and deep draft for sea transport. Ballast tanks, fourteen-foot doors and ramps allowed for debarkation without a dock. The lower deck could hold cargo or twenty tanks; the upper deck held lighter vehicles, weapons, or 160 soldiers—a total of 2100 tons of cargo. Armament consisted of fifteen AA guns. Although referred to as "slow targets," only thirty-nine were lost to enemy fire or mishaps at sea out of over 1300 built.

9 Casualty numbers according to Guthrie and Flanagan. Devlin, in *Back to Corregidor* and *Paratrooper* lists higher numbers for the 503rd: 60 KIA, 303

WIA. Google's totals are 66 and 343.

10 Built in 1942 to train Troop Carrier pilots. The first group through was the 317th Troop Carrier Group, which would deliver every airborne troop in the Pacific, and in between jumps, millions of tons of supplies. The airbase quickly converted to pilot and troop training for CG-4 Waco Gliders, which were towed by C-47s.

11 Letters from William T. Calhoun, DDS, to John Lindgren (fellow 503rd officer) and Jonathan Turner. About 150 or 200 of these were produced in the US. After the war the surplus T-26s and some knockoffs were advertised as the "Tanker" model by gun dealers. Why they were given this name no one knows; they were too big to store in a tank and never issued to tank crews. Chalk it up to advertising.

12 After the war, a senior Japanese Eighth Area Army intelligence officer, Col. Matsuichi Juio, was interviewed. "The Japanese Army," he said, "preferred direct assault, after the German fashion." Of MacArthur's strategy, he said, "This…was the type we hated the most"—attack and seize weak areas, build airfields, cut supply lines, and starve out strong points—"just as water seeks the weakest entry to sink a ship." Thus, MacArthur "gained the most while losing the least." Buna-Gona had cemented the strategy.

Chapter 9

LEYTE
MacArthur Returns

T he Russians, led by Marshal Zhukov, had broken the siege of Leningrad in January 1944, after a million citizens had starved or frozen to death and as many soldiers had been killed or captured. They retook the Crimea, rolled through Hungary, Slovakia, and the Baltic States, but stood idly by in Poland as the Warsaw uprising—counting on Soviet help—was defeated during the summer, and the insurgents were killed by the Germans or carted off to concentration camps. Since February, Merrill's Marauders had been spearheading "Vinegar Joe" Stilwell's campaign to push the Japanese out of Burma. By August, Stilwell's "X-Force"—a conglomeration of American, Chinese, British, Indian, and Burmese troops—were fighting down the Ledo Road to its junction with the Burma Road, which would open up re-supply to the Chinese Army by New Year's 1945. The US Army had swept across France but was up against the Siegfried Line at the German border; the British waited for the Germans to evacuate Athens so they could move back in.

In July, MacArthur and Nimitz—the former through the

166

Solomons and New Guinea and the latter through the Gilbert, Marshall, and Mariana Islands—had converged on the Philippine Islands. FDR met with them in Hawaii, and they and the Joint Chiefs of Staff debated recapturing the Philippines or skipping them entirely and striking Formosa. It turned out the United States would not have enough troops or transport for the Formosa plan until the war was over in Europe, and the Chinese Army was now so ineffective that a linkup from Formosa would be useless. Even once the Burma Road was reopened, the best to be hoped for from China was to continue to tie down a large portion of the Japanese Army. MacArthur, of course, felt he had a promise to keep and a score to settle. In his eyes, deserting the Philippine Islands again while being this close but striking elsewhere would be not only inexcusable but criminal. Furthermore, the largest concentration of Japanese troops outside of Japan and China would be left in the Philippines to harass Allied shipping lanes and protect Japan's own rubber and petroleum supply line from Indonesia. Admiral William Leahy, the President's Chief of Staff (and the only five-star officer in the war) agreed with MacArthur. FDR gave the green light to MacArthur's Operation "Reno" to get a toehold in the Philippines by shooting for Mindanao, Leyte, and—by December 20—Luzon. Bull Halsey meanwhile would turn north to Iwo Jima in January and Okinawa in March.

Marines from Third Fleet landed on Peleliu, 500 miles north of New Guinea and within 500 miles of the Philippine Islands, on September 15, but with an eye towards Japan. They and their Army reinforcements would stall there for two months and suffer forty percent casualties—the highest rate for any amphibious assault in history. The Australian and American armies got 200 miles closer to the Philippines the same day by taking Morotai

Island, one of the northernmost of the East Indies and halfway between New Guinea and the Philippines. Its air bases would be important not only for the Philippine campaign but also for the Aussies' upcoming campaign to reclaim Borneo. Unfortunately for the Allies, Operation "Market Garden," Gen. Montgomery's gamble to get across the Rhine in Holland, failed in the same month, very likely postponing Chinese Gen. Ho's prediction and the American General Staff's expectation of subduing Hitler by Christmas. The Battle of the Bulge would guarantee a delay of victory in Europe. The 82nd and 101st Airborne Divisions would play tremendous parts in both battles, wresting bridges from Panzer divisions in the former[1], and holding the buckling Allied line when the same Panzers broke through in the latter.[2]

The Fourteenth Japanese Area Army defended the Philippines with 430,000 men under Gen. Tomoyuki Yamashita. It was he who had forced the surrender of 90,000 troops in Singapore, thereby earning the nickname, "the Tiger of Malaya." Mindanao (the southernmost island) was garrisoned by the 30th Division, and the Visayas (central islands including Leyte) by the 16th Division, both comprising Lt. Gen. Sosaku Suzuki's Thirty-fifth Army. Gen. MacArthur's intel said 50,000 Japanese were on Mindanao, another 50,000 in the Visayas, and nearly 200,000 on Luzon (the northernmost island). The rest were dispersed among the smaller islands. They were reinforced from Borneo and Formosa, where four carriers, seven battlewagons, two battle-carriers[3], and nineteen cruisers were also stationed. Upwards of 800 planes supported them from a hundred airfields in the Philippines.

Vice Admiral Mitscher's TF 38 (renumbered when Halsey took command of Third Fleet), which had facilitated the Hollandia operation in April and more recently devastated the IJN in the Marianas Turkey Shoot, went to work bombing southern Mindanao in preparation for its invasion, Operation "King I." However, since Yamashita had decided Luzon would be staunchly defended at the expense of the other islands, the Japanese air and naval opposition in Mindanao was negligible and hence completely pulverized. Mitscher destroyed 500 planes and fifty ships.[4] Halsey recommended, the Joint Chiefs approved, and MacArthur agreed to scrap that part of the plan and move the Leyte "King II" invasion, originally slated for November 15, up to October 20. So, Walter Krueger's Sixth Army found itself sailing from Hollandia with Admiral Kinkaid and Seventh Fleet on the tenth. Halsey in the meantime led diversionary attacks on Formosa, 300 miles north of the Philippines, and on Okinawa, 400 miles northeast. On "A" Day (so as not to be confused with "D" Day) Sixth Army once again made a landing, this time on the northeast coast of Leyte, between Tacloban and Palo. There were no nearby airbases for Kenney's squadrons, so Halsey turned south to shield Kinkaid and Krueger.

Joining Sixth Army on Palo Beach was Gen. MacArthur himself. After newsmen got photos and newsreel footage of him coming on shore through the surf,[5] he broadcast his "People of the Philippines, I have returned" speech from a truck the Signal Corps brought onto the beach. It had been nearly a thousand days since he'd left Corregidor. New Philippine President Sergio Osmeña— Manuel Quezon had died in New York a few months previously— returned as well to reinstate the government.

While Nimitz had maintained his base at Pearl Harbor, MacArthur had gotten used to moving his headquarters up: from Melbourne to Brisbane to Port Moresby to Hollandia. Now he turned a mansion in Tacloban, formerly owned by an American but more recently used as a Japanese officers' club, into his new HQ. Barrett McGurn, a *Yank* reporter, had done his own island hopping to try to catch up with the General and wound up in a residence not far away from MacArthur's. "One night," McGurn wrote, "the enemy evidently decided...to eliminate our neighbor." There were twenty air raids that night. After one particularly close strafing attack, MacArthur's aide burst into his office and breathlessly asked, "Did they get you?" Pointing to a bullet hole in the wall above his head with the stem of his corncob pipe, the General replied, "Not this time." Twelve Filipinos and two other correspondents in the neighborhood were not so lucky.

Krueger's X (Maj. Gen. Franklin Sibert) and XXIV (Maj. Gen. John Hodge) Corps battled westward across Leyte Valley against 20,000 dug-in men, half of them from the 16th Division (Lt. Gen. Shiro Makino), which had instigated the atrocities during the Bataan Death March. To make the Americans pay dearly for every mile, Yamashita doubled the defense by pouring reinforcements from Luzon and Mindanao into Ormoc, on the west coast.

Leyte is a large island, 110 miles north to south and fifteen to twenty miles wide, somewhat larger than Rhode Island. The 4000-foot jungle-covered Cordillera Mountains form its spine and separate its coastal plains. Easy access to its eastern beaches and Leyte Valley had seemed ideal for the assault by and re-supply of American troops. From the edges of the beaches, however, the GIs had to wade through swamps into jungles and then foothills even before engaging the enemy. Monsoon season added to Sixth Army's woes by dumping mudslides and fallen trees in its path.

Within a week, to exploit the American struggles ashore with their supply fleet far behind in Leyte Gulf, the Japanese planned what they deemed *Kantai Kessen*—the "decisive battle" of the South Pacific. Japan hoped for the outcome which had eluded them at Pearl Harbor, Midway, and the Marianas—an American defeat so crushing as to convince them they could never win and should sue for peace. For Operation *Sho-Go* ("Victory"), they assembled their largest fleet yet, including all their remaining capital ships, to reinforce Leyte and destroy the American Seventh Fleet. The "Northern" Force (V.Adm. Ozawa), sailing towards the Central Pacific from Japan with their carriers, albeit deficient in planes due to the disaster in the Philippine Sea, lured Halsey and Mitscher back out to sea. A second task force sailed southwest from Formosa past Luzon before turning east, and two more steamed northeast from Singapore via Brunei, to converge on Leyte Gulf with battleships and troop laden assault transports.

Kinkaid, left behind to guard Leyte Gulf, was alerted of the approaching fleets by subs and patrol planes which sank two cruisers off Borneo on October 23. Seventh Fleet, designed merely to ferry and support Sixth Army, had no new battleships or large carriers amongst its warships, just smaller escort carriers, which were old ships topped with short flight decks and a few planes each, the WWI vintage *Mississippi*, and five "ghost ships"— battleships refurbished after being damaged or sunk and raised at Pearl Harbor. Kinkaid knew the transports and LSTs would be sitting ducks and put out an SOS to Halsey. Then Kinkaid, who Halsey jokingly and affectionately called a "fighting fool," brazenly sailed out of the gulf to meet the IJN's seven battleships, sixteen cruisers, and twenty-seven destroyers.

Two days later, southeast of Leyte in the Surigao Strait, Rear Admiral (R.Adm.) Jesse Oldendorf, commanding Kinkaid's Task Group (TG) 77.2, had subs and PT boats line up on either side of the channel, launch their torpedoes at the approaching

"Southern" Force, and skedaddle. Then he executed a classic tactic reminiscent of Admiral Nelson and John Paul Jones. As the Japanese ships barreled through the channel in single file, he "crossed the T" with his ghost ships, which allowed each to fire a broadside against only the forward guns of an emerging ship. All but one Japanese ship were at least damaged, and the battleships *Fuso* and *Yamashiro* were sunk. V.Adm. Shogi Nishimura went down with them. The trailing Japanese reserve task force saw the devastation ahead and turned back.

Northeast of Leyte, R.Adm. Thomas Sprague, with TG 77.4 and the escort carriers, took on the even larger "Central" Force (V.Adm. Takeo Kurita), which had slipped through the San Bernardino Strait north of Leyte and Samar during the night. This force was built around *Yamato* and *Musashi*, the most massive battleships in the world. East of Samar they were met by Task Unit "Taffy 3" under R.Adm. Clifton Sprague (not related to but an Annapolis classmate of Thomas), who warned his captains this could well be a suicide mission. However, his TBM Avenger torpedo bombers and subs sank *Musashi* and damaged *Yamato* while FM-2 Wildcats and F6F Hellcats strafed the fleet. Thinking he'd been tricked and was about to be destroyed himself by Halsey's carriers, Kurita turned tail. Sprague's own chief quartermaster yelled, "My God, Admiral, they're going to get away!" Sprague wisely let well enough alone.

Throughout both battles, Thomas Sprague's escort carriers in Taffy 1 and Taffy 2 had been kept busy fending off a new, terrifying weapon thrown in from Luzon—*kamikaze* (suicide) dive bombers. Born out of the tremendous loss of veteran Japanese pilots, they were piloted mostly by young but fanatical men who had been taught how to take off but not to land. Their job was to hurl their bomb-laden planes into ships. Adm. Oldendorf remarked that "a hail of AA fire" could not stop them. Only the eight-inch guns on cruisers turned some of them away. Hellcats and Wildcats seemed to have better luck.

The next day, Bull Halsey, whose orders from Admiral Nimitz had always been "destroy the enemy," and whose own motto was, "Hit hard, hit fast, and hit often," caught up with Ozawa and took care of the carrier fleet, which didn't have enough planes (barely a hundred) to protect itself. Although the distraction had provided Yamashita time to land some more reinforcements in Ormoc, Japan had lost its big gamble for the initiative, and with it the IJN's last four carriers, three battleships, ten cruisers, eleven destroyers, and 300 planes. The IJN would never recover. By contrast, the USN had lost two escort carriers, a light carrier, three destroyers, and 200 planes. It was Japan's final naval offensive of the war, and, historically, both the largest naval engagement ever and the last between battleships. *USS Mississippi*, in Iceland during the Pearl Harbor attack, had delivered the era-ending broadside.

The same day the Japanese invasion fleet was spotted, and while Marianas-based B-29s bombed Japan (leading to Tojo's ouster), Col. Jones and several staff officers and section heads had left Noemfoor for Leyte to be briefed about the part the 503rd would play in an upcoming operation—"Love III." Mindoro, 300 miles northwest of Leyte and just south of Luzon, would be the next step up the island chain once Leyte's airfields were ready. Planes based on Leyte, in the central islands, would be able to reach both ends of the Philippines. Meanwhile, the 503rd readied itself on Noemfoor, again as part of Sixth Army's tactical reserve.

General Krueger brought in the 32nd Division and 112th Cavalry RCT from his reserve as reinforcements on November 14.

Gen. Yamashita countered with another 25,000 men from Manchuria. Krueger decided it was time to commit the elite of his reserve force, Lt. Gen. Swing's 11th Airborne Division. It consisted of the 511th PIR (Col. Orin "Hard Rock" Haugen, West Point '30), 187th (Col. Harry Hildebrand) and 188th (Col. Robert Soule) Glider Infantry Regiments. With only two battalions per glider regiment, and even with two attached regular infantry battalions, parachute and glider artillery, tanks, and engineers, this division was not nearly as big as the airborne divisions in Europe, which had at least four parachute and glider regiments apiece.

The 511th came to be in January 1943, from conscripted volunteers at Camp Toccoa, where they had seven weeks of BIT, followed by ten weeks of parachute training at Camp Mackall. Like the 504th Battalion, the 511th Regiment had joined, trained, and jump qualified together. The 457th PFAB had also been created in January, at Fort Bragg, and moved to Camp Toccoa in February. The 187th and 188th were constituted in November 1942 at Camp Mackall and activated there on February 25, 1943. They went to Laurinburg-Maxton Army Air Base in July to start glider training. Together with two glider field artillery battalions, an anti-aircraft battalion, and an engineer battalion, these units formed the new 11th Airborne Division, the only one created at Camp Mackall. Joseph Swing, whose report had revived the airborne, was at that time a brigadier general in charge of the 82nd Airborne's artillery. He was promoted to major general and brought over to lead the 11th.

After getting their wings at Fort Benning (Maj. Gen. Swing had all his troops dual certified as glider men and paratroopers), the entire division underwent AIT in the swamps around Polk, Louisiana, for three months before leaving for Camp Stoneman in

April 1944. They arrived in New Guinea in May, where they jungle trained and acclimated near the old camp of the 503rd at Dobodura for five months. They were in the reserve for the Hollandia operation but not used. Noting the climate with which they were dealing, Gen. Swing designed and got adopted a forage cap resembling the ones locomotive engineers wore with a roomier, more ventilated crown—the "Swing" cap. It was manufactured in Australia and issued uniquely to the 11th Airborne (although some showed up in the 503rd as well). He also got ice cream added to the daily menu with the explanation that a bunch of nineteen-year-olds would probably prefer that to three percent beer. (I'm surprised my father didn't ask for a transfer to that outfit!) After the deactivation of the 1st Marine Parachute Regiment, Col. Jones and Gen. Swing had the only remaining airborne regiments in the PTO.

The 11th Division left New Guinea on November 6, 1944, and unloaded on Bito Beach in Leyte twelve days later. They were trucked a third of the way across Leyte to Burauen, which had several airfields nearby. They got their first taste of combat within days when they were thrust into the middle of the line. While the X and XXIV Corps provided pincers on the flanks (X Corps drew the elite Japanese 1st Division), the 11th Airborne cut their teeth by slugging straight ahead through mountains towards Ormoc. They came up against intricate defenses including pillboxes, interconnected caves, log-reinforced trenches, and heavy artillery positions. When night fell, they dug foxholes fifteen feet apart. They used the rubber from their discarded gas mask hoses to cover their dog tags so they wouldn't jingle.

The eastern half of Leyte has no dry season, and the typhoons had hit just before the 11th Airborne arrived. Wounded parachute and glider troops had to be evacuated down steep, slippery trails. Even though local Filipinos helped carry them, many never made it back to the hospital area alive. Men who threw away their soaked woolen blankets during the scorching days had to endure freezing nights. Work on the airfields around Burauen came to a standstill.

The only highway ran around the perimeter of the island. Even that turned into a quagmire. Artillery L-4 and L-5 spotter planes were pressed into service to deliver supplies and even men onto small mesas. A battery was delivered to an isolated battalion by running the only available C-47 back and forth from Burauen thirteen times. Pfc. Elmer Fryer earned the division's first Medal of Honor posthumously when he single-handedly stopped a *banzai* (ferocious all-out do-or-die) attack, dragged wounded friends to safety while being wounded himself, and died killing a sniper with a grenade. Every time they moved up, 11th Airborne built a tent city out of parachutes for a forward base camp. Despite the slow advance, Sixth Army's fifty-mile front closed in on the west coast.

When the 11th Airborne left New Guinea, Gen. Krueger had the 503rd PRCT pack up their camp on Noemfoor as well and board attack transports[6]—*Knox*, *Custer*, and *Comet*—to cover Sixth Army's lengthening supply line. The paratroopers embarked on November 7, Election Day back home. They had already voted—at least those who had gotten through the red tape of applying for a state ballot in time, or ordering a "short" ballot (President, VP, and Congress only) if not—and wondered if their vote would keep them alive, or shorten the war, or even make it back to Frisco. For men trying to stay warm in Northern Europe, dry on the tropical islands, and off the casualty lists everywhere, what went on in Washington was low priority. In the end, only 85,000 service personnel bothered to vote.

The troopers stayed aboard for a week, sitting at anchor while supplies were loaded, sleeping in dry beds, eating full meals (some said they were being "fattened for the kill"), gambling their pay, and spending their winnings at the ships' well-stocked PXs, where Cokes and candy bars were a nickel, and sandwiches and malts were a dime. On the fourteenth they sailed for Leyte surrounded by Kinkaid's fleet. By the time they left Noemfoor, most of the paratroopers in the 503rd had two years of overseas duty. Those who'd been in Panama before forming the 2nd Battalion had three.

Landing near Dulag the day after the 11th Airborne, they pitched their base camp at the Burauen airfields but dug beach defenses against a possible Japanese counterattack. They anticipated being in a joint operation with the 511th—their junior partners—who were rapidly becoming seasoned veterans. Gen. Krueger, in fact, contemplated attaching the 503rd to the 11th, to inject experience and to approximate the airborne divisions in the ETO. Jack Tolson, now on his staff, persuaded him to keep it separate.

What the paratroopers got was non-stop torrential rain. While they dug foxholes that immediately filled with water, the artillerists sighted their guns onto the beach and the gray skies above, and the engineers strung barbed wire and built their next tent city. Miles behind them, repairs and improvements to the airfields dragged because of the continual rain. An occasional parting of the clouds allowed for sunbathing or a rare movie night. The booming of artillery carried across the water from the islands to the east and from the mountains to the west.

As usual, the supplies were already picked over by the time they reached the 503rd. Most days, if not unloading an LST or

177

loading a convoy of 6 by 6 trucks to shuttle supplies to Burauen, Turner and Phillips were in the Service Company sector trying to fend off rain with ponchos and tent halves. Tom recalled, "Max and I were in our foxhole on the beach one day ruminating about what we were going to do when the darn war was over. I said I was going to marry Betty, move out west, and have a couple kids. He said, 'Well, I want to get married too. But I don't know about kids. You go ahead and have the family. I think I'll just be Uncle Max.'"

Kamikazes were now the biggest threats to ships anchored in the harbor and the men unloading them on the beach. Nearly 4000 of them would eventually sink or damage hundreds of Allied ships and account for 10,000 casualties, although unlike the "divine wind" which had turned back the Mongol fleet 600 years before, they would be unable to stop the Americans.

Withdrawal of the escort carriers (kamikazes had gotten the *Saint Lo*) as Fifth Air Force trickled into the limited facilities on Leyte still allowed Japan control of the skies. Late in November the Japanese launched a two-day air raid on the harbor and airfields. During the daylight and at night when the anti-aircraft batteries lit up the sky, troopers in their foxholes watched dogfights overhead in between bomb blasts. Marine Corsairs and Hellcats now finally based on Leyte joined the fracas.

Once again, the only relief in the muddy foxholes and leaky tents between air raids came from Armed Forces Radio, this time with games of the West Point football team, which was undefeated for the first time since the First World War and would remain so for the next two years.[7] On November 11, while the 503rd savored the bed and board of the transports, the backfield tandem of Felix Blanchard and Glenn Davis, consecutive Heisman Trophy winners, ran over, around, and through Notre Dame, 59-0.

It was no mean feat: Notre Dame went 8-2 for the year. On December 2, the same paratroopers huddled under makeshift rain shelters as #1 ranked Army defeated #2 Navy, 23-7, in a game for which, according to MacArthur, "We stopped the war to celebrate." But even the General could not stop the monsoon rain.

By now, it was obvious Leyte's airfields were going to be unusable against Luzon. Whereas the eastern halves of the islands received monsoons continually, the western coasts were for the most part dry from October through January. Mindoro's southwestern corner offered some dry airfields. Operation Love III was imminent. The 503rd was ordered to prepare for an airlift into Mindoro on December 5, but for lack of adequate room to land enough transport and escort planes on Leyte, it was soon cancelled.

That same evening, units from Makino's and the 26th IJA Divisions managed to infiltrate 11th Airborne's rear defenses and bayonet or shoot many sleeping construction and HQ troops. They were joined on the next day by 350 Japanese paratroopers, from the 2nd Parachute Raiding Brigade, dropped near the airfields. There were to be two more airlifts, but they were grounded in Luzon. This is the only known time when paratroopers jumped on opposing paratroopers. Gen. Swing had just finished his chicken dinner and stepped out of his CP in time to see them jump. They wrecked a few planes and a fuel dump near the San Pablo Drome, but rear echelon troops and rifle-wielding Red Legs, led by Swing himself, retook the airfields and held them off until detachments from the 187th GIR and just-arrived 149th IR overran the Japanese positions. Three of the transports had been shot down and crashed on the beach. It took until the next morning for patrols from the 503rd to hunt down and dispatch the survivors. It was to be the only action for the 503rd on Leyte besides dodging bombs, shooting at kamikazes, and trying to stay dry. Makino's 16th Division was wiped out, partially avenging the Bataan and Corregidor atrocities. The others fought on to the west.

On the seventh, the third anniversary of Pearl Harbor, the 511th and 187th were repelling banzai attacks along the front when the last of the American reserve, the 77th Division (called the "Statue of Liberty" Division for its largely New York City, Brooklyn, and Jersey City makeup), landed near Ormoc. Concurrently, the Japanese tried to land reinforcements there. Another sea-and-air battle cost the Japanese most of their convoy and two-thirds of their remaining planes from Luzon. Kamikazes sank two USN destroyers. One of them was the *Ward*, which had sunk a mini sub when it fired the first shot by the American Navy at Pearl Harbor. The 77th took Ormoc on the tenth. A week before Christmas, the 511th cut through to the coast and linked up with the 32nd IR, who had trained in Mojave for Africa but then had battled in the frigid Aleutian Islands instead, only to move on to the infernal tropics. (Their good-service reward would be Okinawa.) The pincers closed from the north and south. Leyte was secured. Troopers of the 511th sat in the warm water of the Visayan Sea and watched chunks of flesh peel off their rotting feet. On Christmas day the 511th finally pulled back to its base camp at Bito Beach while the glider regiments cracked the last Japanese redoubt.

King II had taken 200,000 men from Sixth Army and another 120,000 airmen and seamen to clear Leyte of 65,000 men of the Japanese Thirty-fifth Army. The Japanese had lost at least 56,000 of those, but it is estimated, as in New Guinea, only twenty percent were by combat. The rest succumbed to disease and starvation. Eighty percent of their supplies had been sunk at Ormoc besides nearly fifty transports full of reinforcements, possibly another fifteen or twenty thousand men. Survivors would spend the rest of the war hiding in the mountains and being rooted out by ongoing patrols. Only 800 were taken prisoner. Besides losing four of his divisions, Yamashita had his airpower reduced by half, and the quarter of a million men he'd drawn into Luzon were now without significant naval or air support. The American losses were 3500 KIA, 12,000 WIA, and eighty-nine missing in action (MIA). Over 500 of the casualties were in the 11th Airborne. They had killed nearly 6000 and captured but a dozen of the enemy.

1 As with all Airborne operations, officers jumped into the middle of the fray. Gen. Maxwell Taylor, though wounded, was able to continue commanding the 101st Airborne Division. Among the 501st PIR's casualties was the energetic and popular Col. Howard Johnston, who had commanded them since their activation. After attending the US Naval Academy, he had decided to transfer to the Army. "Jumping" Johnston had earned his wings, made multiple jumps whenever possible during training, ignored danger, and was theatrical—the airborne version of Patton and MacArthur. He was mortally wounded by shrapnel near Nijmegen.

2 The 509th and 551st PIBs, both of which still had a fair number of original Provisional Parachute Group troopers and were attached to the 82nd AB Division, earned Presidential Unit Citations by denying the Germans a breakthrough near St. Vith and thus protecting the vital port of Antwerp. The 101st AB Division earned its Presidential Unit Citation by holding the highway hub at Bastogne although surrounded by several German divisions. It was the first time an entire division had been presented the elite award, fulfilling Gen. Lee's earlier proclamation.

3 Battleships with flight decks replacing rear gun turrets.

4 The downside was that one Japanese ship sunk had 675 US POWs from Bataan and Corregidor aboard. Only eighty-five made it to shore. Filipino

guerrillas rescued them.

5 It was said that the beachmaster, perhaps in a move to upstage the General, refused him docking privileges. MacArthur said it was because he'd taken a deep draft boat and couldn't get in close. Regardless, it made for good newsreel footage.

6 Liberty Ships carrying LCIs and LCMs besides assault troops.

7 Robert Eichelberger, while Superintendent at West Point in 1940, persuaded the Surgeon General to relax the weight restrictions for cadets, thus allowing for recruitment of players who could better compete collegiately. He also replaced horseback riding and drills with modern combat training, bringing the Academy "into the Twentieth Century."

Chapter 10

MINDORO
Doorway to Luzon

Roosevelt had been re-elected for the fourth time, by more than three million votes. The entire armed forces would have had to vote to tip the scales in favor of New York Governor Thomas Dewey. Popular band leader Glenn Miller was lost in the English Channel on a flight from London to Paris. Marshal Zhukov, the hero of Moscow, Stalingrad, and Leningrad, having waited for the Germans to be sufficiently whittled down while they eliminated the Polish Home Guard, decided it was time to move into Warsaw and start his own "liberation war" against the exhausted Germans.

Ever since the December 5 alert the 503rd had been doing their usual prep of weapons readiness, tactics instruction, terrain study, and jungle practice. They got their Christmas dinner—real turkey, potatoes, gravy, dressing, and ice cream—two weeks early. Because of the air lifting implausibility, escorting the Love III invasion of Mindoro had fallen to Admiral Kinkaid. The paratroopers boarded his transports on the eleventh. Their amphibious training amounted to one practice landing later that day, and they sailed the next.

Kinkaid had split Seventh Fleet into three task groups for the 550-mile voyage. "Mindoro Attack Group 9" (R.Adm. Arthur Struble) of VII Amphibious Force carried what MacArthur named the "Western Visayan Task Force": the 503rd PRCT and the 19th Infantry RCT from the 24th Division, aboard transports, LSTs, and LCIs accompanied by destroyers and minesweepers. The "Mindoro Close Covering Group" guarded the flanks with three cruisers, seven destroyers, and two dozen PT boats. The "Mindoro Heavy Cover and Carrier Group" would provide diversionary maneuvers with the old escort carriers, ghost battleships, and light cruisers. The guerrillas on Mindoro had been told to curtail activities. Yamashita had been so focused on Leyte and indifferent to Mindoro that he had only left 1000 men there: a few companies of the IJA 8th and 105th Divisions from Luzon, a couple hundred shipwrecked sailors, and some engineering, air force, and service personnel. Scattered amongst several towns, they were a thin defense for an island half the size of New Jersey.

The convoys started sailing east and south from Leyte towards New Guinea until nightfall when they headed north and west, back through the Surigao Strait. "We got more scared the closer we got to Mindoro and Luzon," Max Phillips admitted, and for good reason. The attack group was spotted late in the afternoon of the thirteenth and, sure enough, a kamikaze raid ensued. Two ships were hit, one of which was the cruiser *Nashville*, the flagship. Brig. Gen. William Dunckel, the Western Visayan Task Force commander, was badly burned. He transferred ships and kept going. His and Admiral Struble's Chiefs of Staff were killed. The commander of the 310th Air Force Bombardment Wing was mortally wounded. Three hundred twenty sailors were killed or wounded. MacArthur had planned to sail on the ship, which he'd been on from Hollandia to Leyte, but his staff had talked him out of it at the last minute. Several landing craft, destroyers, and cargo ships were also sunk, disabled, or damaged. A diversionary bombardment of Palawan to the west, just north of Borneo, convinced the Japanese that the fleet was on its way there. Other Japanese air sorties were intercepted by US Fifth and Seventh Air Forces and Third Fleet so that the enemy lost track of the Western Visayan Task Force.

On "N-Day," December 15, the day before Hitler launched his desperation offensive, *Wacht am Rhein* ("Watch on the Rhine"), that would devolve into the Battle of the Bulge, the 503rd disembarked at 0730 on both sides of the mouth of the Busuanga River, north of present-day San Jose. Filipinos were already lining the shore in anticipation; Admiral Struble had to fire warning shots so they would disperse. There was a short air-and-sea bombardment of only a few minutes. As the landing craft approached the shore, Big Ben Jermolowicz noticed there were cases of beer stacked in the back of his landing craft below the coxswain. "I thought, these sonuva[guns] are gonna wait till we clear the beach and then have a party! To [heck] with that!" When the ramp dropped down, he reached back, grabbed a case, and swung it up onto his shoulder. He picked up his rifle and started for the ramp. "Hey, you, bring that back here!" yelled the coxswain.

"Like [heck] I will!" Ben yelled back over his shoulder. "You come get it!" They waded ashore abreast the 19th IRCT. Amazingly, there was no opposition. The hundred or so defenders had taken off. The 503rd followed the Busuanga River four miles upstream to the tiny town of San Jose (which has since been extended farther south along the coast) while one RAAF and four

US engineer battalions and their equipment landed. Air raids and dogfights continued all day even though Halsey had bombed Mindoro and Luzon airfields just before the landing. Eight of fifteen kamikazes were shot down, but the others got two more LSTs. Exploding ammo on one of them wounded sailors on a nearby destroyer trying to help men in the water. Max and Tom thanked God they were back on land where they were low-priority targets. By nightfall the two combat teams had established a perimeter with a five-mile radius around San Jose's four airfields.

Ironically, a typhoon to the north caused more damage than the Japanese could have hoped to inflict. Three destroyers of Halsey's fleet, which was assigned to protect the beachhead before the airstrips could be made operational, were sunk. Even Halsey, in the battleship *New Jersey*, was tossed around as if in a rowboat. In all, twenty-five more ships were damaged and 200 planes wrecked or lost overboard. Saddest of all to the Navy, 800 sailors who survived the sinkings were lost to the waves or sharks. Halsey notified MacArthur and Dunckel that his fleet would have to seek safe harbor for repairs; he would be unable to cover the beachhead.

Part of the 77th Division, also brought from Leyte, started unloading the Liberty Ships even while the dogfights went on so the ships could get out of danger. The Japanese raided daily and engaged in "nuisance bombings" at night. According to Harold Templeman, the Red Cross rep, there were 343 air raids in the first nineteen days. The fore-sighted Warden pulled the troops back into the jungle, placed the pack howitzers—one battery per battalion— along the tree line in case of amphibious assault, and had the 161st prepare beach defenses including barbed wire, mines, and bunkers for HQ and medical units. Six thousand American and Australian construction engineers worked twenty-four hours a day on the airfields. Unlike on Leyte, within five days an airbase was up and running and another nearly finished. Gen. Kenney's B-25s started flying sorties out of Mindoro. The work was finished none too soon. The very next day, just four days from Christmas, a kamikaze attack, reinforced by planes from Formosa, on an unescorted supply fleet sank or damaged five ships and killed 100 sailors at the cost to them of ten planes.

Japanese planes from Luzon continued attacking supply convoys to, and the bases on, Mindoro. Regardless, in between raids the 503rd got their tent city up with its company streets and— for the first time in months—dry cots. The regiment continued training its replacements, reviewing tactics, and when C-47s were available and skies were clear of enemy planes, staying jump qualified. The men bathed and washed their clothes in the river. Father Powers and Reverend Herb were able to have services in a drip-free tent. Both knew Tom Turner's future father-in-law was a preacher. Moreover, Father Powers came from Oneonta, NY, eighty miles west of Turner's hometown. Tom would kid the priest as he swept out the tent chapel, "Hello there, Father, nice of you to get everything ready for the Protestant service!"

There was another Christmas dinner, flown in from Leyte, which the rear-echelon liberators gladly shared with the local townspeople. The men dug in on the beach, however, had to settle for a single piece of cold turkey delivered from the feast to supplement their usual diet of K-rations. On the day after Christmas, an Imperial task force of two cruisers and six destroyers with air cover attempted a late-night counter strike from Luzon. Max and Tom, who had been sharing another foxhole on the beach throughout the air raids, now anticipated the landing. "There were ships and airplanes and bombs everywhere and we were just praying not to get hit," Max remembered. "In the middle of all the shooting they blew up an ammo ship in the harbor. I don't know if it was a bomb or a kamikaze that hit it, but oh man! That turned out to be quite a Fourth of July show!" Col. Jones had been checking out the defenses and had to take cover in a bunker. The expected landing never occurred, thwarted by night-fighters from the new airfields on Mindoro and Leyte and a handful of PT boats. Twenty-six Allied planes were shot down or crashed trying to get back to Leyte before the battle ended, around midnight, when the Imperial Navy finally gave up the bombardment and headed back out to sea.

On the thirtieth, Gen. Krueger reinforced Gen. Dunckel with the 21st IR, also of the 24th Division.[1] They had lost six killed and thirty-two wounded in a kamikaze raid on the way. In order for the three regiments to expand the perimeter, patrols and "reconnaissance in force" now became routine—not just to flush out any remaining Japanese on the island but to scrounge from Navy and Army Air Force camps across the river and around the airfields. Filipinos were happy to join in patrols searching for Japanese. GIs were happy to get off the beach.

About this time MacArthur put out a public communiqué for the States that the 11th Airborne had "annihilated all resistance within the [Leyte] area." His announcement coincided with news from Belgium that Brigadier Anthony McAuliffe of the 101st Airborne Division (and a West Point classmate of Gen. Miley) had given his famous "Nuts!" reply to the German demand for surrender at Bastogne. Patton's Third Army cut through the Germans to relieve the 101st. The paratroopers naturally denied ever needing to be "relieved." Patton immediately launched a counteroffensive in which Miley's 17th Airborne was tasked with driving the Panzers away from the western approaches to Bastogne. His division would lose a thousand men against the tanks before linking up with the British northwest of the crossroads. By that time, the German offensive had literally run out of gas; they would be pushed back to their starting line along the West Wall in the next month.[2]

MacArthur declared Love III was over on New Year's Eve. He had 12,000 ground troops, 6000 construction and service personnel, and 9500 air and maintenance men on Mindoro. Long range B-24s flew in daily. The 21st started clearing the northeast part of the island closest to Luzon.

On New Year's Day, 1945, B Company of the 503rd was detailed north with a machine gun section to the town of Paluan, where a Japanese radio station with a garrison of troops could warn of American air and naval movements. It could not be bombed because it was situated in a schoolyard amid a neighborhood of bamboo houses. The reinforced company rode an LCI the first sixty miles. As they were debarking, a Japanese plane buzzed the LCI, and the jittery coxswain started to pull out, spilling some of the men into the water and disorienting them in the twilight such that others needed to assume the role of lifeguards.

They trekked the last twenty miles. At one point they crossed a stream full of crocodiles in a borrowed two-man boat. They got the drop on a Japanese patrol after being tipped off by a local boy, surrounded the station at night, and planned to attack in the morning when the soldiers formed up on the school's playground. Untimely firing by guerrillas with guards at a nearby ammo dump spoiled the surprise and B Company had to shoot it out with the garrison of a hundred or more men. They killed twenty-six of the garrison. Four paratroopers were killed and another fourteen wounded during the day long action.

The survivors of the garrison left in the night and were pursued by squads for the next few days. Some of the enemy drowned, others were killed by Filipinos, and some melted into the jungle. The paratroopers had an American flag to raise in the town square. The Filipinos wanted theirs to be on top, but Sgt. Mike Matievich of Wisconsin gave them a verbal barrage and the Stars and Stripes went up first. After destroying the radio station, they took their fallen comrades back to base on the same LCI that had dumped them. The tired troopers let the Navy know what they thought of the previous landing. There was a brief brawl *ala* those in the pubs of Australia before the LCI got under way. PBYs picked up the patrolling squads.

When Company B returned to camp, they learned the 503rd had once again used inventiveness to overcome boredom and acquire more pets. "The natives taught us how to trap monkeys," Turner reflected (for the Filipinos, it was hunting; for the Americans, amusement). "There weren't any monkeys in Australia or New Guinea. The first time we saw them was in the Philippines. We drilled a hole in a coconut, drained it and cleaned it out a little, put a piece of meat or candy in it, and tied it to a tree. The hole was just big enough for a monkey to squeeze his hand in and grab onto the bait. His fist was too big to get out of the hole, but he wouldn't relinquish that snack. We could just walk up and tie a rope around him. Then we'd give him a treat to get him to let go. After that, all we needed was an organ grinder with a hurdy-gurdy."[3]

By mid-January the Mindoro airfields housed three fighter (P-38, P-40, and P-47) groups, two medium bomber (B-24 and B-25) groups, and two night-fighter (P-61 "Black Widow") squadrons. Gen. Kenney could now provide air cover throughout the Philippines, as he had hoped to do from Leyte. Mindoro would be the staging base for US operations from here on out.

Of course, the buildup had come at a price. Between December 3 and January 3, when the impending invasion of Luzon gained their attention, the Japanese Air Force sank twenty-four ships and damaged seventy-four more including battleships, cruisers, escort carriers, Liberty Ships, and LSTs. Three thousand American and Australian Navy, Coast Guard, and Army casualties had been on board. Four hundred seventy-five American troops and airmen had been killed and another 385 wounded on the island itself by the dogfights and constant shelling. The Western Visayan Task Force had lost sixteen of those killed and seventy-one of the wounded. Japan lost fifty planes as well, most of their naval raiders, and 170 soldiers killed on the island. Only fifteen were taken prisoner. The others, including hundreds of wounded, stayed hidden in the jungles. American vessels patrolled around the island cutting off any reinforcement or escape.

MacArthur was just 150 miles from Manila. Operation "Musketeer," liberation of the Philippines culminating at Luzon, was running ahead of schedule. The 511th moved onto Mindoro and joined the 503rd, who were transferred from the Sixth to the Eighth Army. The new army had been raised in June, assigned to Eichelberger, and tasked with setting free the central and southern Philippines, originally targeted by King and Love operations within Musketeer that had been skipped. Six thousand paratroopers anticipated their next jump. They wouldn't have long to "hurry up and wait."

1 The 19th "Rock of Chickamauga" Regiment had suffered casualties at Schofield Barracks at Pearl Harbor, seized the Hollandia Airdrome, and captured "Breakneck Ridge" against elite IJA troops in northern Leyte during a typhoon. The 21st "Gimlet" Regiment, also raised at the beginning of the Civil War, had seen action on the Western plains, at San Juan Hill, and along the Mexican border. They too had fired their M1 rifles at Japanese planes over Honolulu and fought at Hollandia and Breakneck Ridge.

2 By then the 509th had only fifty-five men left, about half of whom had jumped at Oran. The battalion had picked up 1700 Purple Hearts, more than double its size. The 551st was down to 110 men. A handful had been with them since leaving Panama. The two historical battalions, the first to have seen foreign service, were dissolved at the end of January and the men transferred to other airborne divisions.

3 Originating in medieval times, it came to be known as a "barrel organ" and was a common form of street entertainment in the late nineteenth and early twentieth centuries. While the "organ grinder" turned the crank on the hurdy-gurdy to play its melody, a monkey on a leash would dance around and collect coins from the audience.

Chapter 11

LUZON
Liberation

After taking over Manila in 1942, the Japanese had tried to convince the Filipinos that the occupation would be friendly. They touted their Oriental links, painted the Americans as arrogant usurpers, freed Filipino prisoners of war, and promised independence in another year (the United States had not guaranteed the latter until 1946). But they squelched free speech and religion, beat suspected insurgents, seized farm produce, and fomented inflation, like they had in New Guinea, with the infusion of invasion money. The Filipinos had had a developing economy and government under the Americans, and above all else they had faith in Douglas MacArthur, who made clear his affection for the islands by staying on as military advisor to President Quezon even after his tours of duty had ended there and he had retired from the US Army (he'd been recalled to active duty when the war broke out).

The resistance movement, begun along the trail of the Bataan Death March, had a quarter of a million members—a resource MacArthur knew he could use. The guerrillas had built a sophisticated network of militarily organized groups. At least eleven of them were in Luzon. Escaped American and Filipino Army officers ran many of them (often by self-promotion). Coastwatchers, like the Australian Army had implemented, provided MacArthur information about Japanese movements, concentrations, air and naval bases, and convoys. Resistance groups had stockpiled supplies, weapons, and ammunition brought in by American and Aussie subs at strongholds in the jungles and hills throughout the islands. They sent radio messages out as far as San Francisco. They sought out, fed, and recruited stranded and lost soldiers, sailors, and airmen to the groups. Two of the leaders —Raymon Magsaysay and Ferdinand Marcos—would become Presidents. Their willingness to jump into the fight had been evident in Leyte and Mindoro. All this they did at the risk of being tortured to death along with their families.

Tomoyuki Yamashita had dispersed the remaining seven intact divisions of his Fourteenth Area Army throughout Luzon to forestall the inevitable. Other available units were thrown-together remnants of IJA regiments, rescued sailors, and rear echelon troops. As on other islands, he would not contest the beaches. He put his "*Shobu* Group," 152,000 men whom he would personally command, in the mountains northeast of Manila. Another 80,000, the "*Shimbu* Group" (Lt. Gen. Shizuo Yokoyama), were in the southern peninsula and hills east of Manila whence came the city's water supply. The last 30,000, the "*Kembu* Group" (Lt. Gen. Rikichi Tsukada), were northwest of Manila holding the area around Clark Field and the Bataan Peninsula. An additional sixteen thousand IJN troops, mostly sailors without ships yet also many "Special Naval Landing Forces"—Imperial Marines—garrisoned Manila and the islets in its bay.

On January 3, 1945, the "Luzon Invasion Force" left Leyte Gulf in the company of 800 Seventh Fleet ships—a sight that looked to Barrett McGurn of *Yank* like a "steel-covered ocean" and formed a convoy forty miles long—headed by V.Adm. Oldendorf, who had just been promoted after successfully "crossing the T" in these very waters two and a half months ago. MacArthur was aboard the cruiser *USS Boise*. The cargo was MacArthur's battering ram—the 68,000 men of Walter Krueger's always reliable Sixth Army. The divisions had rendezvoused at Leyte Gulf from bases all over the South West Pacific: New Britain, Bougainville, Hollandia, Aitape, the Vogelkop Peninsula, New Caledonia, and Noemfoor. Their mission was "Mike I," the invasion of Luzon. Avoiding the weatherside of the Philippines and bombers from Formosa, they sailed up the west side of the archipelago. There were kamikaze attacks all along the way. Despite the abundance of onboard anti-aircraft guns and fighters from Mindoro, Leyte, and escort carriers, some got through. Battleships and carriers were the preferred targets. The *California*, already sunk and raised at Pearl Harbor, and the *New Mexico* were hit with the loss of the latter's captain and Churchill's liaison officer to MacArthur, Lt. Gen. Herbert Lumsden. The highest-ranking British officer killed in the war, he was blown off the bridge when a kamikaze hit the ship. Cruisers *Columbia* and *Louisville* and carriers *Kitkun Bay* and *Ommaney* were severely damaged, the latter eventually scuttled. The men aboard two transports were lucky to get only slight damage. The worst day saw a dozen ships damaged, crippled, or sunk and hundreds of sailors and soldiers killed.

Despite the shorter distance from Mindoro, parachuted dummies and diversionary sabotage by the guerillas in southern Luzon, and increased activity by navy and air patrols along its southern shores (including a feint by the 21ˢᵗ IR from Mindoro), Yamashita had expected the Americans to land in Lingayen Gulf just as they had in 1899 and the Japanese had in 1941. On the ninth —three years and a week after the Japanese entered Manila— having dropped leaflets to warn the Filipinos to stay off the beaches, Oldendorf began his pre-invasion bombardment. Kamikazes crashed into the cruisers *Columbia* and *Australia* (its fifth hit in a month) and the battleship *Mississippi* while soldiers hurriedly climbed down rope ladders into Admiral Barbey's landing craft. Exploding planes and ships had not been part of their AIT. At 0950, I Corps (Maj. Gen. Ennis Swift—Eichelberger now ran Eighth Army) and XIV Corps (Maj. Gen. Oscar Griswold) hit the beaches. They were met with cheers and Filipino and United States flags at the town of Lingayen. Griswold's 40ᵗʰ and 37ᵗʰ Divisions drove straight south for Manila between rice paddies and sugar cane fields along the base of the western Zambales Mountains. Swift's 4ᵗʰ and 6ᵗʰ Divisions veered east towards the Cordillera and Sierra Madre Mountains to keep the huge force in that direction from harassing XIV Corps and from reinforcing Manila. Kamikazes swarmed again. They sank twenty-four allied ships and damaged sixty-seven before the Americans established their beachhead and supply line. Planes from Third Fleet, Struble's escort carriers, and airfields on Mindoro and Leyte sank thirty-three Japanese vessels and destroyed 450 planes, many of them from Formosa and Borneo. Yamashita had perhaps 200 planes left. He would get no more reinforcements; all available assets were needed to defend the homeland.

I Corps found that Yamashita had prepared the usual connected caves, trenches, tunnels, pillboxes, and for want of fuel, dug-in tanks used as artillery. Their advance slowed as they literally crawled through the hills; to stand up was to invite target practice. XIV Corps marched as if on a parade for a while through towns celebrating and offering their liberators feasts. They too slowed down in the revelry (and the expectation they must be ambushed at some point) until MacArthur had to issue an order to move on. He wanted the port opened ASAP and the prisoners freed from nearby camps before the Japanese could move them or exterminate them. They stepped it up until January 23, when, halfway between Lingayen and Manila, they ran into Tsukada's defensive line around Clark Field, where the Japanese had bombed MacArthur's prewar air force and more recently trained kamikaze pilots. It took another week for the 40th Division to inflict 2000 casualties on the *Kembu* Group and force them to retreat. The Japanese reinforced their lines with men shifted north from the *Shimbu* Group.

On January 25, Sixth Army alerted Col. George Jones to prepare for the 503rd PRCT's next mission. The 11th Airborne had gotten their alert three days before and were already preparing for action. Initial plans to drop the 11th Airborne into southern Luzon to confuse the Japanese were dismissed as a waste of manpower and supplies. At worst the units would be cut off and cut up. Another idea had been to have the paratroopers and glider troops land on Clark Field, but the crated gliders hadn't even been delivered yet and would take many days to build. Maybe the 511th and 503rd could jump onto Clark Field together. There was doubt, well-founded as it turned out, that the infantry would get there before the paratroopers were wiped out. In the end, it was decided to send in the glider troops amphibiously, drop the 511th inland, and have them link up to attack Manila from the south. The 503rd was held back once more; it was needed for a different objective.

The rest of MacArthur's plan to liberate Manila began to unfold. On the twenty-ninth, "Mike VII" got underway as XI Corps (Maj. Gen. Charles Hall) from Eighth Army attacked the west coast of Luzon north of the infamous Bataan Peninsula. Hall's 38th and 24th Divisions were to cut off Tsukada's retreat into the peninsula and clear it out, open the nearby Subic Bay Naval base, and capture the San Marcelino airfield. XI Corps followed a road that snaked through the coastal mountains. The men dubbed it "Zig Zag Pass." They ran into the same dug-in resistance as I Corps had. It was not until two weeks later, when San Marcelino could provide air support, that they began to make headway.

On the thirtieth, a company of the 6th Ranger Battalion from Sixth Army, a few Alamo Scouts (usually used for behind-the-lines reconnaissance preceding invasions), and a couple hundred guerrillas routed, killed, or captured the garrison of the Cabanatuan Prison Camp, sixty miles north of Manila and just south of San Jose. They had trekked twenty-five miles behind Japanese lines to free 522 American POWs who had been there since the Death March. The Rangers carried many of the weakest inmates on their backs, while the Filipinos held off pursuing Japanese battalions until the Rangers returned to American lines.

While XI Corps established its line across the Bataan Peninsula, 11th Airborne began "Mike VI." On January 31, the 187th and 188th Glider RCTs landed amphibiously at Nasugbu Bay, fifty-five miles southwest of Manila, preceded by an hour-long bombardment at 0730 and cheered on by the locals here as elsewhere. This time they were to be the vanguard for Eighth Army. Gen. Eichelberger, as impetuous as Krueger was cautious, did not want to get tied down like the other divisions. He had air cover strafing, Gen. Swing's artillery pounding, and vehicles racing on the road to the first objective, Tagaytay Ridge, from where 11th Airborne would turn north to Manila. The glider troops, trucked from the beach, fought 7000 Japanese defenders for two days to get onto the ridge. Col. Soule of the 188th was wounded in the action but won a Distinguished Service Cross for his leadership in the battle up the ridge before being evacuated.[1]

At dawn of February 3, the 503rd could only lick their chops and watch the 511th load up into Col. Lackey's C-47s on Mindoro. They were going to jump onto Tagaytay Ridge in the rear of the enemy facing the glider regiments. As usual, not enough planes were available so the regiment would be delivered in three lifts, at 0815, 1200, and on the fourth at 0800. Col. Haugen had come a long way since his days as a captain in the 502nd PIB. He was in the lead plane with Lackey and was the first man out. Unlike the Noemfoor drops, there were only fifty injuries and one death (and a few stuck in banana trees) amongst the 1800 paratroopers in the 511th. One equipment drop was made too early, and some following pilots dropped their men over the errant chutes. These had to hack their way five miles through the jungle to the ridge before getting into action. The division reunited on the ridge at 1300, paratroopers climbed into glider men's trucks, and 11th Airborne headed north on Highway 17, the same one XIV Corps was following south. Manila lay between them.

A race to the capital ensued. Gen. MacArthur, tipped off by POWs escaped from Palawan that the Japanese had orders to "annihilate prisoners and leave no traces," had already sent Maj. Gen. Vernon Mudge's 1st Cavalry Division on an errand Patton (and Custer, whose 7th Cavalry Regiment was a part) would have applauded. Even though the 37th Division was by now close to Manila, MacArthur ordered Mudge to "go around the [enemy] or bounce off the [enemy] but get to Manila" and make a beeline for the Santo Tomas University, which the Japanese had converted to a concentration camp. Mudge was up to the task. On February 1, although his tanks, halftracks and trucks were still 100 miles from Manila and had only been on Luzon for three days since finishing their own campaign on Leyte and Samar, he had Brig. Gen. William Chase make a good old-fashioned cavalry charge. For Chase, it was a throwback to his early Army days as an officer in the horse cavalry on the Mexican border and in WWI. He launched a "Flying Column" (actually two) that leapfrogged entrenched positions, leaving them to the infantry. If one column was held up, the other forged ahead. Marine dive bombers protected the flanks and helped clear out river defenses. On the third, while the 511th was coming down on Tagaytay Ridge south of Manila, Chase's 8th Cavalry Regiment came up to the last bridge north of Manila. The Japanese had not blown it, but they had lit the fuses. A demo expert dodged bullets and sprinted across to cut them. Marine pilots dropped a package over the POW camp with a message: "Roll out the barrel. Santa Claus is coming." 8th Cav roared across the bridge, broke down the gates of Santo Tomas, and freed 3785 civilian prisoners, 2870 of them American. The 1st Cavalry Division's motto would forever after be "The First Team."

General MacArthur came to visit Santo Tomas on the seventh, and spoke to many of the internees as old friends, by name. They hugged him, kissed him, and shook his hands. He felt like, for once, he was a "life-saver" instead of a "life-taker." Emaciated soldiers, kept separately from the civilians and barely able to stand, saluted him. All he could say to them was, "I'm a little late, but we finally came."

By the morning of the fifth, the 511th was at the Parañaque

River and the suburbs south of Manila, where they ran into the strongest defense yet, the Japanese "Genko Line." Six thousand fanatic Japanese troops manned pillboxes (some in the middle of the highway), multiple story blockhouses, and naval artillery behind miles of barbed wire. The big guns hit the paratroopers so hard that they wondered if they were fighting the Japanese fleet. Troops planning a surprise assault on a bridge tried to stop a jeep from racing across to no avail. The jeep came under fire and did a U-turn. It was Gen. Swing. "Why didn't you stop me?" he yelled at the troopers, who now had not only lost the element of surprise but were also getting hit. He fell silent when he realized the latest casualties were his own doing. It took a week to capture Nichols Airfield on the left flank, another week to take Fort McKinley on the right, and yet another before the Genko Line finally began to collapse. It would be late February before the airborne joined the armor and infantry in the city.

The 37th Infantry had entered Manila behind the 1st Cavalry (and just six hours ahead of 11th Airborne's arrival at the Genko Line), slowed down only by liberating a brewery along the way where they took beer showers and filled their canteens. They next liberated Bilibid Prison, which held another 1330 POWs and civilians. Across the street at the Far Eastern University, one of the most bizarre scenarios of the PTO unfolded. Sixty Japanese held over 250 hostages. They negotiated with the 8th Cavalry to release the prisoners unmolested in exchange for safe escort through the American lines. On their way out of town, the Japanese soldiers bowed to the cavalrymen lining the streets. With fingers on their triggers, the Americans honored their word.

Yamashita, like MacArthur, didn't plan to hold Manila, not wanting to destroy the beautiful downtown or its highly inflammable and therefore indefensible suburbs. He would have been content to blow the bridges and declare it an open city. But R.Adm. Sanji Iwabuchi, in charge of the Naval defenses, decided to defy Yamashita and fight to the last man. The "Pearl of the Orient" became an inferno after all when Iwabuchi destroyed its water and electrical infrastructure and the nearby houses ignited. A *Time* magazine correspondent wrote that hundreds of blocks "were burned or flattened." MacArthur, seeing the flames and smoke arising, proclaimed, "By these ashes [the enemy] has wantonly fixed the pattern of his own doom." Since the residents had not been evacuated, the Army did not have the luxury of bombing the enemy. The battle for Manila, "Mike V" (II through IV had been cancelled), behind only Warsaw and Stalingrad in destruction and carnage, became street-to-street and building-to-building fighting amidst the rubble of *Intramuros*, the district housing the sixteenth-century Spanish citadel and the once picturesque historical, cultural, and financial center of town. MacArthur's own former home, the penthouse of the Manila Hotel, was torched as his men entered it. By the time they battled to the top of the stairs, his lifelong collection of books, souvenirs, and belongings were ashes. Even a pair of ancient Japanese vases gifted to him by a foreign minister were smashed.

Other American units were approaching Manila via the Pasig River, which divided the city. They used amphibious landing craft as gunboats, as their sons would a quarter of a century later in Vietnam, to take out machine gun nests along the banks. To the north of the Pasig River, refugees built a squalid shanty town in the shambles and ashes left by the Japanese.

XI Corps went about securing the air and naval installations on Bataan Peninsula. Across the bay to the east, Swing's glider troops were clearing the Cavite and Ternate areas south of Manila. Before they were finished with the battle for Manila, there would be 200 killed and 750 wounded in the 11th Airborne Division, most of those around Nichols Field.[2] They would take out 3000 Japanese along their road to Manila.

The 503rd had gotten another alert from Gen. Krueger on February 3, after the 511th was in the air, for a possible jump on Nichols Field to help the 511th break through the Genko Line. They did their prep work—ammo, weapons, supplies, parachutes—but then on the fifth they were told to stand down again. They cursed their superiors and the heavens over being denied another opportunity to fight alongside their brothers-in-arms.

1 Soule, as a Major General in Korea, would win a second DSC for his collection of fifteen medals. He died in 1952 while still in Korea, but from a "traumatic" incident, not in combat.

2 TV's *Twilight Zone* creator Rod Serling was one of Gen. Swing's and Col. Haugen's paratroopers and a Camp Toccoa "grad." He made the jump on Tagaytay Ridge with the 511th. Later, he received severe shrapnel wounds in Manila. His knee would bother him the rest of his life. Like most vets, he declined to talk of his war memories and flashbacks but would use them— particularly their emotional and psychological impact—throughout his stellar TV writing career.

Chapter 12

FORTRESS CORREGIDOR
Rock Force

One operation remained in the quest to free Manila: to open Manila Bay by recapturing Corregidor, the island fortress called "the Rock," which had been the last holdout against the Japanese invasion and from which "Dugout Doug" had so reluctantly left. A tiny island of barely two square miles, it is the first of several which form a natural picket line across the mouth of Manila Bay from the Bataan Peninsula. It lies about two miles off the southern tip of Bataan, some thirty southwest of Manila. Close by but smaller at only 160 acres is Caballo Island. Diminutive El Fraile—the size of a football field—is covered by a concrete and steel fort built by the Army Corps of Engineers. Carabao Island is last in line, only 500 yards from the southern coast of the bay. Early in the century they all had been fortified, crammed with artillery, and called, respectively, Forts Mills, Hughes, Drum (or as its garrison liked to call it, "the concrete battleship"), and Frank. Gen. Wainwright had been compelled to surrender these along with the rest of the Philippine Islands.

Even on a map of Luzon, Corregidor is only a dot. While the islet seemed insignificant, in the forty years the United States had possessed the Philippines, fifty-six heavy artillery pieces and mortars had been emplaced in twenty-three batteries on it to blast passing ships before and after they got into the bay. The batteries were installed on large concrete pads (fifty-foot diameter circles or even larger rectangles) surrounded by concrete parapets, with ammunition storerooms and quarters for the crews below. The largest guns threw twelve-inch, 700-pound, armor-piercing shells sixteen miles. A few were mounted on turntables that provided 360° fields of fire. Some batteries contained mounted three-inch AA guns and .50-cal. machine guns. The batteries were the main reason Corregidor, also considered the "Gibraltar of the East," and its neighbors (with even bigger fourteen-inch guns) were able to withstand attack and keep Japanese forces at bay on Bataan for so long. However, even though some of the cannons were retractable below ground or into cliff faces, they were vulnerable to direct hits while firing and from the air, so one by one they were wrecked. The Shore Defensemen who operated the guns had sabotaged what were left before surrendering so the Japanese couldn't use them. It was not known how many had been repaired or replaced, but some of the big guns had recently dueled with and damaged American warships. Furthermore, Corregidor had an old Navy control panel in a bunker for detonating mines in the harbor. As long as the Japanese had access to that control panel, it was assumed they could blow up American ships that got past the naval guns. Lastly, MacArthur desperately wanted to avenge the sting of ultimately being ordered by the President to leave to avoid his capture, as well as the subsequent surrender by Gen. Wainwright. He sent Gen. Krueger a memo envisioning an attack by vertical envelopment, amphibious landing, or both. Before twenty-four hours had passed, Krueger submitted an assault plan.

From above, Corregidor looks like a polliwog (the always-hungry paratroopers said a pork chop) with its head facing due west towards the South China Sea, and its tail east into Manila Bay, before curving slightly south at the end much like a comma. The end of the tail, Hooker Point, is partially submerged at high tide. Farther up, the tail slowly rises to 100 feet, widens to about 500 yards, and flattens out enough for a short runway, Kindley Field, between shallow palm tree-lined beaches. A little way past the airstrip is Water Tank Hill, the high point along the two-mile-long tail.

The tail ends where Malinta Hill rises from the waist of the island. In the 1930s, the Army had hacked a system of concrete-reinforced, bomb-proof tunnels throughout this 400-foot-high, quarter-mile-long volcanic rock. They had built large arched entrances for the main Malinta Tunnel, wide enough to drive trucks through, on the east and west sides of the hill. The Army had even laid a set of railroad tracks leading in. Over twenty shorter tunnels (or "laterals") branched out from the main. These were used as storehouses for fuel, water, and food; hospital wards; auxiliary headquarters and cryptography rooms; ammunition and arms stockpiles; even living quarters for civilian, diplomatic and government officials (and where the families of MacArthur and President Quezon stayed during the invasion). Two of the laterals had smaller entrances on the north and south sides of Malinta Hill.

The western Malinta Tunnel entrance opens out onto a hundred yards of sand and volcanic grit aptly named Black Beach. From there South Dock, big enough for several good-sized ships, protrudes towards the mouth of the bay. North Dock, somewhat smaller, and from which PT-41 had departed, points to Mariveles at the tip of the Bataan Peninsula. A little fishing village, San Jose, which had been blasted and abandoned, squatted between the docks. This area, the neck of the polliwog, is referred to as Corregidor's "Bottomside."

Roads coming from Kindley Field skirt each side of Malinta Hill above the breakers along 100-foot-high shelves before dropping down to Bottomside. While the two shore roads continue on around either side of the polliwog's head, the road from the tunnel begins to climb a modest slope. The slope levels off at "Middleside," about the same height as the top of Malinta Hill. In 1945, a few gutted prewar barracks and powerhouses, a PX, and two school buildings sat empty on Middleside. After winding along a steeper slope, the road reaches the crown of the head, an undulating mesa atop 500-foot cliffs with sheer drops to narrow beaches. A mile and a half in diameter, the mesa is known as "Topside."

Like many Army posts, Topside had resembled a resort before Pearl Harbor, with rows of white-washed officers' quarters and tended gardens along paved streets, a swimming pool, a nine-hole golf course, tennis courts, a baseball diamond, a hospital, a school, a movie theater, and clubs for officers, NCOs, and EM. The focal point was a 1500-foot-long three-story whitewashed building, the largest barracks in the world, affectionately known as "The Mile Long Barracks." In front of it stretched out the parade ground, on the other side of which was the flagpole—a mast which had long ago been removed from an old Spanish galleon with its rigging still attached. The Japanese had made a point of showing the world that mast when they struck the Stars and Stripes to hoist the Rising Sun.

Most of the artillery emplacements were situated around the perimeter of Topside. In between some of the batteries were deep ravines which carried runoff from Topside down to the beaches. A network of roads connected the buildings and batteries. Before the Japanese attack, the railroad tracks had snaked up from Malinta Tunnel and meandered around Topside to supply the batteries. An electric trolley had taken the American garrison and their families to work, school, the movies, or the beach. The Japanese had ripped most of the tracks out and dismantled the trolley for scrap iron.

Prior to 1944, the Japanese garrison had consisted of only 300 men in three companies from Gen. Tsukada's *Kembu* Group. They supervised 500 POWs, many of whom had wrecked the big guns and were brought back to repair them and rebuild the installations. The Japanese went about the repairs leisurely, thinking not only that they'd never have to defend the island but that it would eventually become a public park for Manila and a retreat for officers. While Gen. Yamashita considered Corregidor militarily unimportant and wanted all available troops on the Luzon firing lines, Adm. Iwabuchi included it in his "last man" Manila defense orders. By the summer of 1944, the POWs had been removed. Perhaps eight or ten of the guns had been repaired. The garrison was increased by two more Fourteenth Army companies and some 300 Imperial Marines of the 31st Special Naval Landing Force (SNLF). They brought along additional AA and heavy artillery. Thus, Gen. Krueger's G-2 section had estimated there to be no more than 850 men on Corregidor, confirmed by reports of escapees, guerrillas, and Alamo Scouts.

Unbeknownst to G-2, Iwabuchi had added more AA and naval batteries in addition to 4000 Imperial Marines and

Construction Troops in October. The latter were commanded by IJN Lt. Takeji Endo, who sped up the repair work and created defenses around Malinta Hill and within the ravines above the beaches. He built a system of tunnels with interconnected, fortified caves, bunkers, and pillboxes around the batteries and down the sides of the ravines with interwoven fields of fire. He stashed 100 one-man Q (suicide) boats, with 500-pound TNT charges in their prows, in caves along the shoreline. He stockpiled ammunition and explosives inside battery tunnels and cavernous Malinta Hill. He converted some of its laterals into barracks since those above ground had been destroyed and were largely unusable.

IJN Cpt. Akira Itagaki, in charge of the Manila Bay Entrance Force, which included Mariveles and the four island forts, had his headquarters on Topside. He was convinced the only possible attack was amphibious and thus concentrated his defenses mainly against the beaches, ravines, and tail end of the island. Gen. Homma's men had come ashore at Kindley Field in 1942, so Japanese engineers had heavily mined the airstrip and its beaches. They had mined Black Beach as well since it was equally likely to be assaulted. It was inconceivable to Cpt. Itagaki that an airborne attack could succeed on the small island.

General Krueger's plan for the assault on Fortress Corregidor came back to Gen. MacArthur quickly for a couple of reasons. First, Krueger was an expert strategist (one reason MacArthur had picked him to lead Sixth Army, besides "he'd never lost") and had anticipated his commander's order. Second, Lt. Col. Jack Tolson, who had overseen the troop train from Fort Bragg and then commanded a battalion in New Guinea (and would one day head up the entire Airborne Corps at Fort Bragg as a lieutenant general), had been transferred to Sixth Army's G-3

(Ops) Section. He had also been working on an airborne operation for Corregidor, which of course involved the 503rd. It was precisely for what Tolson had convinced Krueger to withhold the 503rd PRCT. Their ideas meshed immediately.

Their plan called for the 503rd PRCT to jump on Topside, spread out, and take over the batteries and buildings. A "reinforced" infantry battalion would shortly land on Black Beach, capture Malinta Hill and its tunnels (and hopefully the mine control panel) and make contact with the paratroopers. With Corregidor thus neutralized, the Navy could start steaming into Manila Bay. Joining the 503rd in this "Rock Task Force" would be the 3rd Battalion of the 34th Infantry Regiment[1], which was currently battling through the Bataan Peninsula in the 24th Division of XI Corps. The 503rd and the 34th (Col. Aubrey "Red" Newman) had patrolled alongside each other at Hollandia and had comprised the reserve at Noemfoor. Though they'd been in California on Dec. 7, 1941, the 34th had fought to get off the beach at Biak and through the mountains of Leyte. Their "reinforcements" would be Company A of the 34th, an artillery platoon of three M7 "Priest" 105-mm self-propelled howitzers, two of Gen. Mudge's M4 Sherman tanks, an AA battery, and the 592nd Engineer Boat and Shore Regiment to deliver them. Also to be attached were a combat photography unit for the press and posterity and some signal corps units to allow for communication between the ground troops, the Air Force, and the Navy. MacArthur, likewise, answered the next day: Approved.

Fifth Air Force, now under Gen. Whitehead (Gen. Kenney had been given charge of all Far East Air Forces), began bombing Corregidor on January 23. Whitehead doubled the daily tonnage on February 7. B-24 "Liberators" from Thirteenth Air Force dropped

500-pound bombs leaving 3000-foot plumes of smoke. Seventh Air Force from the Central Pacific added B-24s, A-20s, and newly arrived P-51 "Mustangs" with 1000-pound bombs. Corregidor was so packed with explosives that whenever an underground ammo dump was hit, secondary explosions would race along adjacent tunnels. According to a May '45 magazine article by Maj. Thomas Hardman (Air Force Overseas Staff), Corregidor was "the most heavily bombed island per square foot of any invaded area in the Southwest Pacific." Eight hundred tons had been dropped before the landing and jumps in Noemfoor. Lae had received 1000 tons in two months. Hollandia had gotten 2000 tons over ten square miles. Three thousand tons were dropped on Corregidor's two square miles in twenty-five days.

George Jones had flown to Luzon on February 5, the same day the Nichols Field jump was cancelled. His men grumbled again, but they knew something was finally up when he came back to Mindoro next day with his arms full of maps and aerial photos that Tolson had given him. The question now was, how to get those troops onto Topside? Because of the Japanese destruction three years ago and the more recent bombings, Tolson's photos showed gutted buildings with their concrete and rebar debris fields, broken-off tree stumps, jagged sheets of tin roofing, and rock-strewn bomb craters. Jones climbed into the nose gunner's compartment of a B-25 going on a bombing run to get a look. When he came back, he called Gen. Krueger to consider Kindley Field, which was 800 yards long and relatively intact. Krueger nixed the idea: it was the thinnest part of the island, the battle would be uphill on a narrow front, and the two attacking combat teams would be separated by and vulnerable to fire from Malinta Hill.

The only other conceivable drop zones were the golf course

and the parade ground on Topside, neither over 350 yards long nor 250 yards wide—a fraction of the size of their previous DZs and the smallest, it would turn out, of any airborne jump in the war. Jones had his S-3 section crunch numbers. The transports would be over them but five or six seconds; sticks would be limited to half a dozen or maybe seven men. The planes would have to make three passes to empty out, giving the enemy plenty of chances at potshots. The ocean breeze would be brisk, upwards of twenty mph. A man dropped from the usual 500 feet would float for twenty-five seconds and drift nearly 300 yards—the entire length of a drop zone—with only a couple hundred feet to spare before the cliffs.[2] The drop would have to be lower than ever to avoid having men sail over them. Because of the very same rationale, Cpt. Itagaki had dismissed the idea of a parachute assault, even though Gen. Yamashita had warned him of this often-used American tactic. The paratroopers didn't care where, why, or how, just when?

On the eighth, Col. Jones squelched all rumors with the announcement to the camp that the 503rd had been selected by Generals Krueger and MacArthur to recapture Corregidor. He assembled his staff. It was veteran and hence well-rehearsed. 1st Battalion was still under Maj. Robert Woods, who had been an instructor in the old 504th Battalion before taking over after the disastrous Noemfoor landings. 2nd Battalion would be in the capable hands of Maj. Lawson Caskey, yet another mustang who had completed OCS at Ft. Benning. Hard-hitting Wyoming-bred Lt. Col. Erickson, who had defied the odds of recovering from his wounds from Noemfoor, was back at the head of 3rd Battalion. John Britten was now a lieutenant colonel and XO.[3] Gen. Krueger had wisely loaned Lt. Col. Tolson, the craftsman of the attack plan, back to the 503rd as an Ops advisor and "Deputy" Commanding Officer. Maj. Ernest Clark, S-3, oversaw Operations overall. S-4 Cpt. Robert "Cracker" Atkins was in charge of Supply, and S-6 Cpt. Charles Rambo—another private at Fort Benning—headed up the Communications department. Maj. Arlis Kline still commanded the artillery as did Cpt. James Beyer the Engineers.

Leading the five companies of the 34th Infantry[4] would be Lt. Col. Edward Postlethwait (West Point '37). He had led their fight across the mountains of Leyte (and been wounded) in X Corps and through the jungles of Bataan with XI Corps. His 1000 riflemen and their attached artillery and tanks would add significant firepower to the assault. Postlethwait was already familiar with the Philippines; his first posting had been with a Philippine Scouts Regiment. Though he'd never been on Corregidor, he always hoped he'd get there. He just hadn't expected to have to fight his way onto the island.

The usual sand terrain model was built and set up in the S-3 tent. Col. Jones briefed the battalion, company, battery, and platoon leaders. He brought in coastal artillerymen and soldiers who'd been stationed on Corregidor to point out details to the officers and men of each battery and platoon. Soldiers spent the mornings at the shooting range. After dinner they cleaned and oiled their firearms and sharpened their bayonets and knives. Two hundred fifty replacements who'd only shown up on the fourth were drilled mercilessly to bring them up to speed. Jones had 1st Lt. Lester Levine, the S-1 regimental adjutant, empty the stockade and attach the miscreants to Service Company. They would man the supply lines on Mindoro so that every available jumper was in a plane. This would be their chance for redemption from the Warden (and they would indeed earn a commendation from him).

Captain Francis Donovan, S-2, who had given Turner one of his positive reviews for officer candidacy, got a visit from his newest interpreter, Harry Akune. A Nisei who had enlisted in December 1942 at the Amache Relocation Camp in Colorado, Harry had graduated from the Military Intelligence Service Language School and had been an interrogator with the 33rd Division throughout the New Guinea campaign. He had been promoted to sergeant in Sixth Army G-2 and had landed with them at Lingayen Gulf before coming over to the 503rd on Mindoro and joining Andy Ando in its Intel Section. Akune's brother, meantime, was fighting in Italy with the 442nd, all Japanese-American and the most decorated infantry regiment of the war.

Harry recounted at a reunion, "When we got to Mindoro, I told the S-2 officer [Donovan] I had never had jump training. The officer told his sergeant, 'Take Sgt. Akune out and show him how to jump out of an airplane.' He looked down to sign papers. The sergeant took me over to a tent that had poles holding up the doorway. He said, 'OK, Harry, you stand in the doorway like this.' He grabbed the door posts. 'And you jump. Now you try it.' So I got in there like he had. 'Now jump over this way.' I hopped a few feet out from the door. He said, 'Great. One more time.' I did it again. He said, 'OK, Harry, that's how it's done.' So he made me jump out of that tent twice. That was my jump school. Next day I was on an airplane."[5] Nine of the signal and photo section troops were not jump qualified, either. These men, like Harry, would have on-the-job training.

Colonel Jones was short parachutes—they had been tattered and disintegrated by the Leyte weather and humid salt air. He called Col. Haugen of the 511th who sent him 1500. Hard Rock accompanied them; he'd been wounded in Manila and evacuated to

Mindoro. Jones visited Haugen, with whom he had a long history, the two having commanded troops together back in the 501st Battalion. Jones told his wounded cohort the plan. Haugen had done a stint on Corregidor and, like Itagaki, couldn't believe the plan would work. His last words to his old pal were, "George, they can't do that to you." He died in Hollandia, waiting for his ride home to the States.

Colonel John Lackey brought his 317th TCG of the 54th TCW to Mindoro from Leyte. He had fifty-eight Skytrains available, which he split between Elmore and Hill airfields, close to the 503rd camp. His pilots had delivered every paratrooper in the Pacific Theater from Nadzab to Tagaytay Ridge. He and Col. Jones were also old drinking pals, and their men had enjoyed Aussie beer together in Port Moresby. He agreed "the drop zones left much to be desired" and felt this operation would perhaps be "the greatest misuse of airborne forces yet conceived." Still, the two colonels had the planes and trucks paired and chalk numbered.

On February 10, the colonels had their transport pilots and jumpmasters rehearse low-level jumps on small DZs staked out on Mindoro. On the twelfth, the same men boarded B-25s so they would all see the actual drop zones. The only good news they could bring back to the men was that there were no visible booby traps on the DZs like the sharpened, mined stakes Rommel had planted in Normandy.[6] The lush jungle vegetation that had started to grow back between invasions was reduced around the golf course and the parade ground by the American bombings to leafless, shattered stumps, as though left by a forest fire. The once stately buildings were just cracked, crumbling concrete shells. There was yet more rubble on the DZs and slopes down to the sheer cliffs not far away. Topside, they said, looked worse than

Noemfoor. Thick woods, good cover for snipers and infiltrating troops, remained around the edges of Topside, down the ravines, on Malinta Hill, and along the tail.[7]

The next day, the Air Corps switched its focus to Mariveles to help the 24th Division get into position and assure safe anchorage for the landing craft that 3/34 would use. Landing craft began funneling into Subic Bay. Eight cruisers and fourteen destroyers took over shelling Corregidor. They exchanged shots with and took some hits from Itagaki's reinstalled naval guns. On the other side of the bay, 11th Airborne finally captured Nichols Field.

The 462nd broke down its 75-mm howitzers from the Mindoro beach defenses and packed them and their shells onto the planes' bellies. Engineers and weapons crews stuffed their flamethrowers, bazookas, machine guns, mortars, and explosives into padded bags and coffin bombs to be dropped. Platoons and batteries were rotated through the tent with the sand terrain table to review their roles. Jones issued field orders from Gen. Krueger. They were written with an air of matter-of-factness, as one might write a shopping list or a meeting agenda.

On "D-Day," February 15, 24th Division would secure the Mariveles area, the landing craft would move there, and 3/34 would embark.

On "D+1," the sixteenth, at 0830, the first lift would land on Drop Zones A (the parade ground) and B (the golf course), secure Topside, and prepare to support the imminent amphibious assault. The first lift would consist of: 3rd Battalion and its HHQ; Battery A of the 462nd and the 3rd Platoon of Battery D (with eight . 50-cal. machine guns); one platoon of the 161st Engineers; one platoon of Service Company; the company XOs from the later lifts (to reconnoiter terrain and positions for their companies); and partial staff and medical sections of RHQ.

At 1030, 3/34 RCT, coming from Mariveles, would land on Black Beach, secure Malinta Hill, stop any reinforcements coming from the tail or the hill, and link up with Topside.

At 1215, the second lift would land on DZs A and B and relieve the first drop to expand the perimeter to the north, west, and south. The second lift would be: 2nd Battalion and its HHQ; Battery B and the 2nd Platoon of Battery D; the rest of the engineers, RHQ, and Service Company (except those being used for re-supply on Mindoro).

On "D+2," the final lift would deliver the reserve at 0830. These were: 1st Battalion with its HHQ; Battery C, and the remainder of Battery D. They would "exploit" the area south of the DZs.

By the end of D+2, with Jones' 2962 men and Postlethwait's 1598, the Rock Force would achieve five to one odds, plenty—they thought—to take even Fortress Corregidor.

On D-1, Valentine's Day, the S-3, Maj. Clark, was making last-minute arrangements with Seventh Fleet to have PT boats offshore and Air-Sea rescue units for the men who would inevitably miss the tiny DZs and wind up in the water. He set up liaisons for Navy and Air Force support for the land troops. Turner and other battalion supply sergeants passed out "units of fire,"[8] four rations, two white phosphorus (WP) and two fragmentation grenades, first aid kits, Atabrine[9] pills, two canteens of water—they had discovered that in the tropics one was not enough—and water purification tablets. To those who would be in the first sticks Turner gave double units of fire. He gave every medic as much first aid supply and plasma as he could carry and a loaded .45-cal.

pistol with an extra clip. Given their experiences on other islands, there were no dissensions.

Colonel Jones called for the last 503rd regimental formation of the war. Rather than crisp uniforms on a bright green parade ground, they wore fatigues and dirty jump boots alongside the dry, dusty riverbed. His Three Thousand Thieves stood proudly at attention. After allowing them to be at ease, Jones read them a commendation and good luck message from Gen. MacArthur, then told them he had faith in them to carry out this difficult mission, and that they were about to make history. After buglers sounded *Retreat* and *To the Colors*, the men were dismissed. With supper they were issued rations of six cans of warm Top Hat[10] beer per man.

1 The training battalion for Tom Turner's great-grandson for boot camp at Fort Jackson would be 3/34.

2 Each mile per hour of wind speed pushed a parachutist 2.8 yds per 100 feet of altitude. A 20-mph wind was expected. Resulting drift = (2.8 yds/100 ft) x 500 ft x 20 = 280 yds (backwards) from jump position.

Additionally, each stick's exit time affected its spread upon landing. Forward speed of jumpers = Plane speed - headwind = 110 - 20 = 90 mph = 44 yds/sec. If each stick took five seconds to get out, resulting spread = 5 x 44 = 220 yd spread from first to last jumper in the stick.

The wind turned out to be 20 knots (23 mph), increasing the drift and reducing the spread. In effect, if a stick started jumping when it was directly over its DZ, the first one or two men would likely land in the ocean, and the last one might still be short of the DZ.

3 Lt. Col. Joe Lawrie, XO up to this point, was apparently not on hand for Corregidor, either due to furlough, incapacitation, or reassignment. I have been unable to pin down the reason. Although one source (often incorrect) lists him as XO and arriving with Woods and the third lift, Templeman's roster (the most

used though not completely accurate source) excludes him. Maybe he oversaw the supply operations on Mindoro. Wherever he was, "Little Joe" was not done; he would rejoin the 503rd for its final battle.

4 Besides the attached Company A, the 34th had a "Heavy Weapons" company. Whereas the Airborne battalions pooled their machine guns and mortars in a headquarters "section," regular infantry battalions were assigned a fourth company consisting of two platoons with four .30-cal. water-cooled "heavy" machine guns each, a third with four 81-mm mortars, and some extra riflemen.

5 Transcribed from taped interview, 503rd PRCT Corregidor Day Dinner, Feb. 21, 1987.

6 German: *Rommelspargel* (Rommel's Asparagus). Twelve- to fifteen-foot poles driven into the Normandy beaches and fields, topped with mines and/or barbed wire, to hinder glider landings and kill paratroopers.

7 Corregidor's topography and installations are much the same as they were by this point in the war. The rubble has largely been removed and the jungle has taken over much of what had been cleared, but the skeletons of buildings, the rusting broken batteries, and the Malinta Tunnel are still there. San Jose has been replaced by a hotel. Kindley Field serves as Corregidor's airport. Abandoned to the encroaching elements for years, Corregidor is now a Philippine National Park and a tourist destination (remarkably close to the Japanese aspirations) including memorials, guided tours, and interactive displays in the Malinta Tunnel. It has been revisited by many of the men and women who were there in 1942 or 1945. The most recent, at age ninety-eight in 2020, and the last known to have made the jump, was Richard Adams.

8 The amount of ammo a trooper would be expected to expend in a normal days' fighting: 150 rounds for a rifle, 750 for a BAR, 200 for a Tommy gun, 2000 for a light machine gun, and 3000 for a heavy machine gun. Each mortar crew packed 100 shells, each howitzer crew 300. Every pistol (except Turner's six-shooter) held a seven-round clip.

9 Quinine, most of which came from Indonesia, had been in short supply since the Japanese invasion.

10 Top Hat Brewing Company was one of many which started in the late nineteenth century in the Over-the-Rhine district of Cincinnati, home to a large population of bock-beer-drinking German immigrants. After the war, the company was bought by Schoenling Brewers which then merged with Hudepohl. The company still operates as a subsidiary of Christian Moerlein. Some WWII beers came in "crown-top" cans which had a conical top (similar to a brake fluid can) and a pressed lid instead of the familiar flat top which required a can opener. The cans were colored olive drab to avoid reflective glare and packed in crates padded with straw for shipping. Many of those crates were parachuted to GIs in the Pacific.

Tom with M1 and emergency chute. Hollandia. July, 1944

With Bill Ryle. Pyramid Tent. Port Moresby. 1943

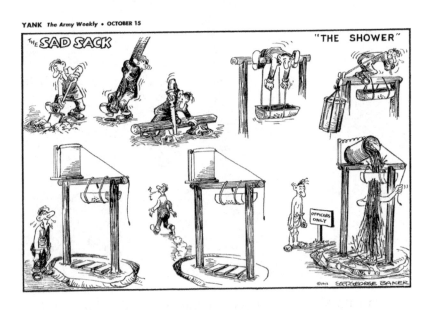

Sad Sack Cartoon. *Yank.* Oct, 1943

Service Co. squad ready for Noemfoor jump.
Hollandia. July, 1944

"The Beard" with Al Runyon at supply dump.
Noemfoor. 1944

PARATROOPS IN MARKHAM VALLEY PROVIDE

THIS picture, which has been acclaimed in Australia as one of the most graphic of the Pacific war, may soon prove to have historic significance, as it records a phase of an operation designed to hurl the Japanese from two of their major bases on the New Guinea mainland. The photograph, taken by a member of the United States Fifth Air Force, shows transport planes dropping one section of the American parachute unit which seized the western inland approaches along the Markham Valley last Sunday. During the same operation, Australian artillery men and guns were dropped, and light artillery was in action within a few hours. First plane to fly over the enemy-controlled landing area contained General Douglas MacArthur. His Chief of-Staff (Major-General Richard Sutherland) and the Commanding General of Allied Air Forces in the South-West Pacific

Page 1 of 2-page spread from *Yank*.
Shadows below troopers who are still airborne.
Nadzab, New Guinea. September 5, 1943

224

ONE OF PACIFIC WAR'S MOST GRAPHIC PICTURES

Area (Lieutenant-General George Kenney) were in other aircraft accompanying the paratroop convoy. In this spectacular picture can be seen the billowing smoke screen laid by Allied bombers to hide the action from Japanese across the Markham River. Hundreds of parachutes, in various stages of descent, stand out against the kunai grass of the landing area. Four transports fly abreast in the middle distance, while near the fringe of the clearing (left) three more planes have just completed dropping their parachutists. By special arrangement with United States Army Public Relations, the block of this picture —provided by courtesy of "The Courier-Mail"—was rushed to New Guinea by air, and was received in "Guinea Gold" office soon after its publication in Brisbane. It is considered dramatic enough to occupy all this week's pictorial space.

Page 2. C-47s staggered up to right for drop.
Smokescreen in background.
Nadzab, New Guinea. September 5, 1943

Drongo's Serenade

I'M just a flamin' drongo,
    Just a lowdown useless wart,
Don't know my left or right hand,
—No brains of any sort;
Just a blot upon the landscape,
But onward I must go;
I'm just a flamin' drongo,
—The Sergeant told me so.

I'm just a flamin' drongo,
Can't seem to keep in step,
Or execute a front salute,
With necessary pep;
Can't swing my arms, keep up my head,
It's always sinking low;
I'm just a flamin' drongo,
—The Sergeant told me so.

I'm just a flamin' drongo,
And thru' weary days to come,
I have the Sergeant's promise,
That things are goin' to hum;
He says he'll make or break me,
He says he won't go slow;
I'm just a flamin' drongo,
—The Sergeant told me so.

I'm a very tired drongo,
Been drilling all darn day,
Until I do it properly,
At drilling I must stay;
And tho' my feet are burning,
And my spirit's sinking low,
I'm still a flamin' drongo,
—The Sergeant told me so.

Page 6 from Memories of Moresby. Anonymous Author. New
Guinea. 1943

226

Ode to a D.I.

HE barks and snarls and curses,
  Till his face grows red and wet;
Calls every mother's son of us,
Names we won't forget.

He waves his arms and splutters,
He grinds his teeth with rage;
Says his Ma could drill the pants off us,
Though she's just twice our age.

He trots along beside us,
Heaps insults on our head;
We take it all in silence,
And wish the blighter dead.

But we always see the day out,
And can joke with him next morn;
We look at him quite calmly,
And think, he's not a bad old prawn.

For we realise this is his job,
A tough one for him, too;
For he's got to turn out men,
From blokes like me—and you!

So we say "Go to it, Sergeant,
Bung it on real thick;
Call us anything you like,
If it's going to do the trick."

"Maybe someday we'll thank you,
As on through life we plod;
And think of all the fun we had
In the Rookie Squad."

Page 7 from Memories of Moresby. Anonymous Author. New Guinea. 1943

227

Typical village stilt home. Noemfoor. 1944

Turner with "Tom and Penny." Noemfoor. 1944

Native family. Noemfoor. 1944

Panama Jones's "3000 Thieves" on patrol. Noemfoor. 1944

Bob Hope's "Southern Exposure" with Patty Thomas,
and sea of wolves. Noemfoor. 1944

Ceremony at ship mast flagpole. MacArthur below flag. Mile-Long
Barracks in background. Corregidor. March 2, 1945

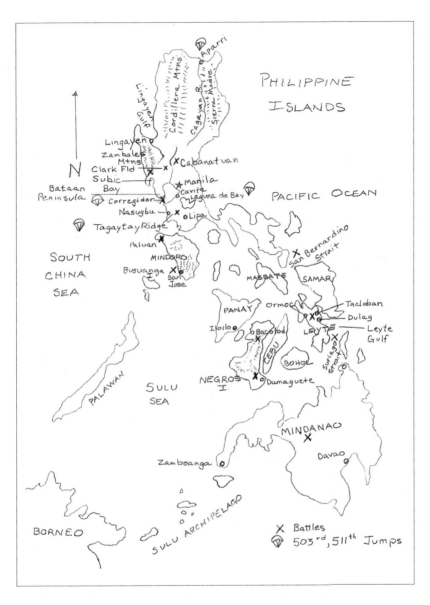

Philippine Islands

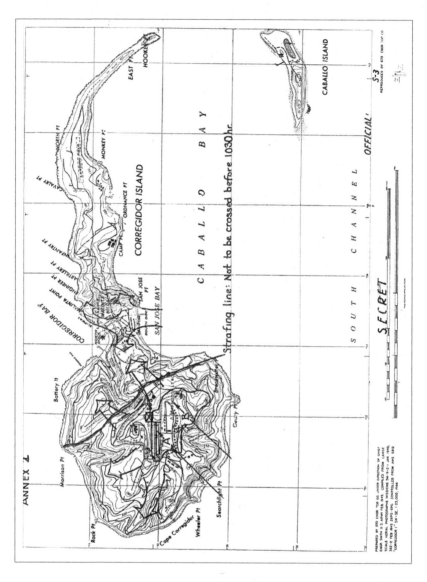

Corregidor map issued to officers by 6th Army. Notations show flight approach path, Drop Zones A and B, sea landing area, and prospective troop movements. February, 1945

Parade Ground Drop Zone A.
Center: officers' homes. Upper left: lighthouse and water tanks.
Corregidor. February 16, 1945

Golf Course Drop Zone B.
Corregidor. February 16, 1945
Postcard from Pete Komer to Tom Turner, 1970s.

Cathedral. Bacolod, Negros. 1945

Filipino money. Invasion, "Victory" (US Printed).

No More Waiting! Home at Last! October, 1945

503rd Association Corregidor Day Reunion Cake
with McNeill's Uniform Patch Design. Buena Park, CA

Tom and Betty Turner. Corregidor Day Reunion. 1978

Chapter 13

TOPSIDE AND BOTTOMSIDE
Assault

T hursday, February 15, 1945, dawned like every other day in the tropics—hot and humid already. Men were starting to stir. Most were trying to ignore their massive hangovers and *Reveille* for a few more minutes of shuteye. Tom Turner decided to do what he knew he wouldn't be able to for some time—take a shower—before he manned the supply dump. The engineers had rigged up auxiliary fuel tanks overhead with shower heads. He reminisced, "It was funny what different soldiers did with their first helmet full of fresh water. The Brits and the Aussies, they brewed tea. French and Italians always made soup. Filipinos and South Americans had coffee. The American GIs, we took a bath." Like most of the guys, he'd already washed his jump clothes in what was left of the river. He put on his only clean underwear and socks, washed out his one extra change, and laid them out on a rock. They would be dry by the time he finished shaving. Off came the Vandyke and the mustache. It would cause some consternation:

"Where's the supply sergeant?"

"That's me."

"Lieutenant told me to see the Beard."

"You're looking at him."

Closer to home, Ecuador, Paraguay, Peru, and Venezuela were one by one declaring war on the Axis Powers. Twenty-five thousand Brazilians were already in Tuscany and would soon spearhead a spring offensive against the Gothic Line at the Apennine Front. Mexico was sending copper, zinc, and lead to American factories. Three hundred thousand *braceros* were working for US farmers whose sons and hired hands were off to war; fifteen thousand Mexican nationals had joined the American Army. *Escuadrón 201*—the "Aztec Eagles"—a hand-picked elite P-47 squadron, was training north of the border. After staging out of Camp Stoneman in March, they would eventually log 2000 combat hours over Luzon and Formosa. In Germany, Dresden was an inferno, having been firebombed the previous two days. The Marines were about to invade Iwo Jima, one of Japan's own outlying islands.

One hundred fifty miles away from the Mindoro base, XI Corps was still battling south through Bataan while bombers exfoliated the jungle ahead of them. The 151st and 34th IRCTs got on Admiral Barbey's LCVPs[1] in Subic Bay, sailed down the Bataan coastline, and came ashore on the beaches at Mariveles. They cleared the area at the cost of a landing craft that hit a mine but had no casualties. B-24s and a destroyer provided ground support. The 151st pushed the few defenders back towards the rest of XI Corps while the 34th got ready for the morrow's mission. Gen. MacArthur had a close call on the peninsula when he had his jeep and some trucks go beyond the front line for personal reconnaissance. Patrolling aircraft assumed the little convoy was Japanese, although there were supposedly none around, and asked for an OK to strafe them. It was fortunate both that the fighters called in first and that William Chase—the old cavalryman had just been promoted to major general and placed in command of the 38th Division at Zig Zag Pass on the seventh—knew MacArthur was out there and refused the order. A few miles south, the Navy's relentless pounding kept Corregidor's defenders in their bunkers and caves.

On Mindoro, deuce and a halfs made dry runs from the tent city to Hill and Elmore airstrips. The men struck the tent camp, save those for supplies and personal belongings, and then picked up and inspected their newly arrived parachutes. Each man spread out his eighty or more pounds of equipment, repacked his musette bag, and stuffed his cargo pockets. They disassembled and oiled their rifles and machine guns yet again. Squads went through the briefing tent for a last look at the sand model and to confirm their assignments. They wrote letters home—for many, their last. Almost all attended Father Powers's and Reverend Herb's services. That night Col. Jones showed captured newsreels of Japanese soldiers trampling the Stars and Stripes and brutalizing POWs. It was an eye-opener for only the newest men. The veterans of New Guinea and Leyte nodded knowingly. Like cavalrymen and their saddles, the paratroopers used their musette bags as pillows for a fitful sleep.

Reveille was at 0430, two hours before dawn on D+1, February 16. There had been no "last supper" or steak and eggs for breakfast, just a coin-flip choice between undercooked powdered eggs or runny pancakes. ("You'd think after four years the Army cooks could get something right...but no.") At 0600 the first lift boarded their trucks corresponding to the numbers on their planes.

Harry Akune left his helmet and equipment on the hood of a jeep for a minute to "take care of business." The driver was the same sergeant who had "jump trained" him the day before. When Harry came back, the jeep and his stuff were gone. He climbed into a truck. He never found his equipment. "I never knew why," he concluded, "but that sergeant didn't like me."

At the airfields the paratroopers were issued life preservers as well as their parachutes since they would be flying over the ocean and then might be blown into it when descending. The flotation devices were called "Mae Wests" after the buxom movie star they resembled when inflated. The parachutes went on over them. Men strapped their rifles to their sides with the reserve chute's belt as they had at Noemfoor. Tommy guns were slung around their necks with the barrel and stock under the elbows to be immediately accessible. At 0645 a thousand paratroopers and paragunners waddled to and pushed and pulled each other up the steel ladders into fifty-one of Col. Lackey's C-47s.

Colonel Jones spotted Father Powers climbing aboard Plane #1. He stopped him. "But I always go in with the first jump," Powers protested. "Some of these men will need me."

Jones insisted, "Not this time. I want the Tommy gun guys on the ground first." He had the priest go to Plane #13, hoping to guarantee him some semblance of protection.

Harry climbed aboard minus helmet, weapon, or equipment. Someone found him a Tommy gun. He had never touched one. Someone else traded him for a carbine and an extra clip and showed him how to stuff it into his harness. "I got between half a dozen guys who showed me how to hook up and check everything. I said, 'What about landing?' They said, 'Don't worry about it. Just act like you're drunk.'"

Tom Turner, Max Phillips, and thirty-seven other Service Company men split into two groups after donning their Mae Wests and parachutes. The first group followed Cpt. Atkins up the ladder into his numbered Skytrain; the rest clambered into the next one. They buckled themselves into the canvas jump seats. The planes began to shake as their 1200-hp radial Pratt-and-Whitney engines revved up. Because of the noise and because most of the men were lost in their own thoughts, very few words were said. Old-timers told newcomers they'd be fine. Every man knew what he was expected to do and how to do it. Most of the men lit up cigarettes with hands trembling from anxiety or excitement. Tom took his pipe out of his jump jacket pocket, tamped down the tobacco before lighting it, then opened his Army-issue pocket Bible to the Psalms.

At 0700 the lead planes from both fields took off. Planes left in thirty-second intervals. Within fifteen minutes, Lackey's transports formed their Vs of Vs and started the hour and a quarter flight to Corregidor. They were flanked by fighters. Up ahead, B-24s, B-25s, and A-20s saturated the island's known gun emplacements and then flew on to bomb Fort Hughes on Caballo Island next door to make sure its 500 defenders would not send help to Corregidor. Meanwhile, the Navy zeroed in on Corregidor's beach defenses. PT boats hammered caves and bunkers around the shoreline. At 0800, while the Japanese hunkered down on Corregidor and Caballo, twenty-five LCMs of the 592nd Engineer Boat and Shore Regiment shoved off with Col. Postlethwait's men and vehicles at Mariveles, where, ironically, the Bataan Death March had begun three years ago.

Even though the two drop zones ran east to west, they had to be approached from a southwest to northeast diagonal because of the wind direction. At 110 mph, each plane would be over its target no more than six seconds. Even if they throttled back to 90 mph, they'd have only eight seconds, be flirting with stall speed and make better targets. They were heading directly into a northeast wind, which would blow the men backwards. Sheer cliffs were within a couple hundred yards of the DZs. To account for wind speed and drift, jumpmasters were to count four seconds after the green lights came on at the edge of Topside before giving the "Go" command and jumping. The planes would require three passes to empty themselves at six or seven men per stick. Thirty miles out, the transports left their Vs and formed two files, one for each drop zone. The left column, flying over the parade ground, would circle counterclockwise after dropping each stick—the right column, over the golf course, clockwise.

They came in at 1050 feet, 500 feet above Topside's highest hill. Lackey, as always, was flying the lead plane. Jones was in it to observe the outcome of their calculations. Erickson was in the door as jumper number one. Five minutes out from the "jump point," Battery Wheeler (near the southwestern edge of the parade ground), the red light came on, and Erickson yelled for the hundredth time, "Ready.... Stand up.... Hook up.... Check equipment.... Sound off.... Stand in the door!" The men bunched up behind Erickson, so much so that his body was turned the wrong way for his exit. At 0833 the green light replaced the red and Erickson saw the concrete battery pass beneath him. He counted off his four seconds, kicked out the first bundle, yelled "Go!" and jumped, with his stick right behind him. The plane peeled off to the left. The second stick hobbled forward into position as the plane circled around for a fifteen-minute trip to the end of the line. Sergeants would lead the remaining sticks. Jones saw a lot of men drifting far off the DZ and heading for the cliffs, Erickson included. The wind had picked up to twenty-two knots, almost five mph more than planned for! Jones radioed the other planes to drop 100 feet and jumpmasters to add four more seconds to the count.

Anti-aircraft guns that the bombers, destroyers, and cruisers missed started shooting. Shells came through the floors of some planes and sent splinters and shrapnel ricocheting around the cabins. Japanese soldiers were starting to appear out of their pillboxes, caves, and spider holes since the shelling had subsided. Several paratroopers were shot or bayoneted before they hit the ground. Others killed or were killed by snipers while still trying to get out of their chutes and Mae Wests. One trooper, with a camera handy while still in the air, got a photo of a Japanese soldier ducking into the underbrush. Fortunately for the cameraman, that individual was more interested in avoiding the action than shooting at descending invaders.

The plane containing 3rd Battalion's demo section had to leave the formation when AA hit an engine. It caught fire and spewed oil past the doorway while the plane lost altitude. Its passengers threw all their equipment out the door as the pilot headed for Manila. Covered in motor oil, they all jumped into a rice paddy, with no injuries. The pilot managed to make it to Nichols Field, which the 511th had just cleared. The men, led to the Mariveles base by Filipinos, would get rides to Corregidor the next day.

As Father Powers hooked up before his plane's second pass, he saw the copilot get hit and slump over. Minutes later, just as his parachute popped open, the padre was hit in the upper thigh just below a cheek. Ironically, his own father had exhorted him,

"Don't get shot in the [backside]," implying not to be turning his back on trouble, and Andy Amaty would one day exclaim at a reunion, "Remember when Father Powers got shot in the [fanny]!" The wounded chaplain then smashed into the naval gun on Battery Wheeler. It cracked ribs and knocked him out but kept him from going over the cliff and perhaps drowning. He awoke groggy and aching in front of a cave. His aide sensed Japanese were inside and pulled Powers into a bomb crater with some GIs in it, one with a broken leg. For a couple hours Powers kept asking, "Where are we?"

Chaplain Herb yanked his risers into his chest for a rapid descent to avoid gunfire on his way down, but in doing so, he slammed into a tree trunk, broke a leg and both kneecaps, knocked himself out, and fell into a crater. When he came to, two medics were putting him onto a door (their stretchers and other equipment bundles had gone over the cliffs) to take him to the aid station. He wound up in a cast from ankles to neck, and after half a dozen surgeries, would wear a thick-soled shoe for his shorter leg.

Sergeant Akune successfully hooked up and bailed out with his stick. "When I finally jumped, that sensation of being out there all by yourself, enjoying looking around, even hearing birds chirping…. It was so peaceful up there—until I looked down. I couldn't believe how fast the ground was coming up!" Harry figured out how to pull one riser, with its connected suspension lines, to spill one side and steer past a tree stump. "They told me, 'Right before you land, pull hard on the risers to slow down.' I did it too soon, and boom! Boy, did I hit hard." Then the wind pulled him fifty yards down a slight slope towards a cliff. He barely stopped in time, got out of his chute and Mae West, and climbed back up, hatless (his fatigue cap had of course blown off in the prop blast). Paratroopers at the top had him in their sights. One of them recognized Harry, or he'd have been a "friendly fire" casualty. They pointed him in the direction of RHQ.

Most of the other first-time jumpers landed safely as well. The photographers, with an assortment of movie and still cameras, started "shooting" as soon as they were on the ground. One twisted an ankle; another cracked a knee. They kept filming from where they sat to get the full impact of the drop and the flurry of action around them. Their work would be praised by film and photo critics.

One of 3rd Battalion's surgeons, Cpt. Logan Hovis, miraculously landed on the parade ground but then was blown across the rubble over to the edge where his parachute finally caught in some trees. He hadn't wanted to manhandle the chute for fear of injuring his hands. It was a wise decision considering the other surgeon had broken a foot and was pinned down by rifle fire.

As Maj. Kline, the artillery commander, approached DZ A, he was hit in the arm and legs by shrapnel from an explosion below him. Unable to control his chute, he got caught in a tree at the end of Officers' Row. Though his feet were touching the ground, his legs were so badly wounded he could not lift himself up to release himself from the chute. He drifted in and out of consciousness until his orderly cut him down and took him to the CP. From there he alternately talked on the radio and coughed up blood until his XO, Maj. Melvin Knudson, arrived to take over. Before long, Kline would be lying on a stretcher, legs wrapped in bandages and an arm in a sling.

When Pfc. Jesse Castillo, a machine gunner with the 161st, hooked up and heard his jumpmaster holler, "Check equipment!" he realized he had not fastened the leg straps of his harness. That meant when the static line yanked the chute, the jolt would fling his body through the harness for a dead fall. The men on both sides got him strapped into the harness. A couple minutes later, when he jumped, he crossed himself as the canopy blossomed and the harness held. Then to his dismay, the man behind him, Jesse's assistant gunner, who had helped Jesse with his own straps, had a malfunction. Castillo could only watch in horror as his teammate plummeted to his death.

Staff Sergeant Doc Landes jumped from plane #2 as the oldest jumper (thirty-eight) onto Corregidor. He landed on one of the officers' homes that lined the golf course. "I crashed through the roof into a room with several Japanese guys in it. They thought I was a bomb or something because they all dove into the corners. I got a hold of my Tommy gun and plastered the room. Then, since I was in [3rd Battalion] Headquarters Company, I started setting up a command post." Erickson later had his men move 3rd Battalion HQ into an old lighthouse, with a better view, on a little knoll between the gutted officers' quarters where Landes had come down and the pock-marked golf course.

The old barracks still had some rooms intact, mostly on the ground floor. Before long 503rd RHQ was up and running. Cpt. Rambo was networking with the base at Mindoro, the battalion HQs, and Gen. Hall of XI Corps (who was in overall command of the sector) via shortwave radio. Gen. Hall gave Col. Jones *carte blanche* for whatever he needed. The medical section already had several rooms full of casualties. The 6th Support Air Party and the Joint Assault Signal Company (JASCO) sections, having survived their first jump, were sending coordinates to the Air Corps and Navy, respectively, for ground support. Cpt. Frederick Pope had his fire direction center ready to spot for Battery A.

Colonel Jones, circling with the rest, determined that the later drops were hitting their marks and jumped out with the third stick. He landed just off the parade ground. Despite the absence of *Rommelspargel* on the DZs, sheared-off tree stumps presented a formidable hazard. He straddled one which scraped the skin off the insides of both thighs and planted a huge splinter in his leg. He gritted his teeth and yanked it out. In retrospect, he felt fortunate it hadn't gotten him higher up. His orderly broke an ankle. They hobbled into the barracks and were offered (for medicinal reasons, of course) some Japanese whiskey that had just been captured.

Battalion CO Erickson, and Sgt. Ben Guthrie and Pfc. Arnie Williams of Company H, were among the fortunate ones to land unscathed. They immediately provided cover fire to protect men coming down behind them. A stick of men from Battery D landed in a ravine, hiked down to the beach, and flagged down a PT boat. One artilleryman was shot going out the door with his stick, another as he landed on the golf course, and another when he got caught in a tree. Other men fell heavily on concrete roofs, broke legs or arms, and had to wait for comrades to climb up and rescue them. Japanese machine gun nests had to be wiped out just to get to the concrete stairwells. One of the last men to jump suffered a streamer and fell into the empty swimming pool.

One bad landing turned out to be incredibly fortuitous. An aide to Cpt. Itagaki had notified him of the LCMs[2] leaving Mariveles and skirting around Corregidor to the west. Itagaki and a few of his staff went to an observation post on Breakwater Point, southeast of the golf course and the lighthouse, and a short way down the cliff, from where he could see the 34th in their LCMs to the southwest of Topside, but not the paratroopers landing above. He was so focused on the boats, probably relishing the thought of blowing them to bits on the beaches, that he wasn't even aware of the C-47s coming in from the same direction. He may have thought they were just another wave of bombers. His disbelief that they could be disgorging paratroopers probably helped. A couple sticks from Company I, whose target was the golf course, were blown completely over the cliffs onto an outcropping only 200 feet above the water, right behind Itagaki's group. They were following a trail up to Topside, came around a corner, saw the cluster of Japanese officers, opened fire, and threw grenades. Itagaki's aide was the only survivor.

Another squad of 3rd Battalion came upon the communications center in the old phone exchange building. They cut every phone line they could see. They had found Itagaki's one weak logistics link: all phone lines throughout the island led to this one communications center near his headquarters. The defenders were now without their commander and lateral communications. All their efforts from here on out would be piecemeal and without coordination. It is the textbook way to lose a battle regardless of odds.

The first lift had met their objectives. They had cleared out all the old buildings around the drop zones and established the operations center in the Mile Long Barracks. Company H (Cpt. Joseph Conway) was flushing out the Middleside barracks and hospital to the northeast of the Mile Long Barracks. Company G (Cpt. Jean Doerr) had a platoon at the top of Ramsey Ravine to the east of the drop zones. They covered the beach and the road coming up through the ravine to Topside. Battery D (1st Lt. Daniel Doherty) had two heavy machine guns overlooking Black Beach as well to aid the pending amphibious assault. Company I (Cpt. Lyle Murphy) held the perimeter of the DZs. The platoon from Service

Company (Cpt. Samuel Smith) was collecting dropped and mis-dropped bundles. Battery A had nearly put together a couple of howitzers (once they collected all the parts, it took half an hour to assemble one) and were starting on others. Two troopers had even climbed a telephone pole and wired an American flag to the top. They got the first cheers of the day. The first jump had had close to twenty-five percent casualties. Jones had expected fifty percent. Any man injured who could walk and hold a gun was patched up and sent back out. At 0930 the Navy and Air Corps resumed bombing around Malinta Hill and the island's tail. Not much later, Col. Postlethwait's LCMs out beyond the destroyers started their half-hour run into the beach.

The C-47s had finished dropping their third sticks and were well on their way back to Mindoro to fetch the next lift. Besides the crews and a few wounded men, Gen. Hall of XI Corps remained on board to see first-hand what progress was being made and to anticipate what Col. Jones might need. Two photographers and two movie cameramen stayed to take aerial shots. Some select members of Service Company had not jumped with the platoon and were flying back to Mindoro. Their job was much like Col. Jones's had been before he jumped. However, whereas he was concerned with troopers, who could manipulate chutes, these men were concerned with para-drops of supplies. Max Phillips explained:

"Your dad [Tom Turner] was the supply sergeant and was assigned the task of re-supplying the ground troops by air. On the first jump there were thirty-five jumpers from Service Company and four 'observers,' one of which was Tom. The four took notice of 'chutists' descent angles for time-compensation for bundle-dropping. This was a huge concern during planning as the jump zones were very small and the wind very significant. After the thirty-five jumpers were on the ground, the plane headed for Mindoro to pick up supplies. At Mindoro there were three additional planes waiting. Each observer was assigned his own plane. Each one then flew to Corregidor, dropped its equipment and supplies allowing as previously noted for the wind, returned to Mindoro, re-supplied, and so on."[3]

Colonel Postlethwait's men had watched from their LCMs as the C-47s circled and the white, tan, and camouflaged puffs of color billowed out. They could see where the chutes were landing on Topside, in trees, on buildings, down the cliffs, and in the ravines. An infantryman exclaimed, "Those crazy paratroopers can keep the fifty bucks!" The 34th passed destroyers and cruisers that were still blasting the beach and dueling with artillery and machine guns in caves. They picked up an escort of rocket launching LCIs which added their salvos. Despite the one-sided bombardment, one of the rocket ships received hits from shore. Some minesweepers which had gone in as close as possible to clear the beach areas fired away as well to provide the final screen.

The LCMs formed five waves of five for the landings, fifteen minutes apart. This landing would not be like Leyte or Luzon, where the beaches had been conceded. The 34th hoped most of the Japanese firepower was concentrated on North Dock, which faced Bataan, or Kindley Field on the tail. Machine guns and mortars opened up from Ramsey Ravine, which faced southeast towards the approaching landing craft. Three LCMs were hit but no one was wounded. The ramps dropped at 1028; the men poured out. Postlethwait had told them, "There's no place to go, once you're there, but forward.... The only reason you will not reach the top of Malinta Hill is because you are dead or incapable of putting one foot in front of the other." Companies K (Cpt. Frank Centenni) and L (Cpt. Lewis Stearns), in the first two waves, sprinted across the beach, avoiding the tips of vehicle mines they could see protruding above the sand, which had been churned up by the bombardment. They started scrambling up Malinta Hill's steep sandy slopes.

Even with the paratroopers' rifle, mortar, and machine gun cover fire from west of the beach on Topside, the Japanese fire intensified with machine guns and mortars from San Jose Point to the east of the beach. Somehow, the following waves had only two men killed and six wounded running the gauntlet to Malinta Hill. Postlethwait's boat itself had forty hits but no casualties until it was empty, and then a mortar round killed the coxswain and a crewman. The vehicles in the later waves started hitting mines, which blew the tracks off one of the tanks and destroyed a 37-mm AT gun, a self-propelled (SP) 105-mm gun, and a truck. The beach was clogged for the following vehicles until a bulldozer could get in to push the wrecks aside. The remaining tank accompanied Company I (1st Lt. Paul Cain) across to North Dock. Company M (Heavy Weapons) set up their mortars and machine guns on the now non-existent fishing village. The attached Company A (Cpt. Gilbert Heaberlin) spread out around the base of Malinta Hill, kept watch on the western Malinta Tunnel entrance, and provided cover fire for Company M and the last of the vehicles—jeeps towing AT and AA guns—trying to get through the mines and wrecks. The infantry could now fight back. While mechanics went about repairing the one Sherman's treads, the other went to work blasting caves near the beach and tunnel entrances into Malinta Hill.

A couple of news correspondents went ashore with the last wave and were immediately pinned down by crossfire. One noticed he was beside an ammo truck, got away from it and crouched next to a tank just as it hit a mine. Two of its crewmen were shot as they got out. He no sooner dove into a bomb crater than a mortar shell exploded over the top. Cowering, he watched from his hole as a medic calmly went about his work of tending to wounded men. The medic blew off his later compliment: "Just doing what I'm getting paid to do."

By noon, Japanese fire was slackening, and Companies K and L of the 34th got to the top of Malinta Hill. Cpt. Centenni looked around, saw his Company K was still intact, and said, "I'll be [darned]. We made it." The last of the infantry's supplies were being unloaded from the LCMs and being replaced by the wounded and dead to be evacuated from the beach assault. Then the landing craft were gone. Col. Postlethwait radioed Col. Jones to say the 34th had met its objectives and was ready to "mop up."

The same time as the 34th was splashing onto the Rock, the C-47s of the 317th TCG were being refueled, superficially repaired, and lined up again on Mindoro's runways. Maj. Caskey's 2nd Battalion had been ready to go since 0830. The second lift went about stowing its bundles and climbing in. The rest of RHQ and most of Service Company (minus the guardhouse detail and the dozen continuing to fly supply) would jump as well. So would "Deputy" Commander Tolson, who had been so instrumental as a planner. Cpt. Henry Gibson, who was about to board with his Battery B, had been born in Tacloban, on Leyte. His father had worked for the US Navy in the Philippines. Later, in high school, Henry (called "Hoot", for the cowboy movie star) had lived in Cavite and had come to Fort Mills for swim meets in the pool, now empty save for some parachutes and a dead trooper.

Due to a last-minute dust storm before takeoff, the second

lift showed up over Battery Wheeler at 1240, almost half an hour late, but the wind had dropped down to its expected level. The changes in altitude and timing seemed to work. Most sticks hit on or close to the targets. Still, there were misses. Tolson landed in a crater and broke a foot. He got it splinted and kept on going. Pete Komer—Turner's buddy since jump school and recently transferred from Company A to Service Company—landed ten feet from the cliffs past the parade ground. Company E commander Cpt. Hudson Hill, who had broken a wrist when he landed on a truck at Noemfoor, dropped onto a roof where his parachute dragged him into a bomb hole. He fell all the way to the first floor and broke some teeth on the pile of debris. He was the lucky one in his stick; the other six were gunned down outside. Another stick of his men missed the golf course and sailed over the cliffs beyond Battery Crockett at the southernmost point of Topside. Hill's XO, Lt. Donald Abbott, noted men in the sticks ahead of him drifting off mark so lengthened his count. Nevertheless, his chute still dragged him nearly to Battery Wheeler, where other men helped him stop. Had he jumped any earlier, he was sure, he'd have gone over the side. Turner's long-time friends, Al Runyon and Johnny Grooms, landed safely and went to work setting up 2nd Battalion's headquarters in the Mile Long Barracks as Maj. Caskey rounded up his men.

By this time the Japanese had well recovered from their surprise and shock. The enemy climbed up the ravines from the shoreline and cliffside caves. They came out of the battery casemates and bunkers, particularly around Batteries Cheney (directly west of the parade ground) and Wheeler and the ravines they overlooked. They fired at the planes; men inside were hit through the floorboards. They counterattacked all around the perimeter. They even used a couple of mis-dropped American machine guns.

A squad of Imperial Marines stood at the edge of the parade ground shooting and stabbing men as they came down. They wounded Sgt. Edward Gulsvick from E Company's mortar platoon. As soon as he hit the ground, he swung his Thompson around and mowed down the squad. He was killed by machine gun crossfire when he tried to attend to a severely wounded comrade.

Fire from pillboxes between Batteries Cheney and Wheeler immediately pinned down some fifty paratroopers from Companies E and F, who were assembling on the field, so they ducked into the buildings at the edge of the parade ground. Two men raced out to help paratroopers still trying to get out of their harnesses while under the fire from the pillboxes. They were shot immediately; one made it back inside. A dozen or more Japanese charged out of Battery Wheeler to bayonet wounded and struggling men on the ground. Caskey's men drove them away with rapid fire from their buildings. The artillery's surgeon, Cpt. Emmett Spicer, was helping some wounded men on his way to the barracks and was in turn mortally wounded. He lived long enough to fill out his own death certificate (minus the time of death) and smoke a last cigarette.

Battery B was scrambling for bundles to assemble guns and even found two of Battery A's. The first few howitzers put into action by Batteries A and B fired point-blank into bunkers and pillboxes, just as they had practiced in Australia. The gunners called this unorthodox method "sniping with a 75." Cpt. Gibson had his men carry one gun up to the second floor in pieces and assemble it there to get a better shot at a hilltop position. One of the gunners, Pfc. John Prettyman, was picked off by a sniper when he tried to get a hanging parachute out of the way. He was awarded a posthumous Silver Star. Machine gun teams set up their fields of fire. 3rd Battalion added to the clamor and helped repel the counterattacks. The perimeter was restored.

The last men of the second lift came down at 1342. Unbelievably, just over 2000 Americans were on Topside. Eleven had been killed on impact with walls or casemates or dragged over the cliffs onto the rocks below; three more had streamers. Twenty-one had been killed by the enemy; fifty were wounded; twenty or more were missing. Most of the latter were hiding in the ravines till it was safe to climb up on top or get down to the PT boats. Seventeen had already been picked up by PTs (from the beaches, mostly; legend has it that two brothers wound up in the water together) and were delivered later in the day to the 34th on Black Beach—they would be the only men in the war to make both an airborne and an amphibious assault on the same day. Two hundred ten had suffered jump injuries. There were countless "walking wounded;" no blood, no treatment. All in all, Jones felt fortunate. His casualty rate was far below expectations, not quite fifteen percent.[4]

Captain Hill, broken teeth and all, set up Company E's HQ at one end of "Officers' Row"—the two-story houses south of the parade ground in which they had earlier taken refuge. The skirmishing there with the batteries and bunkers would continue throughout the afternoon. The engineers set about clearing a small landing strip within the DZs for Maj. Kline's L-5 observation plane to land. Almost 200 men would eventually be evacuated, some by the spotter plane, others later off the beach. Turner and the other three supply sergeants, each at the head of a V of "biscuit bombers" that had been loaded by the stockade detail, hit the mark with their coffin bombs and turned to follow the pack back to Mindoro.

More command posts were being set up amongst the most intact buildings and the barracks. P-47 "Thunderbolts" and destroyers around the island were already responding to the 6th Air Support and JASCO calls to strafe and bomb enemy strong points. The 2nd Portable Surgical Hospital (the forerunner of Korea's MASH units) had its hands more than full. Maj. Thomas Stevens, 503rd surgeon, stripped to his shorts and boots as he worked on the wounded and injured, many of whom were in his own section. A few doors (or holes in the wall) down from Cpt. Rambo's comm center, Harry Akune and Andy Ando were already translating captured documents.

Pete Komer and some other Service Company jumpers had been assigned to assist Red Cross Field Director Harold Templeman. With their help he set up a canteen, as he had on the other islands, in the barracks. They collected four tons of supplies from the DZs including cigarettes, candy, coffee, and toiletries. In the following days it would come to be the only place of refuge, where an exhausted GI could get a cup of coffee and a snack between patrols. When Pete—a master scavenger—was rummaging through rubble in the room that was to be the canteen's storeroom, he found bolts of exquisite Japanese silk. He stuffed as much as he could into his musette bag. There was another stash of *sake* (rice wine), whiskey, and beer. Templeman and Komer delivered most to the aid station for the wounded and medics, and some, with their compliments, to Col. Jones. The rest they kept as a finder's fee.

Heading to RHQ after making the rounds of E Company's deployment an hour after his jump, Lt. Abbott came across a group of 462nd gunners north of the Mile Long Barracks. Their howitzer was ready to go, and they were passing around a bottle of hooch they had also found in the barracks. They offered him a drink. Well within his rights to have them arrested, he simply elected to have them "carry on."

By mid-afternoon, 2nd Battalion began taking over 3rd Battalion positions around the DZs so Erickson's men could expand the perimeter along the northern rim. 1st Lt. Joseph Turinsky's Company D fanned out to the south, where Batteries Geary, Crockett, and Hamilton lay. His platoons sparred with the enemy inside and around the casemates.

Company F took over Officers' Row. 1st Lt. William Bailey set up his HQ at the southwestern end, behind Batteries Boston and Wheeler. Caskey's instructions to him were to clear the two batteries. Boston, a small AA battery guarded by a few Japanese, fell quickly, but Wheeler was a different story. A machine gun in a tower held them at bay despite their using grenades, a bazooka, and a flamethrower.

Hill's Company E was to move north from the DZs. However, Hill was still penned up in the officers' buildings by the firing from around batteries Wheeler and Cheney to the west. He radioed Lt. Abbott, who radioed for artillery support. The SCR 576 walkie-talkies apparently worked better here on the plateau than they had on the other islands: 75-mm shells soon banged into the pillboxes, silenced the machine guns, and allowed Company E to move out. When he finally got his men together mid-afternoon at the northwest corner of the parade ground, his platoon leaders reported they had already lost an officer and thirty-seven men, fully a quarter of his company.

3rd Battalion moved out. Company H worked its way north

to Morrison Hill, Topside's highest point, and James Ravine which it overlooked to the northwest. On the way they killed a few enemies in the Middleside barracks beyond the hospital before finding yet another supply of liquor. Cpt. Conway put a guard on it and told the rest to keep moving. When a platoon got to Morrison Hill, it was able to take Battery Chicago (AA) from the rear and establish a solid position. Company G was already positioned on Middleside, 500 yards west of South Dock. Besides machine gun nests in some old AA pits above Ramsey Ravine to aid the 34th and cover the road that came up the ravine from the beach, Cpt. Doerr had emplacements in buildings east of the golf course. Company I had assembled on the golf course and started towards the southeastern rim of Topside between Breakwater Point (where Cpt. Itagaki had been killed) and Ramsey Ravine to tie in with Company G. One of Cpt. Murphy's platoons had already gone down into Ramsey Ravine, south of the beach, to provide more firepower for the amphibious landing, while the other two stayed on the edge of the rim.

Jones decided there would be no more drops. He radioed his recommendation for a new plan to Gen. Hall: fly Pug Woods's 1st Battalion and the rest of the third lift from Mindoro to Luzon tomorrow, truck them to Subic Bay, and have the Boat and Shore Regiment deliver them to Black Beach. That way, Jones figured, at least there wouldn't be any more parachuting injuries. Woods's men were spending today as the other two battalions had yesterday, reviewing their assignments, sighting their guns, cleaning their weapons, drawing their supplies, repacking their cargo pockets and musette bags, and bundling weapons for the planes.

Late in the afternoon, the Japanese troops around Topside started making uncoordinated, separate attacks from their many hiding places—of which forty-five were later counted within fifty yards of the DZs alone. They began to pop up out of spider holes everywhere. It seemed like a life-or-death game with jacks-in-the-box. Areas that had earlier been cleared had to be won again. Bunkers previously knocked out were refilled with Japanese via Lt. Endo's catacombs. A machine gun nest on a knoll near Wheeler peppered the drop zones where Weber, Hudyma, Phillips, and the rest of Service Company were trying to retrieve the supplies that Turner and their other cohorts had just dropped. Cpt. Atkins herded them back inside. Gibson's second-floor howitzer took out the machine gun nest so the supply section could resume its work. Only five out of the nine howitzers dropped were currently operational: two were damaged and two were still out of reach.

As dusk approached, the 503rd on Topside—as well as the 34th on Malinta Hill—found it nearly impossible to dig in for the certain night counterattacks. Beneath the surface dirt, the island was pure volcanic rock (hence the black beach). Soldiers resorted to piling up rocks and chunks of concrete around bomb craters for breastworks. The procedure after dark was the same as at Nadzab and on Noemfoor, Leyte, and Luzon: don't move, shoot what does, but don't shoot what you can't see. Men in foxholes and bomb craters slept briefly in shifts. JASCO had arranged for destroyers to fire star shells (parachute flares) over the island. The few infiltration attempts on Topside were unsuccessful; as soon as a flare lit up crawling bodies, they were shot. Two did get in as far as the Mile Long Barracks and ran along the front throwing grenades inside until a 2nd Battalion sentry shot them. Japanese mortars plopped in a shell here and there to keep everyone in the rifle pits and machine gun nests on edge.

Around midnight, a duty officer on Malinta Hill had no

more than written "All quiet on Corregidor" in his company journal than firing erupted from the east end of the hill. Mortar fire, previously ranged, was well placed into American positions. Japanese climbed up the east slope and tried to scale the nearly vertical northwest face. Forward squads fought hand-to-hand as they were overrun. Phones were knocked out. Men at the top, as though on Bunker Hill, held their fire till the last second and finally repelled the attack. In two hours of fighting, many squads were reduced to half strength or completely eliminated. K Company was particularly hard hit. Its 3rd Platoon was isolated on outcroppings around Malinta Point and pinned down all night. Some squads would be cut off for days.

At 0300 there was an explosion in the cliff next to Company A of the 34th. It was intended to bury them and block the road but instead it blew rocks over their heads into the bay. A platoon of Japanese waded ashore wearing vests loaded with TNT. Companies A and M eliminated them on the beach before they could cause damage. An almost simultaneous banzai charge from Malinta Tunnel by twenty or thirty Japanese Marines was likewise repelled.

When dawn broke, K Company attempted to relieve its surrounded outposts but failed. Cpt. Centenni, who had been so elated they all made it to the top yesterday, was killed along with three more of his men in the attempt. Half his 200 men were already casualties. There were an estimated 350 enemy dead so far on the Rock. The Americans were fortunate indeed to have disrupted Japanese communications. A coordinated attack from all sectors that first night would surely have wiped them out.

1 Landing Craft, Vehicle, Personnel. The American Army designation for a Higgins boat.

2 At sixty men or a tank apiece, Itagaki would have known this was a significant force approaching.

3 As related by Max Phillips to Jon Turner (12/29/89). Colonel Lackey had assigned a dozen planes for supply. Each of the four observers would be in the lead supply plane of a group of three from Mindoro. When the observer started pushing supplies out the door over Corregidor, men in the other two planes would follow suit.

4 Sources disagree overall, with eight to twenty-one KIA and between five and seventeen killed by landing mishaps. All agree to 210 jump injuries of varying seriousness, three killed by malfunctions, and fifty wounded in action. The "History of the 2d Battalion (Airborne) 503d Infantry" lists two killed by swinging into buildings, and eight KIA near Japanese caves around the cliffs; nine over the cliffs but rescued by PT boats; six MIA. Devlin claims as many as eight were dragged over the cliffs and onto the rocks below. I used Guthrie's numbers, corroborated by the S-3 officer's journal. After all, they were there. There is a consensus of between thirteen and fifteen percent jump injuries and casualties, nearly 300 men.

Chapter 14

MIDDLESIDE
Linking Up

On Topside, D+2, as paratroopers shaved or ate their breakfast rations, their eyes widened and jaws dropped. Out of nowhere came a bright red Ford V-8 Roadster. Japanese soldiers were piled into the front seat and the rumble seat, and more were running behind. They were heading down the road towards Middleside. Once they got over the edge, they could get protection from or take refuge in the many caves along the road. The stunned paratroopers finally unslung their weapons to open fire, and machine guns raked the vehicle and runners. The car crashed and exploded. The runners toppled over one by one.

Thirty miles away in Manila, a unit that dated back a hundred years to the Mexican War, the 148th Regiment of the 37th Division, freed 7000 civilian prisoners at the Philippine General Hospital, another location used by the Japanese as an internment camp. Sixth Army surrounded Fort Santiago, the old Spanish fortress, where 1000 Japanese troops held 4000 Filipinos hostage, again negating the use of aerial bombing. The US artillery began a barrage that would take six days to breach the fort's forty-foot-thick walls.

The Rock Force on Corregidor had yet to link Bottomside with Topside. The Americans guarded the approaches, but Japanese emplacements down the ravines, in the cliffs, and along the beaches prevented any travel. Supplies could not get up to Topside, and wounded men could not be taken down to the docks. Furthermore, one of the messages Akune had translated was one sent out to the Japanese officers telling of Cpt. Itagaki's death. This was crucial info: a naval captain—the equivalent in command to an infantry colonel—would command at least 5000 men. Col. Jones now knew what he already suspected: the Rock Force was facing far more than the G-2 estimate. In fact, a POW captured later would divulge that 3000 of them virtually surrounded the troopers on Topside. Postlethwait's men sat on another 2000 inside and around Malinta Hill. Each regiment was outnumbered by 1000 men. Even more were dug in along the tail.

The 3rd Battalion was to expand the perimeter towards the northern and eastern rims. Col. Jones had pulled Company H back at dusk to reduce the perimeter and solidify the line. At 0730, Conway's men once more attacked Morrison Hill, which had been reoccupied by the Japanese in the night. The battle ended there at 1000 with Conway in control. Company H had two men wounded but killed thirty-seven Imperial Marines.

Jean Doerr and Company G continued to hold the area overlooking Black Beach, Ramsey Ravine, and the road coming up from Bottomside. One of his platoons started combing the slope down along the road.

Lyle Murphy's Company I worked its way past the lighthouse towards Breakwater Point to the southeast and then down the slopes of Ramsey Ravine. One of his patrols heard talking up ahead and prepared for an ambush. It turned out to be a group of eight of the missing men, several of whom were wounded, all from Company E. They were the ones who had landed downhill while Cpt. Hill was falling through the roof. They had tried to fight their way back up and then spent the night eluding Japanese patrols while patching each other up. Murphy sent them towards the barracks. Hill's shot-up company would be glad to see them. Within minutes, Company I was fired on from a camouflaged cave. Machine guns, grenades, and finally an engineer's flamethrower ended the fusillade.

At 0830, the C-47s carrying the third lift flew across the DZs. The Japanese AA was livelier since the Navy and Air Force had not suppressed them this time. They hit sixteen of the forty-four planes and killed or wounded half a dozen crew members. Col. Jones had been correct not to attempt another jump. Maj. Woods had his men jettison the supplies, bundles, and pack howitzers so they wouldn't have to lug them onto the boats or up the hill. They flew on to San Marcelino's airfield where they'd be transferred by truck to Subic Bay and onto LCMs to Corregidor.

Major Caskey's 2nd Battalion swept the southern rim, keying on the one area where the defenses of the 503rd had been thinnest and the Japanese concentration the largest: the vicinity of Batteries Wheeler and Cheney, and Cheney Ravine beyond them to the west. These were positions the enemy had tried to exploit during yesterday's second drop. Battery Wheeler, which housed the huge gun that broke Father Powers' ribs, was 150 yards across and fifty yards deep. Its steel-reinforced concrete walls were immune to aerial and naval bombardment. It had underground chambers for ammo and crews. F Company, like H, had retracted their perimeter in the evening. As elsewhere, the Japanese had moved back in. The fight for Battery Wheeler began anew. Young Lt. William Campbell was the first casualty. When he peered over a ledge for a look through his binoculars, a rifleman zeroed in and waited. When Campbell came up for a second look, he was hit between the eyes. He had a newborn son he would never hold. Trooper Joseph Shropshire led a bayonet charge through white phosphorus smoke. Half a dozen men charged up to the roof of the battery, where they were killed. The company was stopped, like yesterday, by machine gun fire. They threw more smoke grenades and withdrew.

Lieutenant William Calhoun, the Company F platoon leader who had opined on the merits and flaws of the M1 Carbine in the States and tested the "Tanker" model in New Guinea, lined his platoon up for another try. Before they could go in again, Maj. Caskey sent Lt. Joe Turinsky and Company D to take up the assault. Calhoun was disappointed that F Company was not to resume the attack but was relieved to learn that the men killed on the roof had been Japanese, not American. He questioned a planned artillery barrage, doubting the howitzers had enough distance to arc shells into the battery. Sure enough, the shots went over the battery into the ocean. He had F Company pour in cover fire and some more WP grenades; then 1ˢᵗ Lt. James Gifford's platoon charged the battery.

They got up the stairs to the roof, where Japanese rushed up from the casemate below. There was a melee for fifteen minutes around the base, up the steps, and on top of the concrete pad. Company D regained the battery. Over sixty Japanese were killed. Six paratroopers from the 2ⁿᵈ Battalion died and fourteen were wounded. Besides Campbell, two other officers had been hit. Also among the casualties, D Company thought, was S/Sgt. Amleto Pucci, with a bullet hole in the middle of his helmet. When they tried to move him, suddenly he groaned and awoke. The bullet had gone in at such an angle that it spun around between the shell and the liner until spent and dropped out. Pucci had only been knocked out and suffered no more than a headache. He rejoined his platoon when his head literally stopped spinning.

A platoon of Company E was trying to knock out a bunker between Battery Wheeler and the Mile Long Barracks. Their first assault, like Company F's, was beaten back. They called for artillery. Gibson soon arrived with two 75s and their crews. Standing unprotected while bullets zipped past them, they used their nineteenth-century direct fire approach to blast open the door and fire inside. They eliminated nearly 100 of the enemy. Gibson and the two gunners won Silver Stars for selflessly putting themselves in harm's way.

While some squads watched rear areas where Japanese might pop up out of spider holes or supposedly empty emplacements, platoon-sized patrols began a grueling process of eliminating the enemy around the perimeter of Topside one cave or bunker at a time. Companies K and L of the 34th were doing the same thing to get to their stranded men and re-establish their own perimeter on Malinta Hill. Company I of the 34th worked its way up the road towards Middleside while Company G of the 503rd inched downwards. It seemed the Japanese contested every yard of the two-mile road and its switchbacks.

Captain Magnus Smith, the Assistant S-3, recorded that one proven method of reducing a strongpoint such as a cave was for a squad or platoon to approach the position with a bazooka round or a machine gun blast, throw a couple WP grenades in front, and shoot a three-second burst from a flamethrower through the smoke. To ensure the cave would not be reoccupied after the paratroopers moved on to the next, engineers and demolition teams topped off the job with twenty pounds of TNT in satchel charges to blast the mouth and seal the opening.

Doc Landes and some engineers figured out how to wipe out caves in the ravines if TNT wasn't available. "We'd open a five-gallon gasoline can, tie a rope on the handle, and work our way around the mouth of the cave to get above it. The other guys had to be watching other nearby caves for snipers while we did this. We'd lower the can into the opening and swing it forward. We let go on the backswing, and it would crash down into the cave and that gasoline went everywhere. Then a guy with a flamethrower would ignite it."

The artillery emplacements were particularly hard to flush out. Like Wheeler, they were bomb-proof. All the tonnage dropped on them had done negligible damage. Even a howitzer at close range had little effect, and all the while enemy snipers and machine gunners could pick off the attackers. The entrance for a battery was generally through a tunnel that led to a heavy steel back door, usually camouflaged. Once they found it, the gunners shelled the hillside around the door to cause a landslide which sealed it. Then the demolition team would find a ventilation shaft between the door and the emplacement and remove the covering. They wrapped grenades and TNT around a gasoline can with prima (detonating) cord, then put in two fuses, one a few seconds longer than the other. The whole "infernal machine" (so named by 1st Lt. William Blake, head of the demolition section) was let down a short way, tied off, and the fuses lit. The first fuse was long enough for the men to get away and under cover. Near its end it would burn through the cord holding the can, which would then drop while the second fuse ran out at the prima cord. About the time it hit the floor, the whole contraption exploded. What occupants the explosion didn't kill outright were asphyxiated when the fire used up the oxygen inside the tunnels. Some teams actually had conversations through the shafts with their adversaries. Refusing the option of surrender while the fuses were being lit, one presaged, "Oh, you don't want to do that. Very much dynamite down here." Nothing blew up but the gas can. For now.

The twelve supply planes made two runs from Mindoro on D+2, as they would continue to do until the road to the beach could be made usable. Turner was now doing double duty as a communications sergeant. He was in radio contact with JASCO, which was in contact with the Navy. "I was supply sergeant, so I didn't jump with the rest of Service Company who went in on the first couple jumps. I stayed in one of the planes to go back and re-supply the regiment on Topside. While performing this task, whenever we spotted a Japanese strongpoint on the island, we would radio the Navy with the coordinates or position of the bunker or cave or whatever, and they would bomb it so our guys didn't have to grind it out. On one of the supply flights the Navy radioed the plane and told us to back off, that they were going to do some shelling. When the barrage was finished, they radioed the plane back, said they were done, and to continue air supply."[1]

Colonel Postlethwait knew the 503rd was hard-pressed for water and medical supplies. Their two canteens apiece were already empty. Their tongues were swelling and lips cracking. The island had no substantial fresh water source; it had always been shipped in from Mariveles and stored at several locations. Watertank Hill and Malinta Tunnel were both in enemy hands. Two reservoirs on Middleside and Topside were nearly dry. Furthermore, Postlethwait's medical section had just gotten a call from Topside requesting plasma. He loaded up a Sherman tank and the M7s with water cans and medical supplies and had them head up the road to Topside. Caves on both sides of the road spewed fire. Bullets clanged off the armor all the way up. Paratroopers and infantryman fired back at the caves. Cheered on by the paratroopers up above, the armored vehicles made it. Not only did they deliver that load of crucial supplies, they also carried wounded men back down the hill for evacuation. Then the tank turned right around and did it again, only this time firing into the hillside caves as it made the run. Back down below, the tankers tried to count the bullet dents and scratches. They gave up at 200. The tank crew, in the fashion of bomber crews, had painted a name on its sides—*Sad Sack*. It had taken four years, but at last Sad Sack was a hero!

All told, the Army sealed over forty caves along the road to Topside. Blake's demolition team, which had bailed out into the rice paddy and been brought into the beach, stepped up the process. The 34th and the other tank—*Murder, Inc*—sealed off dozens more caves around North Dock and the base of Malinta Hill. Companies K and L likewise inched closer to their stranded men. Though they did not reach them, they made radio contact to tell them they weren't forgotten. The platoon radioed back that they had found a water hole nearby and were still killing Japanese who were trying to get to it.

At about 1330, paratroopers from Company G met up with infantrymen from Company I at a hairpin turn in the road. Col. Postlethwait thought it was safe enough to send two jeeps towing trailers filled with water cans to Topside. Cpt. Atkins had them unloaded and took one jeep and trailer to collect coffin bombs and bundles around the DZs. Col. Jones took the other down the hill.

Like Wellington and Blücher at La Belle Alliance after Waterloo, the two colonels shook hands and had a short discussion. Then Jones drove back up to 503rd RHQ.

The third lift arrived mid-afternoon in LCMs from Mariveles. They were both relieved and disappointed not to have jumped. Despite all the cave closures, machine guns opened up from Topside's east-facing cliffs. They killed half a dozen GIs and a sailor in the tightly packed boats. The landing craft backed off. JASCO made a call. A destroyer moved in and shelled the cliff face.

Weldon Hester, the Red Cross Field Director for the 34th, had been watching the landing when the shooting started. He did "a belly slide" into a foxhole. Three "profane" guys jumped in on top of him but moved out as the firing abated. The boats came back in, and the troops debarked without further casualties although the firing continued. A fourth man, naked, cursing, and dripping wet, now jumped in on Hester. He had been bathing in the surf when the landing began and had been seeking cover the whole time since. He quit cursing when Hester began laughing despite bullets whizzing around. "And to think," the man said, "I could have joined the Navy."

By now dusk was near. Col. Jones sent orders down for 1st Battalion to form a perimeter defense for the night and come up in the morning. 2nd Battalion, centered at Battery Boston, would guard the DZs, surrounding buildings, and Battery Wheeler. 3rd Battalion covered Morrison Hill and Middleside, overlooked the eastern cliffs from Ramsey Ravine down to Breakwater Point, and tied in from that point back over to the golf course. S/Sgt. Walter Baker of Company I and Pvt. Herman Lackey of Company H earned Silver Stars for protecting and retrieving wounded comrades from under the Japanese' noses as the companies disengaged and drew in their perimeters.

The night was quiet until a half hour before midnight, when the Japanese inside of Malinta Hill came out to try to reclaim it. They had climbed nearly to the top when a flare lit them up. K and L Companies blasted them with rifles, machine guns, and grenades. At about the same time, a Japanese suicide squad on Topside detonated a powder magazine beneath Battery Wheeler. It blew chunks of rock and spewed flames hundreds of feet from the openings in the concrete. Men from 2nd Battalion running for cover were surprised to see, lit up by the flames, Japanese running alongside them who had infiltrated but were equally intent on escaping the explosion. Shots were exchanged; a trooper was killed and two were wounded. The Imperial Marines disappeared into the jungle around the rim of Topside. When the smoke and heat finally diminished at Battery Wheeler, Lt. Gifford would find sixty-five charred bodies inside.

The Japanese tried another charge up Malinta Hill at 0300 with the same results. The enemy lost 150 soldiers, but by dawn Company K was down to thirty effectives—eleven of which were still stranded. Company cooks and clerks manned the line. Lt. Gitnik, who had replaced Cpt. Centenni, was dead. He was replaced by Lt. Fugitti, who had gotten a battlefield commission on Leyte. They were out of grenades. Company L split the few they had left with them.

By dawn of "D+3," the Rock Force had already counted 200 more enemy dead than the 850 who were supposed to be there, and no one knew how many more had been sealed up in caves or blown up in the caverns below the batteries. "Mopping up" was going to take a while.

The 1st Battalion of the 503rd PRCT started up the curving jungle-bordered road to Topside at 0500 on Sunday, February 18. The trip was interrupted by skirmishes with caves that had not yet been cleared (usually concealed by foliage or camouflage) or had been magically reoccupied. Richard Pardue wrote in the Company A Journal that "naval and aerial support were active" but there were no further casualties. "Plenty of flies and very hot sun," were his first impressions of the Rock. "The whole place stinks." It took till noon for the first men of the battalion to reach Topside.

As the platoons arrived, Col. Jones had them take up positions looking south across the mouth of the bay, from Breakwater Point, just below Ramsey Ravine along the east rim, as far over to the west as the smoldering Wheeler Battery. This allowed 2nd Battalion to shift to its right and cover from Battery Wheeler around to the north and James Ravine. 3rd Battalion overlooked Bataan to the north, and Middleside and Bottomside to the east. They still held the high ground above James Ravine at Morrison Hill and completed the circle back to Ramsey Ravine. Gaps between the battalions were covered (they hoped) by machine gun fields of fire.

Having finally achieved the linkup, the Rock Force would next be tasked with clearing the famous Malinta Tunnel and the "tail of the tadpole." This would take yet another two weeks, cave by cave and bunker by bunker, to accomplish. But first, the methodical reduction of the enemy's enclosed positions around Topside and its cliffs needed to be completed. Pfc. Fernando Valdez of Company I earned a Silver Star in Ramsey Ravine by foiling a Japanese ambush, killing more than half a dozen while his own wounded and dead squad members were evacuated. Lt. Calhoun of Company F, who had reluctantly given way to

Company D at Battery Wheeler on Saturday, had the task of taking Batteries Smith and Hearn west of the old barracks. Today he was successful. Meanwhile, Company F commander Lt. William Bailey cleared nearby Battery Way and the hill it commanded.

After calling in a preliminary air attack, Company E headed down James Ravine just to the west of Morrison Hill. A typical ravine for Corregidor, it had a lip of ten or twenty feet across the top, dropped 300 feet down to the beach from the Topside slope, and opened to 150 feet at the base of the cliffs on the beach. A road ran down through it almost to the shoreline where it met the road around the cliff face at Battery James. Supposedly, a large underground barracks, a water pump house, and possibly the mine control panel were down there. Lt. Joe Whitson's platoon had gotten halfway down yesterday before heavy fire forced him out. This time two of Cpt. Hill's platoons started down at 0730, one platoon on each side of the draw, but after a while fire from all sides pinned them down. It would take them until late afternoon, with help from P-47s summoned from Mindoro, to extricate themselves.

Jesse Castillo, the 161st machine gunner who had nearly jumped out of his own harness, accompanied some medics to a temporary forward aid station down the slope south of the parade ground. He set up his gun in a shell hole and immediately exchanged fire with Japanese near the cliff. His gun jammed. "I leaned over it a little to clear the jam," he recalled. "All of a sudden I felt like somebody hit me on the side of my head with a hammer." A bullet had ricocheted off the casing, shattered his cheekbone, and sent bone slivers up into his eyes. Some men took him back to the medical section, where Maj. Stevens told him his war was over. Like his colleague George Kojima, he had gotten a "homer."

Jesse said that later on, as he was recuperating from reconstructive surgery, "The doctor told me it would be three weeks before he'd know if I could see. I still had the eye over the other cheek. When the three weeks were up, I said 'OK, Doc, today's the day you're supposed to tell me if I can see.'

"'OK,' said the doctor, 'I'll be right back.' He came back with a little flashlight and shined it in my eye. He kept saying, 'Do you see anything? Do you see anything?' I kept saying, 'No, no, no, no.'

"Finally, he got tired and he said, 'Well I guess that eye is gone. The only thing we can do is remove it and give you two plastic eyes so you'll have a good appearance.' And you know, that's the only thing that came out right. For a long time, these ladies kept coming up and telling me, 'Gee, what beautiful blue eyes you have!'"[2]

On Bottomside, a detachment from Company A of the 34th ran across the beach under fire at North Dock and up Malinta Hill with water, extra machine guns, and ammo for K and L Companies. They brought down casualties. The Navy assisted Company L by blasting caves on the southeast side of the hill, where several heavy naval guns had been installed, aimed at the tail. They would have soundly defeated the landing at Kindley Field proposed by Col. Jones. Fortunately, the situating of the guns on the far side of Malinta Hill had made them useless against the beach landings. Company I worked along the road around the north side of Malinta Hill as far as Engineer Point, where the Air Corps helped them advance with napalm and high-explosive bombs. Company I then relieved Company K, which still had not been able to reach its furthest outpost at Malinta Point, just beyond Engineer Point.

Two problems were worsening. Most of the water containers that were dropped by the two-a-day supply flights, even from 100 feet, had been broken open or gone entirely over the cliffs. Troopers were emptying enemy canteens. They even filled up with slimy water left from the last rains wherever they could find it. What Postlethwait had sent up was already used up, mostly for the wounded. Little did the Americans know, the Japanese shared the same predicament. Having neglected to repair the water system, they had relied on a few springs in the ravines, which had either been closed by bombardment or were out of reach where the Americans were patrolling. The water tank and Malinta Tunnel supplies were almost gone and unavailable to the Imperial soldiers around Topside anyway. They were left with getting juice out of ration cans and collecting trickles of water in the tunnels.

Secondly, as noted by Company A's Pardue, huge flies were feasting on the hundreds of Japanese corpses. It seemed to one trooper that "they were reinforced by flies from Bataan and Caballo." Men couldn't get their rations opened before swarms covered them. They tried to cover up with their ponchos, like they had in New Guinea, to eat. Cracker Atkins remembered reading that DDT had been useful elsewhere in the Pacific. He called his counterpart, the G-4 of XI Corps, to see if it were available. Soon a B-24 flew a crop-dusting pattern over the island. That solved one problem, although the effect on the paratroopers' health appears to never have been questioned. Then, late in the day as the patrols returned to their company defensive areas, they were surprised to find a full canteen and three days' rations awaiting each man. Col. Postlethwait had sent supply trucks up the road using Maj.

Woods's battalion for protection. More importantly, he had sent up the 18th Surgical Portable Hospital to help Maj. Stevens's overwhelmed medical section in the Mile Long Barracks. The same trucks carried casualties down to the docks.

As dusk approached, the 503rd shored up its perimeter again. D Company, who had been patrolling the south rim, sidled to the west to make room for the 1st Battalion and got situated along the rim between Batteries Wheeler and Cheney. Companies D and F were supposed to tie into each other at Cheney Ravine, but due to the shifting of the companies just before sunset, the difficulty of digging in, and the ban on movement after dark, a gap several hundred yards wide had been left between Company F, north of the ravine, and Company D, south of it. It was impossible for them to support each other. 2nd Battalion HHQ, 500 yards back from both companies, was either unaware or unconcerned.

Later that night, Col. Jones had a staff meeting. At 2200 he lay down on his bed of parachutes on the concrete floor for whatever sleep he could get. It was a short nap. Half an hour later, F Company's pickets in their shell holes near Battery Grubbs sensed movement down the slope around Battery Smith and Grubbs Ravine beyond it. Shots rang out. Soon the men with Bill Calhoun farther back at Battery Hearn braced when they heard marching and chanting. A star shell lit up what looked like a battalion of Japanese—500 or more—marching in column four abreast up a trail out of Grubbs Ravine. They were supposed to be getting into position for a surprise attack but made so much noise they gave themselves away. Many, probably having imbibed a healthy dose of *sake* to bolster their courage, appeared to be drunk and were throwing up. Company F picked off as many as possible before the flare died out. The mortar platoon weighed in. Another flare: Calhoun's machine gunners opened up, but determined soldiers (or those prodded by their officers' swords) continued to march up the trail and infiltrate between flares. The combined fire finally dispersed what was left of the column, which retreated down the ravine or into the bordering foliage.

The attack at Battery Hearn was finally fizzling out sometime after midnight when the newly arrived 1st Battalion got its Corregidor initiation on the eastern rim of Topside. As at Battery Wheeler last night and Malinta Hill the night before, the Japanese exploded a munitions tunnel, this time between Breakwater Point and Ramsey Ravine directly under Company A's CP. Twenty paratroopers of Battalion HHQ and Company A were killed or injured by the explosion. A rock flew through the roofless barracks and landed beside Col. Jones. Then the troopers watched another jaw-dropping performance. Twenty Imperial Marines who had survived the blast marched out of the glowing hole, sat in a circle, and with a single command committed mass *hara-kiri* with hand grenades held against their chests. More mysterious was why they hadn't charged out and tried to take some more Americans with them.

The dust and smoke were finally settling about 0130, but Company A's Cpt. William Bossert would have to wait till daylight to sort out his casualties. It was about then that a second attack force—but this time from Cheney Ravine—began to climb up and out onto Topside. Double the size and stealthier than the first group, they passed undetected around and between D Company's rifle pits and as far as their mortar platoon, which had set up in a crater to the rear. The Japanese were positioning for another rush. Men posted around the batteries and in foxholes in between, already on edge from the earlier action at Battery Hearn north of them and the explosion to the east but seeing nothing on this moonless night, started shooting at underbrush that rustled.

1st Lieutenant John Lindgren, the mortar platoon commander who'd joined the regiment after Nadzab, sensed something up ahead and had a couple 60-mm rounds launched. The brief explosions confirmed that enemy soldiers were moving on the Cheney Trail. Rifle fire picked up all around. Lindgren realized they were being surrounded in the pitch darkness. "I didn't give much hope for getting through it," he told author Patrick O'Donnell. "They were swarming all over the place.... I told [my men] to get out of there...." He got separated from the platoon and found himself beside the company CP bunker with Lt. Turinsky, a corporal, and another lieutenant. There was nowhere else to go; behind the bunker were the sheer cliffs of Wheeler Point. They, too, fired at shapes and sounds.

Within minutes, Lindgren recalled, Turinsky was shot dead, and the corporal was wounded. The other lieutenant took the corporal into the bunker, which also served as the forward medical station, leaving Lindgren alone. He felt he'd been there "two hours" listening to the shooting and tramping, ready with his carbine, when he was joined by yet another lieutenant, Gifford, who had captured Battery Wheeler yesterday. He was dragging a wounded trooper, Pfc. Art Sanchez, to the bunker. Sanchez was a BAR man, so the two lieutenants used his weapon to guard the bunker and, with a picket line of stragglers, ward off assailants who got past the other platoons. Many of the attackers, Lindgren noticed, had no rifles but spears made of bayonets attached to the ends of bamboo poles. After fending off one attack, Lindgren wiped the sweat off his face. When a star shell went off, he saw blood on his sleeve. He had lost his helmet and gotten grenade fragments in his forehead.

Now Calhoun's men heard chanting again and began to barely make out shapes coming over the rim of Grubbs Ravine. The Japanese had sobered up and regrouped to give it another try. This time they ran into Lloyd McCarter. Pvt. McCarter, in Calhoun's platoon, had already earned a reputation as a ruffian. He'd been a reckless, fearless brawler in Australia. He'd been busted and done time in the Barbed Wire Hotel. Most recently he'd been Away Without Leave (AWOL) on Mindoro and saved from the supply detail by Calhoun, who talked Jones into letting him use McCarter as a scout. He had destroyed a machine gun nest within a few minutes of landing on Corregidor. He was point man in the attacks on Batteries Boston and Wheeler yesterday and Cheney and Hearn today, at one time taunting the Japanese to "come out of there and fight!" Now, McCarter jumped into a ditch next to the road and wracked the column with his Tommy gun every time he could make out a target. When the gun overheated, he went back to his squad for a BAR. When it ran out of ammo, he got a dead paratrooper's M1.

Neither company could call for help or warn RHQ that it was in danger of being overrun because the radio net went silent at night so the enemy would not hear any chatter. However, Andy Amaty was now a comm sergeant in 1st Battalion. Already rocked by the ammunition blast, he heard the battle escalating a mile away. He got permission to at least call the Navy. He told O'Donnell that he had begun arguing with a fire direction radio man on a destroyer to put up more star shells. After being told that the captain was trying to save them for tomorrow, Andy swore back, "If you don't fire those shells, there isn't going to be a [expletive] tomorrow!"

About 0600, in dawn's twilight, a final wave of Japanese, the remnants of the ones who had attacked Hearn and Wheeler earlier, screamed "Banzai!" and surged out of Cheney Ravine right into the withering fire of Company D. The paratroopers largely stayed in their foxholes and fired as the charge rolled around and past them. Only those out of ammo dared come out to fight hand-to-hand. Some of the attackers, along with many of the infiltrators who had waited for this moment, jumped the foxholes, permeated the perimeter, crossed the parade ground, and got as far as the Mile Long Barracks. They threw grenades inside, missing Cpt. Atkins but wounding four Service Company men. The rest of Service Company, who had up to now only dodged bullets on the DZs, got their chance to shoot back. Many were on the second and third floors from where they fired down into the swarm. Col. Jones took out three of the enemy in front of RHQ with his carbine. A machine gunner had an Imperial Marine grab the barrel and try to yank it away from him. He pulled the trigger to get him off so he could lay into the attackers. The high tide of the infiltration made it to Battery Crockett and the golf course where outposts of 1st Battalion, already smarting, stopped them.

McCarter was in the thick of it again. The operating rod on his M1 (which ejects the spent shell and chambers the next) finally broke from excessive use. He stood up from his spot next to the ravine to pinpoint Japanese machine gun and mortar positions for counterfire. In the last moments he was wounded and taken to the rear. Later in the morning his squad would count thirty-five dead Marines where Lloyd had been posted and a hundred more down the road killed by the mortar and machine gun fire he'd directed. When he came to from anesthesia at an Army hospital (he had nearly bled to death before being evacuated) and saw a nearby MP, he asked, "Good God, what have I done now?" Expecting a court-martial, instead he was invited to the White House, where President Truman would award him the Congressional Medal of Honor for holding off half the banzai attack nearly single-handedly.

With daylight faintly limning at last, the isolated companies called for support. Radios squawked, and the howitzers and 81-mm mortars thumped. A hundred or so of the infiltrators were spotted in a railroad cut behind Calhoun's line at Battery Hearn. Battalion's heavy mortars and Battery D's fifty-cals finished them off. Finally, this attack, like the others, sputtered. After the firing died down, 250 Japanese dead were counted along Cheney Trail. More lay scattered around Topside. Among them was Lt. Endo. His disjointed double-barreled attack by 1500 Marines, the equivalent of three battalions, had been broken up by McCarter and Company F on the one flank, Company D at "Banzai (Wheeler) Point," and Service Company and Company A at its furthest reaches.

As it was, Japanese troops lurked around the buildings, under stairwells, and in basements and had to be flushed out all morning. None surrendered. More paratroopers were lost. The final tally for Endo's banzai attack was thirty-three paratroopers dead and seventy-five wounded against 400 Japanese dead.[3] It could have been much worse. Lindgren later wrote that if Endo had used the trail through the center of the ravine between Companies D and F instead of the trails along the sides leading directly into them, he'd have split the seam, gotten his men on Topside unmolested, and completely overrun the 503rd.

The howitzers, now lined up across the parade ground, fired down the hillside and into Cheney Ravine to discourage any more movement from that direction. "The most beautiful sight in the war," Amaty reflected decades afterward, "was that dozen 75s hub to hub blasting that ravine." Col. Jones, not wanting a repetition of the battle in front of headquarters and certainly not near the medical section, pulled D Company back to the edge of the parade ground, where they would remain until the regiment left Corregidor.

This was the first occasion on which prisoners had been taken. Col. Jones had even offered three days of R and R to anyone who brought one in. Akune said there were none for the taking. "Most prisoners that were brought in were wounded. Almost all fought to the death; very few surrendered. One, who had been unconscious, started talking to me when he woke up. When he noticed an American medic walk by, he realized he'd been captured and clammed up." He had, however, informed Harry that Lt. Endo had called for another attack by a thousand men the following night. Another prisoner jumped Harry. It took several MPs to subdue him. "Eventually, they had to eliminate him," Harry said. "As the man's life faded away, he was clinging to me, as if clinging for life." He later saw a GI give a cigarette to a badly wounded and suffering prisoner. Harry never forgot this singular act of compassion in an otherwise heartless struggle where no quarter was given.

1 As related to James and Jonathan Turner.

2 Jesse believed, although blinded for life, that the wounding had saved his life —perhaps because, instead of the one shot, he'd have been the target of a hailstorm of bullets and grenades in no time. He did get married after being evacuated to the States for surgery and convalescence. At a Corregidor Day Dinner of the 503rd PRCT Association one year, Jesse proclaimed, "This is my

anniversary!" He was, of course, referring to losing his sight but leading on the guys, who hoisted their drinks and gave him a hefty cheer.

3 Sources disagree again. There were perhaps as many as 100 paratroopers wounded and 500 Japanese killed. Lindgren said fourteen paratroopers had been killed and fifteen wounded in Company D.

Chapter 15

TAIL OF THE TADPOLE
Mopping Up

The 503rd spent Monday the 19th hunting through every crevice, building, and gully again in the endless task of rooting out the last of Endo's men and strengthening the perimeter. Patrols came upon bands of five or six or even a dozen or more Imperial Marines in ravines, craters, and caves. There was even a machine gun nest under one of the old trolley cars that required a marksman with a bazooka to destroy. Individual bodies had to be checked: after a patrol went by, an apparent corpse would squeeze off a shot or lob a grenade from behind. One squad had to rescue a trooper who got jumped by four "dead men." Company D delightedly found two of their own thankful men in a cave near Wheeler Point where they had hidden, wounded, since the first day.

Hudson Hill sent his platoons back down into James Ravine. Destroyers and fighter-bombers called in by JASCO and the 6th Support Air Party helped them get all the way down to the shoreline this time. They fulfilled their three-fold mission. They came across the beachside barracks with its guards away from their machine gun posts—probably inside the barracks avoiding the shelling. They killed sixty-five Japanese who rushed out of the barracks entrance and sealed many more inside when they blew it up. Then they found the pump house but reported that it had been destroyed beyond repair. At last, after dispatching the guards outside a beachfront cave, they discovered the all-important mine control panel, complete with a hundred switches, six power batteries, electrical leads, and cables dropping underground and out to the bay. Company E's demo section packed the cavern with TNT and blew up the entire system.

JASCO soon sent out a call: the Navy could now safely enter Manila Bay. Minesweepers had cut loose dozens of mines already (most laid years ago by the US Navy) to be blown up by trailing destroyers for gunnery practice. Cpt. Hill's men would spend three more days clearing out James Ravine and kill nearly 500 of the enemy (half of them sealed up in caves) at the expense of thirty-five more officers and men.

A paratrooper from Company F was shot from a tunnel in Way Hill. His platoon threw grenades into the tunnel and charged into an adjoining cavern where they overwhelmed twenty-seven Imperial Marines who had been dazed by the concussion. In Grubbs Ravine, whence Endo's preliminary attack had come, another of Company F's platoons called for their mortar squad to eliminate a group of sixteen Marines at the edge of a large bomb crater who had them pinned down. Heavy machine guns from Battery D shot down twenty more Marines so that the third platoon could move on and finish securing the ravine.

Company H moved from their perch on Morrison Hill through Middleside into a ravine west of North Dock to neutralize a fortified pre-war cold-storage facility called the "Icehouse," whose defenders were still denying full use of the road and were sniping at the 34th on Malinta Hill and Company G on Topside. Two platoons finished the job in much the same manner as on Topside, via the vent shafts. They added a new wrinkle by lighting old tires and stuffing them in. The noxious fumes drove the soldiers outside where they were easily shot or captured. Meanwhile, H Company's third platoon attacked a troublesome supporting machine gun nest in a nearby cave. Its tenants wound up blowing up the cave, which was a powder magazine, along with four paratroopers whose bodies were never found. However, the road to Topside was now unobstructed.

Late in the afternoon, LSTs arrived at Black Beach filled with jeeps, trucks, AA guns, supplies, and the remainder of Service Company, including Turner and the other men who'd flown the two-a-day runs. Now they set to work unloading the ships. With the Icehouse no longer a threat, a pipeline started bringing supplies —first and foremost, water—up the road and casualties down for transport to hospital ships. One of the evacuees was Lt. Col. Tolson, who, like MacArthur, was disappointed to be leaving Corregidor. Not surprisingly, he wanted to see his plan through to the end, but his splinted and swollen foot required proper attention. He and his West Point classmate, Ed Postlethwait, said their goodbyes. The dead paratroopers were removed from the island's movie theater, which had been repurposed as the morgue by GRS.[1] Bulldozers dug large trenches to bury the many Japanese corpses. Flies and thirst hadn't been the only problems. Not only the soldiers on the Rock, but sailors on warships in the bay, were nauseated by the pervasive stench of death.

The night attack that the prisoners had foretold never happened. However, a Company C sentry shot an infiltrator. A sergeant who awakened from a dead sleep rushed over to check out the problem and was himself mistakenly shot as an infiltrator. Others, thinking they were under attack, started firing at shadows and more supposed infiltrators. Several troopers, including the popular sergeant, were killed. Some cursed and some wept for having shot their own friends.

By the twentieth, the Rock Force had killed over 1800 Japanese, 1400 of them by the 503rd, but the end was still not in sight. The paratroopers resumed their tedious task of destroying pockets of the enemy on Topside. Company L of the 34th continued to probe out towards the stranded platoon of Company K. They called on a destroyer to suppress enemy fire so they could advance. Lt. Cain had Company I try to smoke the enemy out of Malinta's tunnels. That didn't work. The smoke just leaked out fissures and vents. Another destroyer shelled the eastern entrance to Malinta Tunnel and caused a landslide which sealed that end.

From Topside, Company I of the 503rd finally made it to the bottom of Ramsey Ravine and South Dock. Murphy's platoons found and destroyed nineteen of the TNT-laden Q boats in caves near the beach. The others had been used against landing craft and patrol boats at Mariveles. Who knew why the rest hadn't been used to stop 3/34 or 1/503 from landing? Some others of Erickson's men knocked out a gun emplacement at Battery Point, Corregidor's northernmost tip, using TNT and a WP grenade down the copula. A mile and a half directly south, Cpt. Bossert's platoons finally cleared out Batteries Geary, Crockett, and Hamilton on their way down to Geary Point. The Company A log, again nonplussed, noted "snipers in caves and bunkers. Casualties light except for [last night's] explosion."

Planes that had been staging above, waiting for calls that

never came, announced that their two hours' worth of fuel was up. Before leaving, they dropped their bombs and strafed areas in the ravines that the Navy's guns couldn't reach. K/34, still short its stranded platoon, climbed back up onto Malinta Hill between Companies I and L so they could start sweeping towards the eastern end together. They knew they were sitting on a powder keg with its tunnels packed with munitions. Every night they had feared it would blow.

On the night of the twenty-first, about 2130, the explosion the men on the hill had dreaded came. The Japanese inside tried to blow open the eastern entrance. They succeeded, but a back-blast triggered more explosions. Malinta Hill rocked as flames shot out of crevices in the rock, the tunnels, and their vents above. The blast was heard, seen, and felt on Bataan. An avalanche of dirt and rocks on the south side came down on the entire 3rd Platoon from A/34, who were guarding the entrances. More than 100 Japanese came staggering out of the tunnels in varying degrees of stupor or terror, apparently for a planned but inadvertently disrupted banzai attack. They were annihilated or driven back in. Fifty more marched out only to be mowed down. Five or six hundred dashed out of the reopened eastern entrance and headed for the tail of the island. Finding the buried men of Company A in the rubble at night was impossible. In the morning, a former Colorado mountain climbing instructor led the search party. All but six of the platoon were dead or seriously injured. The six were reassigned to other platoons.

Topside still was not secure. Company F was closing caves down in Grubbs Ravine near the north shore road when Japanese appeared out of the lower caves to ambush Calhoun's platoon. They killed three of his men and wounded six before Company F's mortars drove them back inside. The other two platoons, following

289

trails on either side of Calhoun, used flamethrowers on the caves. The demo team counted seventy dead Japanese in the caves before sealing their tombs.

Company G was moving along a road in a ravine about 1100 when a Japanese Marine jumped out of the bushes, ran to a rusting cement mixer, and climbed in. Someone threw in a grenade. The troopers were astonished to see the Marine climb out, covered in blood, and start down the road toward the beach. No one had the heart, and they were too dumbstruck anyway, to shoot him.

On February 23, a week after landing on Corregidor, the Sherman tanks closed the last entrances into Malinta Hill. The 34th spent the day clearing the roads of the rocks and debris caused by the explosion, so that the 503rd could pass through the next day and at long last begin reducing the tail of the island. A man found dog tags in the rubble from a buddy who had been stationed there when the war started. Someone else found a wallet from a man in K Company who had lost it going up the first night when he left his pack to help carry ammo. He was grateful to get his wife's picture back.

E/503 patrolled the last third of a mile of the perimeter, from Searchlight Point to Wheeler Point along the cliffs south of Battery Wheeler, which had changed hands half a dozen times by now. The company's strength, after Endo's attack and the subsequent days clearing James Ravine, was barely fifty percent— Hill had four officers and seventy-one men left of the six officers and 137 men he jumped with. One platoon advanced along the narrow beach, and one along the pitted coast road part way up the cliff, in search of caves. When the platoons came to a blind corner at an outcropping labeled "Unknown Point" on their maps, they called for the Navy to shell the other side before they advanced. Around the corner the beach-level platoon came upon a cave with a concrete parapet in front. Bullets were exchanged. Given a bad firing angle, the platoon leader, Lt. Lewis Crawford, got his men to the front below the parapet by continually firing inside while moving. Grenades flew out, followed by a dozen soldiers screaming, "Banzai!" They were all killed in a few seconds. Inside were forty-seven more killed by the naval barrage and non-stop gunfire. Crawford's casualties were luckily only five men wounded by grenade shrapnel.

Up above, Lt. Roscoe Corder's platoon came up to a similar cave but with a concrete-lined tunnel that led deep into the cliff. This was the tunnel through which troops were fed into Batteries Wheeler and Crockett every night. Corder's men got close to the opening before its occupants started shooting. A group made a banzai charge out of this cave, fortunately throwing their grenades far out from the cliff (perhaps blinded by sunlight) and then bunching up at the parapet. They were all killed, but fire kept coming from inside. Corder's machine guns and grenades could not quell it. There was a lull; then another dozen charged out, led by a sword-wielding officer. They fought hand-to-hand with paratroopers who had climbed up over the parapet. One trooper got badly slashed by the sword. This fight had barely ended when two of the troopers left standing were shot. Then, over twenty Japanese came on so hard that the first few flew over the ledge and down the cliff. One grabbed onto a paratrooper who stabbed him with his knife to avoid being pulled down the cliff. Another paratrooper was knocked over the edge by the surge but clung to a bush. The rest of this group was dispatched as well. Cpt. Hill's company, now out of ammo, withdrew while firing their last rounds and carrying their wounded down towards the beach. LCMs picked up Company E and took them to Black Beach. The bodies of two dead men left behind were never found.

H/503 had patrolled from Battery Point down to the beach at North Dock on the twenty-second. Arnie Williams, Ben Guthrie, and their platoon mates had spent the rest of the day picking their way through the sand and disarming mines, which claimed the life of one paratrooper. Today they would have another harrowing experience. A rifleman fired into a cave at an enemy soldier. His shot missed the man. There was a mighty "whump" inside behind him. The hillside lifted up and knocked down everyone on it. Flames incinerated the rifleman and two others. A landslide buried several more men. They were extracted, but four were dead and one was severely burned.

While the Rock Force was literally digging out in preparation for their final advance, over on Luzon, Company B of the 511th flew out of hard-won Nichols Field, which the bulldozers had barely finished leveling, for a unique parachute operation. They had been pulled out of the Genko Line on the eighteenth, as the battle for Manila broiled. Augmented by a machine gun platoon and an engineer squad, they were flying in C-47s—who else's but Col. Lackey's—towards the Los Baños College of Forestry campus, forty-two miles southeast of Manila on the southern shore of Laguna de Bay (Laguna Lake). The Japanese had converted the college into another internment camp. Unlike the others, Los Baños had a high concentration of religiously oriented internees: preachers, priests, missionaries, nuns, and seminary students, besides some civilian professionals, a few Navy nurses and servicemen, and some of their families.

The prisoners had been praying all along that the Lord

would send "angels from Heaven" to rescue them. At 0700 on the twenty-third, their prayers were answered. As the prisoners lined up for the daily head count, and all but a skeleton crew of the guards began their morning exercise routine, Company B dropped out of the sky. Along with their recon platoon, which had infiltrated in the night to mark the DZ, they immediately attacked the few armed guards before they could fire a shot and then the rest as they scurried for weapons and cover. Within twenty minutes all two hundred forty-some guards were dead. Most of the inmates had hit the dirt as soon as the shooting started; some grabbed children and scampered inside. One inmate, as well as one paratrooper, were wounded.

The rest of the 1st Battalion and Battery D of the 511th had motored across the lake on Amtracs[2] and set up a beachhead. The empty Amtracs were driven through the gates of the compound and filled with internees. Filipino guerrillas blocked the roads from surrounding towns to stop Japanese reinforcements. The 1st Battalion of the 188th GIR, with two of their pack howitzers and a tank destroyer battalion, left the battle in Manila to keep Japanese troops in the 8th "Tiger" Division from counterattacking across the San Juan River, which emptied into the lake.

The Amtracs made two trips across the lake to take the internees and their liberators back to safety. The 188th disengaged, with two dead and two wounded, and headed back to Manila. This perfectly planned and executed operation rescued 2150 internees. Unfortunately, the Japanese murdered 1500 locals for retribution.

Despite being what is still considered the most successful airborne operation in history from planning, execution, and casualty perspectives, the Los Baños raid got little press attention. Simultaneously, 1700 miles to the north, US Marines were battling on another tiny island of which no one had ever heard. Newspapers across the States featured what would become the most iconic photo of the war, taken by Associated Press photographer Joe Rosenthal—six Marines raising the Stars and Stripes on Iwo Jima's Mount Suribachi. Halfway between the Marianas and the Japanese Islands, Iwo Jima would be an important B-29 base for the planned invasion. Four Marine parachute battalions saw action, although for amphibious assault and as regular infantry. The grueling month-long battle would be the only time in the Pacific when American casualties exceeded Japanese—26,000 to 21,000—a stark preview of what the assault on Japan itself would cost.

In the fight for Manila, the 37th Division was finally able to storm the breaches of Fort Santiago. During a truce, the Japanese released 3000 women and children hostages. They had slaughtered the men. The 145th IR, clearing out the last of the tunnels, would find the bodies stacked up in the dungeons the next day. US artillery and tanks destroyed the old fort and most of the remaining garrison. The government buildings downtown now became Iwabuchi's last bastion.

Late in the day on Corregidor, a tank and the 81-mm mortar section of the 34th cleared the north road around Malinta Hill of enemy interference. As A/34 passed the Hospital Entrance, they were met with another banzai attack. The tank and riflemen ended it quickly. The infantry moved on while the tank blocked the entrance and engineers blew it up yet again. This column finally made it out to Engineer Point and relieved the remnant of K Company's stranded platoon, who had held their ground for seven days.

At 1600, Maj. Clark, the S-3, gave Col. Jones an updated report. The US casualties were: 118 KIA, 314 WIA, and ten MIA.

Japanese casualties were: nearly 2500 KIA and two prisoners. Oblivious to the headline-grabbing action elsewhere in the Pacific, Jones issued orders for the final phase beginning in the morning: Woods's 1st Battalion would go past the 34th and lead the advance down the tail end; Erickson's 3rd Battalion would follow in reserve and eliminate any hotspots Woods bypassed; Caskey's 2nd Battalion would continue patrolling Topside; the 34th would stay put to keep an eye on Malinta Hill and the beach. Cpt. Gibson climbed Malinta Hill looking for an old observation post. The 34th were well-acquainted with it by now and led him to it. From there he could see the entire tail of the island and would direct fire for the 462nd.

That night, at 0330, Malinta Hill erupted for the last time. The Japanese made this the end-all—seven consecutive explosions with flames and Japanese pouring out everywhere. Some of them were already dead, flung out by the blasts. The rest were instantly targeted and killed.

Promptly at 0730 on D+9, February 24, 1/503 stepped off around Malinta Hill, which was still smoking like a volcano. The artillery provided the men another "beautiful sight," now in line across the parade ground facing east. They laid down a rolling barrage to soften up the path out in front of the advance. A patrolling destroyer and some bombers chimed in. Company A, led by Bill Bossert, covered the southern half of the advance. Col. Jones accompanied them. Companies B and C, led by Captains Wert Cate and John Rucker with a tank apiece, traveled along the north half. There was yet another banzai rush out of the hospital entrance, which the early morning blast had reopened. This time a tank killed five paratroopers mixed up in the melee. Engineers blew the entrance closed for what they hoped was the last time.

A machine gun nest stopped the advance after only a few

hundred yards. T/Sgt. Robert Heyer of Company B charged the nest and destroyed it. Not much further, near Artillery Point, one of Company C's platoons was ambushed. T/Sgt. John Boyle fought off the enemy while the platoon was extracted. Meanwhile, back on Topside, at its easternmost point, Cape Corregidor, Company D got pinned below the sheer cliffs. Pfc. Clifton Puckett fought this battle single-handed so his comrades could withdraw. All three of these men earned Silver Stars. None of them would live long enough to receive his medal.

The 1st Battalion got moving again at 1100. Its trail was lined with caves. Bossert (who would also earn a Silver Star) was able to have the destroyer seal most of them up with its five-inch shells. He noted, "It was an exhilarating luxury to have a destroyer attached to a rifle company." An officer with a samurai sword and a squad of men came out of one of the caves. They all came to attention for a moment, then charged into certain death. Quite a few Japanese were dug in around Water Tank Hill, where Gibson now used the empty concrete tank to zero in the howitzers. The battalion attacked but even with artillery support was repelled.

Colonel Jones decided to dig in for the night. Woods chose a large bomb crater for his CP. His staff, Cpt. Rucker, some sergeants, and a couple of radio operators were in it with him. Jones said he needed to get back to Topside—one of MacArthur's aides was there to plan a visit for the General. Woods suggested that, between enemy snipers and jumpy troopers, "You might not get back alive, Colonel." Jones was barely back on Topside, about 2100, when, ironically, a mortar barrage hit Woods's area. He and several of the men in the crater were killed. Rucker lost an arm. Medic Lester Pinter defied bullets and mortar shells to help wounded company members, thereby earning a Silver Star. Maj.

John Davis, the XO, took over the battalion. Davis called in the artillery. It was a good call. Five hundred Japanese were forming up on the hill for a banzai charge to follow the mortar attack. The barrage killed half of them. When the other half finally attacked at 0330, Company A killed a hundred more before the rest fled back up the hill or towards the tip of the island.

At dawn, Davis positioned his men for a flank attack upon the hill. He prefaced it with a call for preliminary artillery and naval fire. At 1045 his men started up the steep sides to flush the few buildings and flanking batteries and to deal with whatever survivors there might be. After securing Water Tank Hill, they carefully advanced another 700 yards, stopping just short of Kindley Field at about 1630. They had to clear a path through the mines around the runway. The Navy's PT boats had spent the day chasing down hundreds of Japanese who, apparently convinced the island was lost, tried to swim to Bataan or Caballo.

While the 503rd inched along the tail, LCMs delivered the 2nd Battalion of the 151st IR (Maj. Paul Lemasters) and Company B of the 113th Engineer Combat Battalion to Black Beach. Leaving their tanks and SP howitzers, 3/34 packed up and took the new battalion's places on the LCMs. The 151st seamlessly picked up where the 34th left off. They would stay on Corregidor and continue to mop up remnants of the enemy even after the 503rd left. The 34th were not through—only off to rejoin their parent 24th Division on Mindanao to begin liberating the Southern Philippines. In their ten days on the Rock 3/34 IRCT had accounted for 800 of the enemy dead. It had taken forty-two of Col. Postlethwait's men being killed and 163 wounded. He had lost the equivalent of an entire company. Maj. Clark's numbers now showed that with 500 enemies killed today, the total was 3703. It didn't assuage Col.

Jones. He had lost sixteen more paratroopers.

The twenty-sixth was one of the few drizzly days in Corregidor's driest month. First Battalion followed the two tanks and another barrage (which helped blow up more of the mines) across Kindley Field to Monkey Point, coming to within 2000 yards of the tail's end. About 1100, heavy fire came from a concrete-lined tunnel which before the war had been the "Radio Intercept Tunnel."[3] Don Abbott said it was unmistakable—there was a "forest of antennae" on the hill. The Navy had reported seeing a hundred or more men crowd into the tunnel yesterday. Company B had just sealed the emergency exit. Company A and *Murder, Inc* were working on the main entrance. Maj. Davis, Cpt. Bossert, and a sizable number of men from Company A were on the hill above the tunnel; Companies B and C were scattered on either slope or along the shoreline roads.

Jack Herzig, a staff sergeant in B Company, had been one of the men sent on the Paluan mission on Mindoro. Jack was standing next to a telephone pole, eating a bite of K-rations and talking with his lieutenant, Winfield Samuels. The tank fired an armor-piercing shell at the steel door. Just like with the rifle shot on Topside a couple days ago, the hill exploded. Whether it was detonated by the tank or the men inside, no one knows. Herzig described the blast to Patrick O'Donnell. "Samuels was swept out of my vision by a large boulder.... Flames burst out of the doorway of the shaft behind me.... Only a few guys stood up. Everything and everybody was covered with a shower of dirt and rocks. The green ponchos of the battalion HQ were no longer green—many were red." Four secondary explosions were touched off along the trail. Boulders, concrete, dirt, and bodies flew up in the air. A rock injured a trooper on Topside. A boulder totaled the motor of an ambulance farther up the tail, but the driver thankfully escaped injury. Debris landed on the deck of a destroyer a half-mile out to sea. The tank tumbled end-over-end like a football for fifty feet and landed upside down. The one surviving crew member had to be cut out with an acetylene torch. Davis flew thirty feet but luckily only had the wind knocked out of him. Bossert's chest was crushed. Sgt. Boyle, who'd earned a Silver Star the first day of the mop-up, was among the dead. Men hundreds of yards away were bleeding out orifices or had limbs shredded. Others were unbloodied but dead from concussion. Herzig was undoubtedly saved by the pole shielding him from the blast.

What had been a knoll was now a thirty-foot deep crater, 130 feet by seventy feet (about the area of a football field between the goal and twenty-five-yard lines). The Japanese were estimated to have lost between 150 and 200 in the blast. For the first time, they took out an equal number: fifty-two paratroopers were killed and 144 wounded in the 1st Battalion. Most were from Company A, who had already lost six men at Black Beach, at least a dozen in the explosion their first night on Topside, more men scouring Geary Point, and some staff members in the mortar barrage two nights ago. A sergeant was now the company commander. Company A effectively ceased to be. Herzig concluded, "For a long time after that, everybody flinched at any loud noise."

Jones came down immediately. At noon he sent 3rd Battalion through what was left of the 1st, who were frantically digging comrades out of mounds of dirt and administering first aid. It took two hours to evacuate the wounded to Topside, and another two to move the dead to Black Beach. Guthrie said the dead were lined up along both sides of the road by the beach, a few feet apart, for over thirty yards. GRS would have another busy day.

Erickson's men stopped at the end of Kindley Field to dismantle booby-traps and more mines. Erickson called a halt for the night there. Everyone wondered who would get blown up next. Thank God, they thought, when nothing happened. Company A returned to Topside and made the notation in their logbook: "only a few men left."

The 3rd Battalion was a mile from Corregidor's East Point when they started out on the morning of February 27. They lined up across the tail from Cavalry Point to Monkey Point with Company G on the left flank, I in the center, and H to the south. Not far down the road a machine gun opened up from a cave. S/Sgt. Ernest Debruycker crawled to it under fire and threw in a WP grenade. An alert Marine tossed it back out where it burned the sergeant badly instead. Wounded as he was, he took another grenade, and waited a second this time before throwing it successfully. A flamethrower and TNT finished off the cave while friends took Debruycker to the rear. He would recover and be awarded a Silver Star. Pfc. Arvle Maxwell, of Company G, dragged a wounded man through crossfire from several caves to safety with one hand, while firing his Tommy gun with the other. He too got the Silver Star.

The tail end narrowed to about 100 yards across. Company I took the lead. Pfc. Stanley Crawford was killed while knocking out another machine gun nest manned by six soldiers. He got a posthumous Silver Star. At 1630, Cpt. Murphy's men stepped into the ocean. They cheered and yelled and applauded. They drenched each other with helmets full of water. Even then it wasn't over. Shots rang out from the little chunk of volcanic rock and coral, Hooker Point, another hundred yards away in the surf. Everyone scrambled for cover. They exchanged shots for two hours while they waited for low tide and sunset. Then a platoon with two flamethrowers splashed across the gap and killed four Japanese who, with nowhere to go, nothing to fight for, and death the only other option, refused to surrender.

While Company I cleared the tail end of Corregidor, someone on Topside noticed smoke in the Mile Long Barracks. It was coming from the ammunition stockpile, where WP grenades had spontaneously combusted from the tropical heat. Phillips, Turner, and the other Service Company men tried to get the grenades away from piles of ammo and TNT. In doing so, many burned their hands. Johnny Grooms, who'd shared the near-fatal motorcycle ride with Tom at Fort Bragg, and a few more from nearby 2nd Battalion HHQ pitched in to play Russian Roulette with the TNT. They finally had to high-tail it when fizzling grenades touched off mortar and artillery shells. Col. Jones meanwhile had been evacuating the barracks. He was particularly worried about the dispensary and the medical section a hundred yards away. He had men from RHQ moving out the wounded. Just as Jones got the last man out the door, the TNT went off. The blast blew out several concrete walls, and the concussion threw Jones to the ground "like a guy pushed me in the small of the back." Tom and Max got another fireworks show like they had witnessed at the beach on Mindoro. Fortunately, the only casualties were a captured Japanese jeep and a shipment of new uniforms stacked beside it. Jones had hoped to ship the jeep home as a souvenir. "The explosion," he later recalled, "was not unusual on Corregidor, only the Japanese had nothing to do with it."

On the last day of February, as many as 200 Japanese tried swimming to the mainland. Most were shot and some certainly were lost to sharks. A handful gave in and allowed themselves to be rescued by PT boats, but when one pulled a pistol on the crew, all further rescue attempts ended. Along the cliffs at Wheeler Point, a platoon from Company D trying to seal the pesky tunnel entrance to the batteries above was cut off by Imperial Marines. In the firefight, three more troopers were killed and five wounded. The platoon was rescued by LCIs. North of Battery Wheeler, however, Company F found a treasure trove in a bunker: more liquor and a horde of new clothes, all of it probably looted from stores in Manila. No doubt Pete Komer's silk had come from the same source. Paratroopers tried on some of the outfits, but a bright yellow shirt tipped off a lookout at RHQ. Col. Jones sent down an order to get back into uniform.

Flies had regenerated to the nuisance level again. Atkins made another call. DDT was shoveled out the doors of C-47s. A crewman mistakenly shot a Thompson out the door at a Company D patrol. They angrily called the Air Support unit to tell them next time they'd shoot back. The 503rd then sat back and watched "the Caballo Show," starring some graceful and flashy P-51s. Mustangs had only recently been introduced to the Pacific after lengthy and reputable service in Europe. This was the troopers' first look at them.

In their thirteen days on Corregidor, the Rock Force had used just short of twenty tons of explosives to close nearly 500 caves. The Rock Force had 205 men give the ultimate sacrifice, 725 wounded or injured, and nineteen missing.[4] The latest count was 4500 enemy dead and twenty prisoners. The Navy claimed to have killed 1000 would-be escapees. Who knows how many had been blown up, buried, drowned, or eaten by sharks.[5] Japanese continued to refill caves and bunkers and dig new holes. Battery Wheeler would continue to be a thorn in the side since 2nd

Battalion had been unable to seal the tunnel entrance in the cliff.[6]

By March 1, the Navy was anchoring ships in Manila Bay. At 1000 the next day—the third anniversary of the activation of the 503rd—PT 373 and three others landed at North Dock. Gen. Douglas MacArthur returned just as he had left. In his retinue of a dozen were Generals Krueger and Hall and several staffers who had been with MacArthur when he left in 1942. Col. Jones met them at the dock. The General said, "Well, Gentlemen, it has been a long way back." P-47s were bombing Fort Hughes next door as the men chatted.

They piled into jeeps. The first stop was at the western entrance to Malinta Hill, from which MacArthur had made his promise to return. He walked inside, as though inspecting it, even knowing it was not yet secure. Then the convoy continued out to Monkey Point, where the most recent debacle had occurred. Next, they took the jeeps up the road to Topside. Paratroopers lined the road, still bordered by dense woods and countless caves, all the way up. Their uniforms were torn, the herringbone material stiff and stained with dried sweat; many were blood-soaked. Despite the cordon of troopers along the route, Jones and MacArthur's entourage held their collective breaths and kept their eyes open. There were plenty of enemy snipers left should any desire a prime target.

The little convoy drove out to Battery Wheeler, the site of the see-saw battle and so many casualties. The General stopped to gaze, hands in his back pockets, across the bay towards the Bataan Peninsula. He stopped at a bombed-out shell that once was his office, and another, his home. Then he headed for the parade ground. Engineers had leveled off the area around the mast with their bulldozers. Parachutes still hung in the trees, on the sides of buildings, and over the cliffs.[7]

At 1100, MacArthur stepped out of the jeep. An Honor Guard of 336 men was drawn up in formation, backs to the Mile Long Barracks and facing the old mast, while the rest "minded the store." Amid the formation were Col. Postlethwait and a detachment of the 34th who had been returned for the day. Those near the front had new uniforms—the ones that had survived the ammo explosion in the Mile Long Barracks a few days ago. At the command sergeant's roar, as a man the Honor Guard came to attention. Col. Jones announced, "Sir, I present to you Fortress Corregidor."

The General pinned a Distinguished Service Cross on Col. Jones's breast and then read his recommendation for a Presidential Unit Citation (which would be quickly approved and issued). In part he said:

> [Rock Force's] magnificent courage, tenacity, and gallantry avenged the victims of Corregidor of 1942, and achieved a significant victory for the United States Army.

Looking up at the leaning mast and its tattered rigging, he finished with, "I see the old flagstaff still stands. Have your troops hoist the colors to its peak and let no enemy ever haul them down." On cue, Cpl. Donald Bauer of Dayton, Ohio, raised the Stars and Stripes as a pair of buglers played *To the Colors*. An AP Wire Photo of the ceremony, taken by one of the first-jump photographers, would appear days later in the *New York Times* and would go into Betty's scrapbook.

With that, the entourage got back in the jeeps, drove down

to the dock, boarded the PT boats and were off. As they sped away, MacArthur raised his iconic Filipino field marshal's cap, with its gold braid and crushed crown, held it over his heart, and mouthed the words, "Thank you." A couple of minutes later, a GI killed a sniper near Malinta Tunnel. MacArthur would soon claim in a press release that the island assault by the 503rd paratroopers had proved "the day of the fixed fortress is over."

Across Manila Bay, the last Japanese defenders, still refusing to surrender, were finally blasted, along with the downtown office buildings they held, on March 3. In the month since the cavalry stormed into Manila, 16,000 Japanese and 6500 Americans had been casualties. One hundred thousand Filipino civilians—one in seven of Manila's population—were killed by American accidental fire, starvation, disease, or outright Japanese vengeance and murder. The battle for the island of Luzon cost the Japanese over 200,000 men dead from combat, starvation, or the elements, and 9000 taken prisoner. The Americans had 10,000 killed and more than 30,000 wounded.

In the next week, the Rock Force killed 118 more Japanese but lost four more of their buddies. Gen. Hall returned on the sixth to present Silver and Bronze Stars and Purple Hearts to the men who were still there. On the ninth he wrote to Gen. Eichelberger:

> The performance of the 503d Parachute Infantry RCT in the capture of Corregidor has been recognized by a Presidential Citation which was bestowed upon all members of the organization by General MacArthur....
>
> The job, in my opinion, was the best handled of any that I have seen in my career.... Colonel George M.

Jones knew his job and the tools with which he had to work.... The organization clearly showed that it had been well trained, that its personnel was of a high type and that it was willing and anxious to fight.

On March 7, an American reconnaissance platoon in Germany crossed the Rhine on the Ludendorff Bridge, which the Germans had neglected to blow up, at a town called Remagen. Thousands of Americans would pour over the bridge in the next few days before it finally collapsed from incessant bombing. The next day, D+21, LCIs pulled into Black Beach on Corregidor. The 503rd PRCT boarded with all their gear for the return trip to Mindoro. Arnie Williams, one of the few men who had made it all the way to the tip of Corregidor, got onto the same landing craft which had taken him to Mindoro the first time. "We'd had at least fifty men jump injured or wounded, and ten or more killed. The Navy men recognized us Company H guys, and started asking, 'Hey, where's so-and-so?' We could only say, 'Well, he got a homer,' or 'He didn't make it.' I was the last one on. I counted eighty. We went onto that Rock with a hundred and fifty-six."

When the 503rd landed at their old base on the ninth, Tokyo was being firebombed. The base commander on Mindoro announced a welcome, or perhaps a warning, over the camp PA: "Colonel Jones and his Three Thousand Thieves have returned."

A survey team would come in September to see what might be salvaged from all the ordnance left on the Rock. Their conclusion would be: nothing. It would not be till New Year's Day, 1946, that the last twenty of the island's garrison, smartly dressed and led by a young officer shouldering a sword, would march up out of a ravine to surrender to a GRS sergeant. They had found an American newspaper on a nightly foray that convinced them the war was over, and they had decided that surrendering would be in keeping with the Emperor's will.

1 I once questioned a vet what "GRS" after the regimental number on his WWII baseball cap stood for. "A job you wouldn't want," he informed me. "Graves Registration Service. We were in charge of identifying and properly burying the dead from all over the battlefields." Dog tags were the easiest form of ID. If they were gone, wallets, laundry markings (usually initials and last four digits of one's serial number) or other personal items helped. A buddy might be nearby to make an ID. Sometimes the process required taking fingerprints or even making dental charts. Soldiers buried in snow or mud, or who had concealed themselves well before being killed anyway, were particularly hard to find. GRS trucks carrying the bodies had a permeating odor, of course, which always resulted in their being given right-of-way through convoys and formations. GRS men also picked the burial sites, some of which would become National Cemeteries, near the battlefields on every continent and many islands. Lastly, GRS collected and catalogued personal effects to be sent home to the families. They had done the same job in WWI.

2 Amphibious Tractors: Landing Vehicles, Tracked (LVT). These could transfer power for use on water or land. Over fifty of them were used in this operation.

3 Some forty Navy codebreakers had worked inside the tunnel before the war and therefore had high-level information. They had been escorted away on subs during the Japanese invasion to avoid their being captured and divulging what they knew to the Japanese. Their continued work deciphering Japanese messages resulted in the American victory at Midway.

4 Again, these are Guthrie's numbers. He further specifies: 163 of those killed were paratroopers, as were 285 of the wounded. 331 troopers were injured (i.e., jumping or non-combat) and 7 missing. Flanagan gives 210 and 790 overall, with 5 missing. Templeman lists 169 KIA for the 503rd PRCT. So does a

regimental history compiled by Don Abbott, along with 531 WIA (which I find more likely than 285) for the 503rd with 38 and 153 for the 34th. If Abbott's numbers don't already include non-combat and jump injuries, then his Rock Force aggregate would easily exceed 1100 casualties. Breuer gives the highest totals with 223 killed and 1107 wounded or injured. Within the 503rd PRCT, 150 of the casualties were artillerists or engineers.

5 Recent Japanese sources list as many as 6650 soldiers on Corregidor. A statement by a Japanese PFC stationed there (one of only fifty survivors) claimed there were 6800.

6 Troopers who revisited the island were at last shown the tunnel, along with some others they had not known about, by tour guides. "No wonder we couldn't keep the enemy out of those batteries," one commented. "They could have blown us all up."

7 The troopers had been told the parachutes were government property and were to be left alone. Regardless of orders, MacArthur's entourage helped themselves to a number of parachutes, riling the men, some of whose pals had been killed while still in them. On a trip to Corregidor decades later, a vet came across one of the tattered chutes still there. He cut off a riser and took it with him, figuring if the Army wanted it, they'd have taken it by then.

Chapter 16

NEGROS ISLAND
The Worst for Last

Once again, Tom Turner ordered replacement equipment while procuring and stockpiling supplies (as usual, largely clandestinely pilfered from the Air Force and Navy). The 503rd welcomed friends back from hospitals and trained a few hundred new paratroopers—teenagers fresh from Ft. Benning. Still, there were not enough men to bring the companies back to full strength. While he recuperated from a bout of malaria, Pfc. Thomas McNeill of Company G designed a new regimental uniform patch which incorporated the just-won battle for Corregidor. A large white eagle spread its wings beneath a parachute labeled "503." Its talons grabbed the tail of a red polliwog-shaped island inscribed with "The Rock." The picture lay on a blue background with "AIRBORNE" in yellow capital letters across the top.[1]

On February 23, the 511th and 188th had no more than sprung the internees from Los Baños (and been appropriately nicknamed "the Angels") and were returning to Manila, when they were turned around again. The rest of the 11th Airborne caught up, and the 158th RCT was attached. Now they joined XIV Corps, which was given the new assignment of rooting over 50,000 Japanese troops of Lt. Gen. Shizuo Yokoyama's *Shimbu* Group out of their entrenchments in the mountains south of Manila. The procedure was island-fighting doctrine by now—one cave, bunker, hilltop, or bend in the road at a time. The division, already under strength, would spend until May 3, the day after the Russians captured Berlin, securing Southern Luzon. Ironically, their final mountain-top battle would be near Lipa, from where the Japanese paratroopers had taken off to attack the airfields defended by Gen. Swing's troops on Leyte. In three months on Luzon, the 11th Airborne Division would kill 9500 and capture 128 Japanese. Their losses would be 517 killed, 1300 wounded, 133 jump injuries, and three missing. The 5000 guerrillas who proudly marched and unflinchingly fought alongside the airborne troops would account for 2400 more Japanese casualties.

Before the battles for Manila and its bay were over, Gen. MacArthur had decided the Central Visayas and Southern Philippines should be liberated in a series of operations, "Victor" I through V, which would replace the "Mike," "King," and "Love" operations that the General had cancelled when he stepped up the Musketeer timelines. The Japanese forces there could neither be reinforced nor evacuated, and he could have elected to let them die of attrition, as he had elsewhere. However, the islands' air bases and ports would be useful for attacking Borneo. Additionally, the Chiefs of Staff were already projecting an invasion of Japan, which would require bases for twenty-two divisions to be brought from Europe. Lastly, he feared that the Japanese, left to their devices and bloodlust, would slaughter the populace.

MacArthur, presuming Gen. Krueger had Luzon well in

hand—the General had a knack for premature proclamations of victory—stripped Sixth Army of its 40th and 41st Divisions and transferred them to Lt. Gen. Robert Eichelberger, who had commanded I Corps in New Guinea. Since Eichelberger's recently formed Eighth Army had no airborne units, MacArthur also had Krueger release the 503rd, which the latter did very reluctantly. Krueger wrote in his order to Jones that their departure from his command was a source of "deep regret". Thus reinforced, Eighth Army, which originally included the 24th, 31st, and American[2] Divisions, was to liberate the rest of the islands. The General sent his prospective schedule to Kinkaid. He forwarded it to Adm. Struble, who had directed the landings at Normandy, Leyte Gulf, Ormoc Bay, Mindoro, Subic Bay, Mariveles, and Black Beach on Corregidor. Now he planned the delivery of troops for the Victor assaults and the firepower to protect them.

The 41st invaded Palawan (Victor III), the westernmost island and within reach of the East Indies, on February 28, and then the Zamboanga Peninsula (Victor IV), which protruded from the western coast of Mindanao, on March 10. Panay (Victor I, which would include northern Negros) was invaded by a regiment of the 40th on the eighteenth, and Cebu by the Americal Division on the twenty-sixth. Three days later, two more regiments of the 40th landed in northwestern (Occidental) Negros. On April 2, the 41st Division's remaining regiments started hopping through the Sulu Archipelago towards southern Borneo to complete Victor IV. Bohol was invaded on the eleventh, and southeastern (Oriental) Negros on the twenty-sixth, both by troops from Cebu (the last three collectively, Victor II). On most of these islands, the defenders quickly withdrew into the interior jungles and mountains, having been ordered to carry on guerrilla warfare against the Americans. Thirty-fifth IJA commander, Lt. Gen. Sosaku Suzuki, whose headquarters had been on Cebu, was killed April 19 when he tried to escape to Mindanao on a boat that was attacked by aircraft.

Eichelberger did his own version of leapfrogging. As soon as it was deemed possible for the local guerrilla factions to contain and even whittle down the Japanese contingent on an island, the Americans would pull out and invade another island. On Zamboanga, two companies of the 24th Infantry Regiment, who were to capture an airfield, found the Filipinos already in control of it. Marine Corsairs moved in, soon followed by the 41st Division (who had been kept busy on Palawan locating the remains of 123 American POWs executed by the Japanese). Guerrillas controlled most of Panay by the time the 40th Division dropped off a battalion on its way to Negros. The Americal Division found that the Filipinos had killed all but a few hundred Japanese on Bohol. In each case, these divisions were quickly reassigned. The costliest and most protracted battle, however, was on Mindanao (Victor V), which MacArthur had originally bypassed for Leyte. It required the 24th and 31st Divisions, and later the 40th, from April 17 until the war's end to secure the island. The three divisions would lose over 800 killed and 3000 wounded to eliminate 13,000 of the enemy. Negros would prove to be nearly as difficult—and not necessarily because of the enemy.

At dawn on March 24, while Operation Victor was in full swing, the final parachute jump in Europe, and largest ever— involving close to 17,000 paratroopers and glider men along with their vehicles and artillery—lifted off runways in England and France aboard 3000 transports and gliders. Operation "Varsity," a joint venture of the US 17th Airborne and British 6th Airborne

Divisions, comprising the XVIII Airborne Corps, spearheaded the Allied Rhine crossing at Wesel. The river assault, codenamed Operation "Plunder," was faced by 85,000 Germans of Army Group H, which included the German 1st Parachute Army, used simply as infantry ever since Crete.

At 1000 hours, following an artillery barrage and Air Force bombardment (timed to cease and avoid the friendly fire fiasco of Sicily), the airborne corps jumped and air-landed east of the Rhine to secure the forested heights northwest of Wesel, from where the German artillery commanded the crossings, and then the bridges over the Issel River beyond the heights. The 507th PIR, now commanded by Col. Edson Raff and first in, was dropped two miles north of its DZ. On their way south, they overran an artillery battery and killed or captured the gunners. The 513th (Col. James Coutts, West Point '32) jumped for the first time from Curtiss-Wright C-46 "Commandos," which had a door on each side and carried a full platoon. They too missed the mark and came down surrounded by German infantry and artillery. Then British gliders began landing around them. The Yankees provided cover fire while the Tommies exited and unloaded their supplies and vehicles. The combined force battled through the emplacements, knocked out two tanks and two artillery regiments, captured a town and several hundred Germans, and secured two bridges across the Issel. Glider men from the 194th GIR (Col. James Pierce) knocked out forty-two guns and ten tanks while capturing 1000 Germans.

Major General Miley, who had made so many airborne innovations early on, and who had been the 17th Division commander since its inception, engaged in combat immediately upon landing. Dropped two miles from his DZ, like Raff, and pinned down in between German batteries by machine gun fire, he helped three nearby privates set up and crew a machine gun. They took out a battery that was firing at the Americans crossing the river and then got on their way to the assembly area. Late that night, he and Lt. Gen. Ridgway, commander of XVIII Airborne Corps (but who had trucked across the Rhine), were returning to American lines from the British HQ, when they skirmished with a German patrol. Even Ridgway became a rifleman. According to Miley, it was because the general "was the last man standing." Everyone else had hit the dirt. He was wounded by a grenade as he reloaded his carbine behind his jeep, which fortunately took most of the blast. It was the stoic pitching in of commanders like these which made the paratroopers "willing to follow them into [hades]." Airborne casualties were higher than at D-Day: the 17th had 1300, the 6th had 1400, and 200 planes had been lost or damaged. They had, however, captured 3500 Germans and killed an unknown number while meeting all their objectives. A general in the German 84th Division said the airborne drop had a "shattering effect" on the defenders.

After linking up with Patton's armor,[3] the 17th Airborne Division captured the manufacturing town of Essen, including the Krupp[4] arms factory and its owner, who was miffed that the Airborne troops made him move out of his mansion to be held in the gardener's cottage! As Ike and Churchill observed from west of the Rhine, Gen. Montgomery's Second British Army barreled across. American paratroopers climbed onto British and American tanks to pursue the fleeing enemy into the Ruhr pocket. One trooper, on a "liberated" horse, yelled, "Hi-ho, Silver!" (The Brits didn't get it, never having heard the radio program, *The Lone Ranger.*) Meanwhile, exploiting the Remagen bridgehead to the south, the 101st Airborne held the Germans at Düsseldorf to prevent their escape, and the 82nd seized Cologne. The West Wall was crumbling. On the Eastern Front, the Russians would enter Danzig and Austria five days later.

Among the pages of *Knickerbocker News* articles devoted to the immense European operation and ongoing Pacific campaigns, Betty came across a small snippet. It seems a patrol mopping up in New Guinea had routed some Japanese in a skirmish. Native carriers accompanying the troops started shouting, "Hubba Hubba!" They had picked up the college cheer from Cpt. Bob Connolly, a former football star and line coach for New York University.

Having returned to Mindoro barely two weeks before, the 503rd was alerted by Eichelberger on March 25 that they were to be backup for the 40th Division, which had recaptured Lingayen and Clark Airfields on Luzon. The 40th, commanded by Maj. Gen. Rapp "Dash" Brush, had left Lingayen Gulf on the fifteenth for its assault on Occidental Negros, scheduled for the twenty-ninth. Vice Admiral (since December) Barbey and his VII Amphibious Force picked up the 542nd Engineer Boat and Shore Regiment, which would land the men and vehicles on the beaches. As in Leyte and Luzon, Gen. Yamashita's strategy was to delay the American advance to the Japanese homeland. Gen. Suzuki had managed to amass 15,000 men on Negros by pulling as many troops out of Leyte as he could before the Americans controlled the entire island. This force included several independent battalions and a couple platoons of the 2nd Air Raiding Battalion (a remnant of the parachute unit that had dropped on the 511th on Leyte and later fought in Luzon). Lt. Gen. Takeshi Kono commanded the troops on Negros. All but a third of his men, from the 77th Infantry Brigade, were poorly equipped, but he had made the most of his force by stockpiling supplies and preparing his defensive lines.

Negros, situated between Panay and Cebu, is 135 miles from top to bottom and fifty across, about the size of Rhode Island. Like so many other tropical islands, it has razor-sharp kunai grass plains on the coast and jungle-covered mountains inland. Bacolod, in the northwest corner, is the "Occidental," or Western, capital, and Dumaguete, in the southeast, the "Oriental", or Eastern, capital. At the time, a coastal road ran up the west coast, through Bacolod, around the northern end of the island, and all the way down the east coast to Dumaguete. The road was the only way to get from one capital to the other, because they were separated by an 8000-foot mountain range, reminiscent of the Owen-Stanleys in New Guinea. The Central Visayas, moreover, had sugar plantations wherever kunai grass could be cleared. The plantations used the road to deliver their products to the ports. Bacolod, in addition to its port, had an important Japanese air base.

Brush's 185th RCT sailed across the Panay Gulf and came ashore at Pulupandan on March 29; the 160th RCT (less a battalion left on Panay) followed the next day. There was no preliminary bombardment, nor was there any opposition. Lt. Col. Salvador Abcede, leader of the local guerrillas, met Gen. Brush and informed him that the Japanese were mostly in the mountains to the north and northwest, except for some around Dumaguete. The division immediately followed the coastal road north and within two days controlled Bacolod and its surprisingly undefended airfields. Then the division spread out to seek out the Japanese. The 185th kept its flank on the coast road as it moved eastward. The 160th stretched to the south of the 185th. Armored units scoured the road to the far side of the island to contain Japanese movement.

On April 4, the 40th Division ran into Kono's line along the north central foothills. They had constructed strong defenses: the all too familiar tunnel-connected bunkers, artillery hidden in caves, countless tank traps and mines. Brush concluded this was not going to be a walkthrough as on other islands. He called Eichelberger for the reserve. Since the airfields and bridges were already in American possession, there was no reason for the 503rd to risk parachute injuries. On the eighth, Col. Lackey flew the 2nd and 3rd Battalions, for the last time, to Iloilo, Panay. They took LCIs to Bacolod, debarking on the ninth. The 1st Battalion, which had suffered the worst on Corregidor, remained on Mindoro to continue rebuilding and training the newcomers. Don Abbott, who had been a private at Ft. Benning, a mustanger first lieutenant in Company E, and its XO on Corregidor, was transferred to Company A as its new CO. He had been evacuated off the Rock to a hospital in Manila with jaundice. His work would be cut out for him training nearly an entire company of replacements while still recovering.

The two battalions of the 503rd marched north on the road and took up positions on the left flank so the other regiments could sidle south. They sparred hand-to-hand with Japanese patrols immediately, on the first night. A destroyer put up star shells to help stem infiltration. Come morning, the three regiments advanced in line, soon trudging uphill. Oddly, the 462nd PFAB came under divisional control and was mostly denied the paratroopers while shepherded by the infantry, who already had an inherent artillery brigade of five battalions, a tank company, a 105-mm SP cannon company, two mortar companies, and two AA batteries. Only Battery D's fifty-cals were delegated to the parachute battalions. Already denied the advantage of surprise, unlike Lae and Corregidor, their attacks would be the frontal assault against carefully prepared defenses welcomed by the Japanese.

An unforeseen handicap was that Eichelberger, perhaps influenced by the rapid fall of the other islands, had ordered only fifteen days' supplies rather than the prescribed sixty. What resupply there was had to be by air because of the broken terrain. The quartermasters and S-4s resorted to hiring Filipinos to pack in supplies and trading parachute silk for fresh eggs, produce, and chickens. The sweltering heat and unrelenting humidity made every yard of the uphill battle through foothills, valleys, and mountains miserable and costly for the troopers.

The 40th Division, however, shortly after engaging the Japanese, dug itself in, surrounded itself with barbed wire and booby traps, and decided its plan of attack would be to lob artillery shells into enemy positions and determine formulaic casualty counts. Still, Brush (whom Krueger had tried to get dismissed more than once) refused to release to the 503rd its own artillery. Why Col. Jones didn't vehemently protest, or go up the ladder for overriding authorization, can only be surmised as old school unwillingness to breach the chain of command. The paratroopers continued to slug it out and count bodies in the mountains. The strategy reeked of their misuse on Noemfoor and of the 511th on Leyte. The infantry apparently considered the Airborne little more than cannon fodder.

The 503rd locked horns with Maj. Gen. Takeo Manjome's 102nd Division. Rather than cave by cave or bunker by bunker, this battle was fought ridge by ridge. Without proper artillery support, the paratroopers were left with mortars and machine guns to try to soften up direct assaults, or when the rare occasion presented itself, flank attacks. The Japanese, always on the high ground, seemingly got in the first shots of every engagement. The Filipinos who brought in supplies would carry out the wounded and dead. 3rd Battalion surgeon Cpt. Hovis felt that "too many of the casualties were old-timers."

John Reynolds, from D Company, recounted to author O'Donnell that each day seemed the same, but one in particular he had never forgotten. His platoon had just taken one hill and moved on to the next. The Japanese were "dug in," with "interlocking fields of fire" that were "impossible to flank...." The platoon got onto the second hill easily—too easily—but then came under heavy fire from rifles, machine guns, and knee mortars. A mortar shell killed one of Company D's first replacements and their new CO, a young lieutenant. Within minutes, two more privates were wounded, and the lieutenant commanding the machine gun platoon was killed by a sniper. As Reynolds hugged the ground, it occurred to him he had a good chance of being killed this day—his mother's birthday. Another platoon arrived, helped take the hill, and carried down the casualties. John concluded, "The Japanese would kill ten men a day, and pretty soon that adds up to one hundred dead men."

In mid-April, word was passed up from Regimental Headquarters, back near Bacolod, that President Roosevelt had died in Warm Springs, Georgia, near where some of the 503rd had once furloughed. The news was a gut-punch second only to the surrender on Corregidor at the beginning of the war. There was no time to grieve. Maj. Davis's 1st Battalion arrived on the twenty-third by boat from Panay, to where Lackey had flown them, along with replacements for the other battalions. Abbott's Company A went into battalion reserve. The others went immediately into the line. A replacement for Company H was killed before he even got to the CP. At night, veterans shared foxholes with newcomers to ensure that the protocols were followed and the young blood was preserved.

On the twenty-sixth, the 164th IR of the Americal Division, also in reserve, landed near Dumaguete and soon linked up with 40th Division's recon company, which had traveled nearly the entire coastal road. The 164th went into the hills after 1300 Japanese troops of the 174th Infantry Battalion, who were not actually under Kono's command; their parent brigade and commander were on Cebu.

Three days later, American GIs in Bavaria north of Munich were both dumbfounded and revolted when they liberated the Dachau concentration camp. The awful unbelievable rumors of torture, excruciating death, and mass murder reported all along by escapees proved to be true. Three hundred sixty miles to the northeast, with the Red Army closing in on the *Führerbunker* the last day of April, Hitler and Eva Braun, his wife for a day and a half, committed suicide. Hitler's Axis cohort, Benito Mussolini, had been executed in Italy two days before.

On May 1, the Australian 7th Division, old friends of the 503rd from New Guinea, assaulted Borneo and its oil fields.[5] The next day, Berlin fell to General Vasili Chuikov and the Russian juggernaut. The 101st Airborne and 3rd Infantry Divisions headed southeast to Bavaria, where it was thought the Germans would stage a last stand. All they found in the Alps were Field Marshal Kesselring and fine liquor at Hitler's Eagle's Nest and the Nazis' bounty of stolen art at Neuschwanstein Castle and the Altausee salt mine. On the seventh, German Chief of Operation Staff Alfred Jodl surrendered the rest of the German Army. The new President, Harry Truman, announced "Victory in Europe" (V-E) Day on May 8, 1945.

The 503rd continued their frustrating, and at times, futile, hilltop battles for another month. By now they were carrying supplies, ammo, and weapons through the jungles along the mountain trails by tying them onto poles and holding the ends on their shoulders. At 3000 feet, it was usually cold, made all the more so because of their acclimation to heat. By the middle of May, between casualties, exhaustion, and sickness, most companies were down to half-strength. Service Company platoons, with next to no supply to manage, relieved platoons up front, so battle-weary men could get a few days rest behind the lines. Platoons that were rotated out of the mountains back to the base camp relished a shave, clean clothes, dry tents, baseball games, hamburgers, pork chops, and Top Hat beer. Others continued to suffer: Father Powers, having tried to carry on while still recuperating from his broken ribs, was now wracked with the alternating sweats and chills of malaria.

Death, they had learned, was random. You could be careful; you could be wild. Either way, you could be dead. A trooper lagging behind his squad hurried to catch up. "I don't mind dying," he puffed, "but I don't want to die alone." It was as much prophecy as wish. The next morning, his squad found him and his partner dead in their foxhole, victims of infiltrators.

Turner was down with a bout of malaria on a day he was supposed to lead a patrol. His assistant squad leader took out the patrol. "He was a little guy," Turner recalled. "They were ambushed but the bullets went over his head. The guy behind him got it pretty good. If I'd been in the lead, it would have been me."

Constant vigilance and strain took a toll on decision-making as well. Turner made what he later called his "stupidest" mistake of the war. Having advanced across a hill with a platoon, he realized he'd left a clip at his previous position. "Not knowing when I might get more ammo, like a fool, I went back to look for it. I could've been shot or captured," he admitted.

No one was safe behind the lines, either. At an Association meeting thirty years later, Arnie Williams talked about getting hit while on a detail. "I wasn't doing anything heroic at the time. We were low on supplies, and I was coming back when I got wounded —shot through the leg. I was carrying a case of beer." [There followed a round of raucous laughter topped off with a call from the back of the room, "That's REAL heroic!"] Arnie finished with a chuckle, "I swear there's nobody else that can say that!"

In early June, Gen. Kono withdrew far back into the mountains, where he would hold out for two months. Now came the tropical rains, freezing at night but turning into morning fog and afternoon humidity. "Dash" Brush, apparently content in his barbed wire fortress, sent a few guns of the 462nd up the hills along the roads carved by the 161st. The engineers, filling in tank traps with bulldozers to extend roads, were picked off by snipers. A single sharpshooter at one such trap accounted for twenty-two airborne casualties. So, additional troopers started riding shotgun.

John Romero, point man on a patrol for Company E, described a duel he had with a sniper. "I'd shoot. He'd shoot. We did it again. Neither of us could zero in. Finally, I waited an extra tick after one shot and got him when he came up."

Jerry Ross, from Battery B, remembered a fight for one ridge where Turner flirted with death once more. "It was one of those days where we took the ridge in the morning, then the [enemy] got it back in the afternoon, and we got it again at dusk, and then fought off the infiltrators all night. The snipers started shooting in the morning. They picked off the officers and the first sergeant. Your dad [Turner] all of a sudden realized he was the ranking soldier on that ridge. So he told us, 'Look, I'm going up there. You guys find out where the [heck] the fire is coming from and get them.' So with us all lying there watching the trees and bushes he stood up on the ridge and yelled, 'I'm the [expletive] company commander! See if you can hit me!' There was silence. The snipers must have fallen back to their unit on the next ridge."

On the tenth, Generals MacArthur and Eichelberger visited Negros. Gen. Brush, who would eventually be awarded the Distinguished Service Medal (although it is doubtful that any paratrooper would have voted for it) announced that the last enemy line had been overrun. How he knew that from behind his enclosure is up for debate, but he convinced his bosses that the "mopping up" stage had arrived. MacArthur did award medals to three troopers of the 503rd while generally congratulating the 40th for their stellar campaign. Eighth Army Chief of Staff, Gen. Robert Shoe, went all the way up to the forward positions. He asked a tired, disheveled 503rd paratrooper how things were at the front. The trooper just stared blankly. When the general came back, wounded by a sniper, the trooper asked him the same question.

By now Col. Abcede's 14,000 men controlled most of the island and, it was thought, outnumbered the Japanese. MacArthur pulled the 40th Division out in mid-June, to back up the 24th (which Postlethwait's beleaguered men had rejoined) and 31st Divisions, having an equally hard time of it in Mindanao. The 164th left Dumaguete on the twentieth. A 503rd company replaced the latter, and a platoon from the 161st accompanied them to build a water purification facility. At last, the paratroopers got all their howitzers back to break up enemy strongholds and press their advantage. Col. Jones took the spotter plane from a Bacolod airfield into the mountains to watch for Japanese movements and to drop grenades on them.

The guerrillas began relieving entire companies to be rotated out for R and R. A man might get flown out to Mindoro or spend a few days in Bacolod. There were cock fights, sight-seeing trips, night clubs, and of course, alcohol and girls. Turner and Phillips went into town. Filipinos they passed on the street would bow or nod and say, "Japan man bad man; American man good man." The two would nod back and answer under their breath, "Yeah, you said that the other way around a couple months ago." They were just leaving a jewelry shop when the shopkeeper became very excited and animated. The local gendarmes appeared and herded all the nearby shoppers back inside—the owner claimed he had been robbed. Tom and Max turned their pockets inside out and waited patiently while the police did their obligatory search. Finally, they were convinced that the GIs were not the culprits. The two walked away, shaking their heads while they pointed at each other and laughed, "American man good man!"

Max escaped death's dice roll one last time. In late June, "rotation of old men" back to the States for leaves began. Leaves had been authorized by the War Department two years previously, but with a constant shortage of men on hand in the PTO, the leaves had been perpetually postponed. Now, with enough Overseas Service Bars (one for each six-month period abroad), battles, wounds, and medals, a soldier could be sent home. Scheduled for a rotation flight out of Bacolod, Max gave his seat up to a trooper begging to get out early, apparently to meet his wife in Hawaii. The C-47 never made it; it was shot down on the way back to Mindoro. Max's generosity to a fellow trooper saved his own life. By now, the men were growing callous about their buddies' deaths.

They mourned the losses, of course, and wondered why it hadn't been themselves, but they were equally glad it wasn't.

The Tenth Army of Lt. Gen. Simon Bolivar Buckner, whose father had surrendered Fort Donelson to Ulysses S. Grant eighty-three years previously, secured Okinawa, the last in the chain of outlying Japanese islands, on June 22. The battle was another omen of the upcoming invasion of Japan; some companies had 110 percent casualties. There were 55,000 US Marine, Army, and Navy dead, wounded, or missing. One of them was Buckner himself, the highest-ranking American officer killed in the war, in the last few days of the battle. The most widely shared loss—to those who had not received a dreaded telegram—was Pulitzer Prize-winning news correspondent Ernie Pyle, whose reports from the fronts across Africa and Europe had been eagerly read in papers and tuned in on radios for the last three years. He was killed by a sniper soon after arriving on the tiny island of Ie Shima, a few miles from Okinawa. 26,000 more troops succumbed to combat fatigue and sickness. The Japanese lost 120,000 soldiers and an indeterminate number of civilians. Many of the latter died by suicide, others from being used as human shields by Japanese soldiers trying to infiltrate or get away.

Japanese envoys, at last beginning to see the writing on the wall, tried to persuade Russia, with whom they'd had a non-aggression pact since 1941, to broker a peace treaty. The Russians, however, now that they were done fighting the Germans, had deliberately not renewed the pact. Itching for one last land grab, Stalin had been transporting trains full of soldiers to the Manchurian border as fast as the Japanese shipped theirs home to defend against the inexorable assault. Moreover, the Japanese somehow expected to hold onto their gains throughout any negotiations, but the Russians knew that the Americans would settle for nothing less than unconditional surrender. There would be no deals.

On Luzon, Gen. Swift's I Corps had continued to press Gen. Yamashita, who had retreated northwards with his *Shobu* Group and the puppet Filipino government. Gen. Hall and XI Corps had crossed the island to cover Swift's right flank and to reopen Manila's water supply. They spent two months attacking what turned out to be the wrong dam. The river had been diverted years before the war. Finally, they captured the correct dam, and the water flow was restored, but not before disease was rampant throughout the city and its many refugee camps.

General Krueger expected Yamashita to use the northeastern coastal town of Appari to evacuate the wartime politicians and the large number of men he had left. Krueger sent a task force from the 37th Division along the coastal road to capture Appari while the bulk of the 37th Division followed the Cagayan River towards its mouth at Appari. He had Gen. Swing mount what would be the last airborne operation of the war. "The Angels" of 1st Battalion, two additional companies, a battery of artillery, and a company of engineers took off on June 23 for Camalaniugan Airstrip, south of Appari. Col. Lackey carried the troops, codenamed the "Gypsy Task Force." Gliders, for the first and only time in the PTO, carried artillery and jeeps (but no troops besides gun crews). After landing, the thousand paratroopers were to work their way south towards the 37th Division to catch Yamashita in between. They suffered seven percent jump casualties, due to flooded rice paddies, the typical debris-strewn field, and a twenty-five mile-per-hour wind—stronger than the 503rd had experienced on Corregidor (but without the cliffs). Leaving the injured at the airfield, the Gypsy Task Force marched thirty-five miles in three days with only sporadic opposition before linking up with the 37th. Appari was already under control of their task force. Yamashita had withdrawn into the mountains west of the river. A week after they had left their camp at Lipa, the Gypsy Task Force returned.[6]

Although Eichelberger told MacArthur that operations had ceased in Negros as of June 20 and Mindanao as of June 30, Americans and Filipinos were still fighting to liberate the islands. There were clashes between patrols on both islands through August. The paratroopers spread around Negros were coaching and advising the Filipinos how to keep the Japanese bottled up without losing a lot of men. Jerome Mandel, a young 2nd lieutenant replacement in Company B, said he "saw the last man killed" in the 503rd. When their patrol approached a hut in a valley, a Japanese rifleman fired out a window, hitting another lieutenant, Turpin, in the head. The paratroopers demolished the building and the sniper in it. More disconcerting to the company was a suicide by their oldest enlisted man, known as "Pop," by lying on his own grenade. In a few more weeks he'd have gone home to his wife.

Tom Turner was transferred to 2nd Battalion HHQ and promoted to staff sergeant "by order of Col. Jones" on July 24. He had plenty of catching up to do with Grooms and Runyon. As "Battalion Supply Sergeant," with a rocker beneath his chevrons, five Overseas Bars (he'd have six by the time he came home) on his sleeve, and the Combat Infantryman's Badge over his pocket, Tom would be sending home well over $100 a month even before jump pay. Troops were arriving daily in the Philippines from Europe in the build-up for the Japanese invasion. The first assaults were scheduled for November.

On August 6, the world was astounded to hear from

President Truman that a single bomb had destroyed an entire city, Hiroshima, in Japan. When the Japanese government refused to surrender, another city, Nagasaki, was incinerated on the ninth. The men on Negros didn't know about either until the thirteenth. By then, the last three-quarters of a million Japanese were being driven out of Manchuria by double their number of Russians. On the fourteenth, Emperor Hirohito persuaded the war leaders to surrender to avoid extermination. President Truman proclaimed, "Victory over Japan" (V-J) Day on the fifteenth. More high-point men were pulled out of the ranks to go home. They were replaced by kids who'd barely finished BIT and jump school.

George Jones had already flown home on the eighth. Lt. Col. Joe Lawrie took over as regimental commander. Jeeps with loudspeakers, leaflets dropped over Japanese entrenchments, and white-flag consultations with Japanese interpreters announced the surrender of Japan. Patrolling and skirmishing continued; mutual distrust kept the Japanese from believing the Americans and the Americans from offering grace to the Japanese. Eventually, on August 22, the fourth anniversary of the 503rd's existence, it was made known to five emissaries of Gen. Kono's staff at 503rd RHQ that the official end of the war would be 1000 hours on September 2, 1945, when Generals MacArthur and Wainwright would sign the papers with Japanese delegates on board *USS Missouri* in Tokyo Harbor.

Accepting their fate, the Japanese dutifully marched out of the hills throughout the island starting on August 30. The first column of 1600 men was led by Gen. Kono. He and his officers lined up across from Lawrie and his staff, and then presented their swords to the American officers. "They were very neat and orderly," according to Andy Amaty, who thought the soldiers surrendering with Kono were all that were left. They were not. Jesse Gandee, XO of Battery D, 462nd PFAB, said another column of soldiers came out of the mountains "resembling Army ants."

Lieutenant James Mullaney of Company H had a "very uneasy" drive in a jeep with Cpt. Joe Conway (two of the company's eighty to have left Corregidor on their own two feet), along the coast road between several companies of Japanese, followed by women with children and more companies of soldiers. He later received "a beautiful sword...130 years old" from a "docile little man...." As he held the sword, his eyes welled up as the faces of all his friends who had died from Nadzab to Negros flashed through his brain.

Over the next month, a total of 5900 Japanese surrendered.[7] The Army suspected yet another 600 had not. Isolated skirmishes would persist until October. Wherever they surrendered, the Japanese were kept in stockades, little more than pens with a strand or two of barbed wire. One group stayed in a lumber yard. Some were surrounded by GIs, some merely by Japanese guards armed with clubs. There were a handful of escape attempts—by delirious prisoners. Mostly the guards were there to prevent the Filipinos from getting at the Japanese and exacting reprisals. Weapons were neatly stacked and then torched. An engineer in the 161st said they later had the prisoners break up rocks to resurface the Bacolod airstrip while awaiting their turn to return home.

Negros had cost the 503rd PRCT 144 men killed and 370 wounded. Over 1000 more suffered from heat exhaustion and tropical diseases. The 40th and Americal Divisions had lost 226 killed and 655 wounded. Between them, the Americans killed 4000 Japanese. Almost that many died of disease and exhaustion. James Nagy, a sergeant in Company D, was of the opinion, shared by many of the 503rd PRCT veterans, that the mission on Negros was "their most difficult one, certainly the longest, and in terms of overall casualties, the costliest."[8] It proved to be, as Col. Lackey had predicted of Corregidor, "the greatest misuse of airborne forces yet conceived."

The Army estimated over 10,000 Japanese had been killed by the 503rd PRCT during its campaigns.[9] Three hundred ninety-two paratroopers are on the rolls as having paid the supreme price. Exemplifying the losses to the combat team over the course of the war, Ben Guthrie said that Company H had left Fort Bragg with 120 men. Of that original complement, seventeen were left on Negros after V-J Day.

The 503rd was broken up on Negros. The old-timers finally got their trips home. The rest were absorbed into the 11th Airborne for the occupation of Japan. The airlift with C-46s, C-47s, and B-24s began on August 11. Gen. Swing flew with Col. Lackey in the first C-54 (updated four-prop version of the C-47) to land in Atsugi Airfield near Tokyo. Offered a handshake by a Japanese three-star general, Swing scowled until the general dropped his hand. Harry Akune was amongst the first planeloads of the 511th. Allied POWs had just been released into one of the hangars, set up for their reception. The way they carefully ate every morsel, even though a feast had been spread out for them, impressed Harry. By the fifteenth, Swing's entire division was in Okinawa, and two weeks later, in Tokyo. Gen. Swing led the honor guard that welcomed Gen. MacArthur to Japan. Ironically, Swing's troops on parade saluted the General as he stood in front of the Imperial Palace, precisely where Tokyo Rose had once predicted he'd be executed when captured. Thankfully, the 11th Airborne would only be an occupation force, not an invasion force. They would return

Stateside in 1949, after spending four years in Japan.

In 1946, the United States indeed granted the Philippines sovereignty. Fort McKinley became Fort Andres Bonifacio[10]. Part of the fort contains the Manila American Cemetery. It sits on a knoll and overlooks both the Manila skyline and Laguna de Bay amid Luzon's mountains. Twenty-five mosaic maps of the Asiatic campaigns are on display in the visitor center. Its 17,184 graves, forming concentric arcs of white crosses and Stars of David, are the most of any overseas WWII cemetery.[11] In it rest the dead American soldiers, sailors, and airmen from battles in China, Burma, New Guinea, the Philippines, and dozens of other islands, besides several thousand Philippine Scouts who fought alongside the Americans on Bataan. There are twenty-nine Medal of Honor winners and twenty pairs of brothers. Most impressive, at the center of the radiating rows of crosses and stars, is a semicircular monument with 36,000 carved names—service members whose bodies had not been recovered (a few have been found since). Among them are the five Sullivans who went down with the cruiser *USS Juneau* as well as the men lost in Corregidor's explosions.

General George Jones was there when the cemetery was dedicated in 1948. Many of his paratroopers from New Guinea and the Philippine Islands were interred there. He spoke these words over them:

> History will record what you did here, this hallowed ground shall be your tomb and the hearts of a free people forever filled with gratitude shall be your monument.

1 Guthrie states that Cpt. William Bossert designed the new patch while recuperating from the explosion at Monkey Point. Since Guthrie mentions that Bossert's intent was to include the 462nd PFAB and Company C of the 161st AEB, I think he may be referring to the third rendition. This has a white shield on which an inverted blue triangle (vertical assault) pierces the topmost bastion of a blue pentagonal fortress (five combat missions—Nadzab, Hollandia, Noemfoor, Corregidor, Negros). The triangle contains three white parachutes, for the "Three Winds of Death." (A 1987 edition of the Association's newsletter, *The Static Line*, claimed they represented the three Pacific campaigns in New Guinea, Leyte-Luzon, and Southern Philippines.) Inscribed on a blue banner at the bottom is "The Rock."

2 Contraction of American, New Caledonian Division. Created from a task force originally sent to New Caledonia (east of Australia, north of New Zealand) shortly after Pearl Harbor, it was the only division activated outside the States and without a number. It became the 23rd Division after the war.

3 Patton, after racing to relieve Bastogne, was incensed that Montgomery claimed credit for winning the Battle of the Bulge by holding his end of the line —when in fact he had actually withheld British support while the US 99th Division denied the Germans the Elsenborn Ridge, the only sector in which the Germans failed to advance. Deeming Ike and Monty too cautious, Patton then covered another eighty miles from the Luxembourg border across the Palatinate region to the Rhine from March 13-19. Although Eisenhower had halted Bradley's army to allow Montgomery's to cross the Rhine first in Operation Plunder, Patton got across the Rhine at Oppenheim on the twenty-second, a full thirty-six hours ahead of Monty, then turned north to meet him. As in Sicily, the audacious Patton had traveled two sides of the triangle to the deliberate Monty's one.

4 Alfried Krupp's family had manufactured Germany's heavy artillery, tanks, and battleships not only for both world wars but its armaments all the way back to the Thirty Years' War. They had also provided steel for American railroads and the top of the Chrysler building. Alfried was tried at Nuremberg for knowingly supplying the Nazis despite the Treaty of Versailles' ban on rearmament, embracing the use of slave labor to do so, and accepting illegally

seized assets in defeated countries. He served only three years of a twelve-year sentence before being released by a general amnesty from the new West German government. Allied orders to break up the company were evaded and his holdings and fortune were returned to him. He died in 1967 and the company eventually dissolved in the '90s. His father, Gustav, who had married the Krupp heiress and taken on the Krupp name, would have been the only person tried for war crimes in both world wars (Big Bertha which had pounded Paris was built by Krupp), but he was found unfit for trial due to a stroke and the onset of senility during the war. He died in 1950.

5 The 9th Division reinforced the attack on June 10. They had the Japanese in a pincer, as at Lae and Hollandia. Japanese forces on the island were defeated quickly thereafter.

6 The 541st PIR would arrive in the Philippines soon after the superfluous Camalaniugan mission. They'd been a training unit at Ft. Benning since 1943 and had seen thousands of men come and go through their ranks. They were another proud elite unit anxious to finally get into the fight. Expecting to join 11th Airborne, they were devastated, upon arrival, to find out the regiment was to be disbanded and the officers and men distributed throughout the 11th Airborne to counter its losses. Sadly, even more of the 11th would be lost due to crashes *en route* to Okinawa and Japan.

7 On September 19, Gen. Tomoyuki Yamashita led the remnant of his *Shobu* Group out of their mountain bastion on Luzon. Yamashita had elected not to subject himself to *hara-kiri*, because "someone else would have to take the blame." 40,000 men surrendered with him, and as many as another 25,000 surrendered to the Philippine Army. He was tried and executed as a war criminal in 1946.

8 503rd PRCT Association Newsletter, 1989.

9 Public Relations Office General Release 49, 25 September 1945. Headquarters, United States Army Forces Western Pacific, Manila. This document also listed the surrender numbers for Negros and Luzon.

10 The top revolutionary commander against Spain in the 1890s.

11 The National Memorial Cemetery of the Pacific at the Punchbowl Crater in Honolulu holds more than 61,000 American service casualties from WWII, Korea, and Vietnam. 13,000 of them are from WWII. Ernie Pyle was one of the first interred, on the anniversary of V-J Day, 1949.

Chapter 17

THE STATES
Homecoming and the American Dream

S taff Sergeant Thomas Turner got his "R and R" group order on September 12, 1945. He had ninety-six service points. Only two men on the list of thirty-five (all New York or New Jersey bound) had more. He left Dumaguete and the Philippines the next day, ten days after turning thirty-two. He landed in California on the thirtieth. "When I came down the gangplank," he recalled with a sigh, "I dropped my duffle bags and kissed the ground." He had left the United States nineteen days shy of three years before.

He took another cross-country train ride, one of forty-four million such trips taken by the sixteen million service personnel during the course of the war, but instead of getting boring this trip got more exciting. He was discharged at Fort Dix, New Jersey, on October 9. He walked through his parents' front door the next afternoon. Betty was already there, waiting for him. "He was dark tanned and skinny," she remembered, "and his eyeballs were yellow from the Atabrine." Somewhere he'd lost his OD go-to-hell hat with its light-blue infantry piping and parachute patch; he had borrowed an artilleryman's red-piped cap.

Most of the paratroopers left Negros for home or Japan by early November. Even though he had been one of the first to join the 503rd, Lt. Col. Joe Lawrie was the last man of the regiment to leave Negros. The 503rd PIR was deactivated at Camp Anza, near Riverside, California, and its regimental flag encased on Christmas Eve, 1945.

The 503rd was reactivated in early 1951 at Fort Campbell, Kentucky, as part of the 11th Airborne Division, but was not involved in the Korean War. In 1956 it moved to Germany with the 11th. In March 1957, the 11th was inactivated, and the 503rd came under the 24th Division as an "Airborne Battle Group." The 503rd returned to Fort Bragg and was reassigned to the 82nd Airborne Division two years later. In 1963, the 1st and 2nd Battalions were transferred to the 173rd Airborne Brigade in Okinawa.

When the 173rd was deployed to Vietnam in May 1965, the 503rd Airborne Infantry became the first significant US Army ground unit (some Marine regiments and Army "military advisors" preceded it) to see combat. The 3rd and 4th Battalions were subsequently activated and came over later. The 503rd fought several battles in Vietnam, where eight troopers won Congressional Medals of Honor. The regiment won three more Presidential Unit Citations as well as a Meritorious Unit Citation, while the 173rd earned its own Presidential Unit Citation at Dak To in the highlands. The brigade's 10,000 casualties in Vietnam were five times the total airborne casualties in Korea, four times those of the 11th AB in the PTO in WWII, and more than either the 82nd or 101st in the ETO. One of the last units to leave, the 173rd was withdrawn from Vietnam in August 1971. The following January, the 503rd

was inactivated and the troops transferred to the 101st Airborne Division.

1/503 and 2/503 were reactivated in 1986 and attached to the 2nd Infantry Division to patrol the Korean DMZ (where Tom Turner's great grandson now pilots Black Hawks as a Warrant Officer for the Air Assault Brigade of the 2nd). 2/503 was deactivated in 1990 when 1/503 became an "Air Assault Battalion," but it was reactivated in 2001 and joined 1/503 back in the 173rd Airborne Brigade, this time in Italy. Both battalions participated in Operation "Iraqi Freedom." In 2007 they were deployed to Afghanistan, where 2/503 earned another Presidential Unit Citation for heroism in October 2011. The 1st and 2nd Battalions of the 503rd currently remain on duty in Vicenza, Italy, and proudly watch over the retired WWII battle flags and the disbanded 503rd PRCT Association's flag.

Years after the bullets stopped whistling and the bombs stopped exploding, the men who survived the island battles overcame not only physical handicaps, like George Kojima, Hudson Hill, Jesse Castillo, and Reverend Probert Herb had to do, but also deep spiritual wounds. Previously regarded as "shell shock" or "battle fatigue," and often with a negative implication of weakness or even cowardice, these emotional scars have only become diagnosed within the past half-century as signs of Post-Traumatic Stress Disorder (PTSD). Nightmares, tremors, and flashbacks were common to the veterans. One told Kevin Maurer that for a long time he couldn't eat a bowl of soup: by the time he got the spoon to his mouth, the shaking of his hand had emptied it. Another, watching the mock pirate battle outside the Treasure Island casino in Las Vegas, suddenly was overwhelmed by the terror of real battle. He turned his wheelchair around to leave (having suffered a life-long wound as well) only to come face to face with a group of Japanese tourists. He saw them as armed, uniformed enemies. His first instinct was to run them down.

Tom Turner had a flashback of his own after open-heart surgery. When I came into his hospital room, he had just awakened from anesthesia and was thrashing around in the bed. "The [enemy] have caught me! I gotta get oughta here!" he was saying wild-eyed through clenched teeth as he kicked and yanked the covers and tried to rip off wires and tubes. His trigger had been waking up and seeing a Japanese-American nurse. It took me, my mother, and several doctors and nurses all afternoon to convince him he was home, and the war had ended twenty-five years before.

Some behaviors were due to the ingrained training. My mom told me that when she and Dad walked in the park or down a street, he would constantly scan treetops. He was not birdwatching; he was looking for snipers. One day a ne'er-do-well harassed them and tried to pick a fight with Dad, probably looking for an opportunity to grab Mom's purse. Betty said, "You can take this guy, Tom." He responded, "Yeah, until his two jamokes across the street jump in." He had already reconnoitered and declined the bait. He was not about to be ambushed in New York.

Tom added the Colt Peacemaker to his collection of antique firearms he'd started before the war. An avid hunter before his service, Dad never shot at anything other than a paper target afterwards. The paratroopers told most of the battle stories in this book (or borrowed from others) only after decades of suppressing the memories of seeing their best friends and even the enemy brutally maimed or killed in indescribable ways. Thank God they were finally able to choke down the tears and tell Devlin, Maurer,

O'Donnell, Brokaw, Stephen Ambrose, and others their stories so that they would not be lost from history. Their remembering and retelling the funny events, pranks, and jokes *ad nauseum* were their way of coping before the scientific world and veteran help organizations figured out how to give them back normal lives. Mostly, they figured it out themselves.

Max Phillips was true to his foxhole prophecy. He married a UCLA grad, Irene Ross, and they had no children. After getting a law degree from Pacific Coast University, in Long Beach, California, he became a successful Farmers Insurance agent, adjuster, and eventually, claims superintendent. Irene had a government job in Los Angeles with a very high clearance rating, though she was never allowed to say exactly what she did. When they bought their house in Long Beach, not far from Boeing, Hughes, Douglas and other aviation facilities, there were still camouflage coverings over the buildings, oil refineries, and naval installations along the coast. Max died in 1991 and was buried in his home state of Minnesota. His obituary verified that his given name was, indeed, Maximillian Philippi Wermerskirschen.

Karl Landes had already used his vast education to start up a highly successful import business in New York, KHL Flavors, before the war. When he returned from the Pacific, he took up where he had left off. He traveled the world looking for medicinal herbs and plants from which to extract ingredients for pharmaceuticals. He branched out into herbal teas, dried flowers, potpourri, herbs, and spices. KHL Flavors is still family owned today and run by his nephews. He always traveled first-class and stayed in luxurious accommodations for the reunions. Never one to sit idly, thirty years after the war, well past retirement age, he was still teaching university chemistry classes. Besides the German accent, he never lost his dry sense of humor. I was honored to be invited, as the son of one of his best friends, to his room at a Palm Springs reunion, where he told me of the incidents written here.

Pete Komer brought his stash of expensive Japanese silk home. Decades later he had his daughter's wedding dress made from it. Once, when Tom Turner switched planes in Detroit, Pete met him at the airport. He had brought along his album full of wartime photos and articles so they could spend the short layover time reminiscing. On a vacation trip back to Australia and the Philippines, he sent Tom a postcard from Corregidor with one of the Signal Corps photos on it. He made a special trip to California for Tom's funeral and stayed in Betty's extra room so she would not have to be alone for at least a couple days. Pete was laid to rest in 2005.

Father John Powers attended a religious retreat in Rhode Island after his discharge in October 1945 but before being reassigned in the Albany area. He wrote Tom Turner, "You get sort of dried up spiritually—as well as mentally, etc—in our uncle's Army." Although unable to make "the big event" when he was invited to Dad's wedding, he promised to "say a few prayers that the good Lord will bless you and Betty." Eventually he became a monsignor, and he worked with the Veterans Administration to continue to look after his flock. He and his "Protestant son" kept in touch until Tom's passing in 1979. The Monsignor retired the next year to Palo Alto, Ca.

When Jesse Castillo got back to the states and was recuperating from his "homer," he told his fiancée, Florence, that if she didn't want to spend her life married to a blind man—in effect less than she had bargained for—she could walk away, and he would understand. She told him, "If you think you can get rid of me that easy you have another think coming. If you don't marry me, you will get awful tired of me following you around and sitting on your lap." They married, raised four kids, and built very lucrative real estate and restaurant businesses. Jesse passed away in 2004.

Arnie Williams, like many others, moved west from Iowa, where his father owned a large tract of land, to Mentone, California and started over with his wife, Jeanette. He was a mainstay at the 503rd meetings and reunions, and always one to tell a good story with a choirboy smile.

Ralph Leyva settled in East Los Angeles with his wife, Amanda. He was among the first to answer my request for recollections and encouraged me to get hold of Andy Amaty, "a real good storyteller." Ralph made me aware that the men graduated jump school on different dates, but with the same shared sense of panic. He was a president of the 503rd PRCT Association in Southern California.

Harry Akune, while with the 11th Airborne, reconnected with his family, most of whom had stayed in Japan. When he was discharged, he decided not to go back to California, where he felt he wasn't wanted. He lived with a friend in Nebraska before eventually returning to California. After years of anger about the internment camps, he at last "reconciled himself" to being a proud American. "Sometimes," he told Patrick O'Donnell, "we take freedom for granted, but when you lose it, you really appreciate it." He considered the 503rd his family and remained active in the Association. A letter from Jack Herzig, representing the 503rd PRCT Association, and a personal request by then retired General George Jones resulted in Harry's being inducted into the Military Intelligence Hall of Fame.

Chaplain Probert Herb was an Episcopalian priest. He never got married and eventually retired to Florida.

Andy Amaty and his wife, Ginny, were fixtures at 503rd meetings and reunions for decades. Many Association meetings were at their beautiful home in Burbank, California. At a Bob Hope book signing in the nearby (and oft-used movie locale) Galleria Mall, he stood in a long line of customers snaking throughout the mall, waiting to get Bob's autograph. A bookstore employee came down the line, listing what each customer would like inscribed in the cover of his or her book. Andy said simply, "Remember Noemfoor?" The employee soon came back and said, "Mr. Hope wants you to come with me." They went to the front of the line. Andy sat next to Bob, and they talked like old foxhole partners while Bob signed books. In another chance encounter, at a wedding reception, Andy met the Navy radioman he'd yelled at to shoot flares on Corregidor. The old sailor at last knew who "that crazy paratrooper" was that gave a Navy captain orders. Andy died as every trooper would have had it: he manned the registration table in the hospitality room at the 503rd Association's 55th Annual Corregidor Day reunion in 2000 and saw all the old gang for the last time. He gave an interview to Patrick O'Donnell for his upcoming book *Into the Rising Sun*, including several incidents recounted here, and then had a fatal stroke the next day as he got ready to go home.

John Lindgren married a French lady named Claudia. They settled in Laguna Hills, an upscale neighborhood of Orange County, California. He was always involved with the Association, eventually writing articles for its website about his experiences. As an officer he had been called both respectfully, "Senator" for his professional bearing, and sarcastically, "Jungle Fox" for his heavy-footed lack of stealth. It was to John that I first broke the news of my father's passing. Always the platoon leader, he got all the 503rd Association members in Southern California (and some from out of state) to Dad's service. John passed away in 2005.

Don Abbott left the service in Fort Lewis, Washington, not far from his home in Portland, Oregon. He settled in Santa Rosa, California, as a computer programmer. He later wrote articles for the Association's website and refuted quite a few mistakes in previous unit histories. He retold many of his stories to authors of books about the 503rd. Don also presided over the Association. He was laid to rest in Portland in 2005.

Henry "Hoot" Gibson, though born and raised in the Philippines, had graduated from high school in New York. He found his sister, still living in Manila, at the end of the war. He retired from the Army after the Vietnam War. He lived until 2008.

Lieutenant General Joseph Swing commanded the 11th

Airborne until 1947, then headed up the Army War College before commanding Sixth Army. Upon Swing's retirement in 1954, then-President Eisenhower appointed him Commissioner of Immigration. He died in 1984.

Colonel John Lackey, whose planes dropped every Army paratrooper in the Pacific Theater, later served on the Armed Forces Staff College faculty. He died in 1956 while still in the service.

Colonel Edwin Postlethwait got his paratroopers' wings after the war, retired from the Army in 1967, and became a financial planner in North Carolina.

Joe Lawrie remained active throughout the Korean and Vietnamese Wars. He was Commander of the 82nd Airborne Division in Vietnam (1965-7), just before his retirement as Major General. Amongst his decorations were the Silver Star and the Legion of Merit. He died in Texas, at the age of 95, thirty years to the day after Tom Turner.

Lieutenant General John Tolson, III, was on the staff of the Air University of Alabama after the war, with the 325th Airborne IR during the Korean War, and with the 82nd Airborne Division afterwards. As he had been with the Airborne in the South Pacific, he continued to be a top proponent and developer of the Army Aviation (helicopter) program and was Commandant at Fort Rucker (1965-7). He was CO of the 1st Cavalry (Airborne) Division in Vietnam (1967-8), where he formed units of hard-hitting helicopter-borne air-cavalry troops. He began the Army's first drug rehabilitation program while with the XVIII Airborne Corps (1968-71) at Fort Bragg. He retired in 1973 as deputy commander of the Continental Army Command. He passed away in 1991 and was buried at Arlington National Cemetery.

Brigadier General George Jones spent thirty-three years in the Army. After the 503rd was inactivated, he served as the Director of Training for the Parachute School at Ft. Benning, an observer for the Bikini Atoll atomic tests, Chief of Staff of XVIII Airborne Corps, and G-3 for IX Corps in Korea. Then, as Commandant of the Special Warfare School at Fort Bragg, he transformed the mere notion of Special Forces into a highly trained unit. Later, he was Commander of the 66th Military Intelligence Group in Germany, Deputy Commander of the 3rd Infantry Division, and Chief of Staff of Fifth US Army. He was Commander of the Yukon Command near Fairbanks and retired in 1968 as Deputy Commander of the US Army in Alaska. Before leaving Alaska, he got an MBA and embarked on a second career as a financial planner and investment advisor in Tucson. The Warden passed away in 1996 at age 84 and was buried at Arlington Cemetery.

Major General William H. Lee, the man who started it all, had a heart attack shortly before D-Day which required him to give up command of the 101st Airborne Division to Maxwell Taylor, the 82nd Airborne's assistant commander, who led the division through the rest of the war. Lee never fully recovered and died in 1948.

Tom Turner married the preacher's daughter, Betty Dockter, in November 1945, just about the time he had expected to jump into the charnel house that would have been the battle for Japan from which only one in ten GIs could hope to get home in one piece. They moved to Pasadena, California, where there was a population boom and a housing shortage, so they lived for a while in a trailer park (now a Target parking lot) on Colorado Boulevard. The Turners and the Phillipses, who drove up from Long Beach, would play Monopoly all night New Year's Eve and take turns holding a spot on the curb for the Rose Parade. Sometimes they golfed, visited local attractions like Busch Gardens and Will Rogers Ranch, or attended radio or TV shows in Hollywood together.

Tom was in and out of the Veterans' Hospital for several years with malaria flare-ups, during which he would shiver while Betty threw blankets on top of him "and even climbed on top myself" only to have him throw her and everything else off in a raging fever. She said he had nightmares for many more years after that, and that he was never healthy after the war. Still, he managed to take drafting classes in night school while working in Betty's grandfather's glass-decorating shop in nearby Glendale. Since her New York lab certification didn't apply in California, she became a bank teller in downtown Pasadena, and later a school district secretary in Orange County.

They bought a house a few miles east on Route 66 in Glendora, where they started raising my brother and me, and then in Anaheim, within sight and sound of the Disneyland fireworks. Tom retired as a mechanical draftsman, after having worked for several architectural firms and finally for an electronics company. He did some panel light system design work for an Apollo space capsule and the Disneyland Space Mountain attraction as two of his last projects.

One day, in a foxhole on some island, Dad had made a vow

to his Maker that if he ever got back home, he would never complain again. He never did. The closest he ever came, despite layoffs, plans gone haywire, and rapidly declining health, was, "I should've stayed in the tropics. I could've been king of the coconuts!" Doc Landes had told him he thought Tom had diabetes when they left the Army. Tom's doctors did not make the same diagnosis until twenty years later, when it was already rampant. When he lost a leg to the insidious disease (after withstanding several days of gangrene with no more fuss than gritted teeth), the old Airborne athleticism and determination took over: he finished the several-months-long rehab program with his prosthesis in a matter of weeks so that he could stand beside his first grandchild when she was baptized.

Tom was briefly president of the Southern California 503rd Association—and was the first to go, shortly after retiring. Having already had a heart attack and a triple-bypass, he had another attack on the way to church. It was providential that no one else was involved when his car left the road; Sunday morning traffic was light, and Betty had not felt right that morning and stayed home. It was February 25, 1979—the 34th anniversary of D+10 on Corregidor and a week after the Association's annual reunion. At the memorial service, the pastor opened the small New Testament-Psalms Tom had carried throughout the war, remarking that "It still has the smell of the jungle." Then, alluding to the lifelong bonds tied on the beaches and in the jungles, he read scripture from John 15: "Greater love hath no man than this, that a man lay down his life for his friends." The veterans knew it; they had lived it.

Many of Dad's Association friends, local or not—Lindgren, Phillips, Landes, Kojima, Amaty, Komer, Ando, Williams, Matievich, Patterson, Castillo, Akune, Jermolowicz, Leyva,

Sanchez—were there to bid their old pal farewell, carry the flag-draped casket, and salute during the playing of Taps.

BATTLE AWARDS OF THE 503RD PARACHUTE INFANTRY REGIMENT (WWII)

Battle Streamers: New Guinea
Luzon (with Arrowhead for Corregidor Assault)
Southern Philippines

United States Presidential Unit Citation: Corregidor

Philippine Presidential Unit Citation (awarded 1950)

AWARDS EARNED BY TOM TURNER AND MANY 503RD PARATROOPERS

Marksman and Bayonet Qualifying Bars
Parachutist's Badge
Combat Infantryman's Badge (CIB)
    ("for being engaged in active ground combat")
Distinguished Unit Badge (for Corregidor)
Bronze Star (later awarded to CIB recipients per order of Omar
    Bradley)
Asiatic-Pacific Campaign Medal
    (with 3 battle stars: New Guinea, South Philippines,
    Leyte campaigns; and with Arrowhead: Corregidor assault)
Philippine Liberation Medal (issued by Philippine Government)
American Defense Medal
American Campaign Medal

National Defense Service Medal

World War II Victory Medal

Good Conduct Medal

Honorable Service Lapel Patch and Pin
("Honorable Discharge" or "Ruptured Duck")

Purple Heart (killed, wounded, or injured in combat)

Six Overseas Service Bars (each for six months abroad)

Acknowledgments

Of course, this book would not have happened were it not for Thomas E. Turner, whose ability to find humor in nearly any dismal situation and whose knack for telling a story with a good punch line inspired this work. An incalculable thanks goes to my mom, Elizabeth Dockter Turner, who religiously kept the scrapbook throughout my dad's service, from before Pearl Harbor till well after V-J Day. I often verified conflicting information from several sources by finding one of her clippings or souvenirs with the date, who was there, where they were, or why. Other items prompted more research. For example, Col. Kinsler's certificate and the Albany newspaper clipping convinced me that Tom, who had been in the cadre to form the 503rd Battalion, was nonetheless one of the last to get his wings before the regiment's staging train ride to California.

Christian, your great grandpa would be proud to salute you as Pilot in Command and for continuing the Army Airborne/Cavalry tradition you both embraced. Seeing where your paths converge, yet seven decades apart, strikes me as miraculous. You are both, as your boot camp commandant said, "Part of something bigger."

Thanks go to Eric and Brian Hodges, my brothers-in-law,

both Navy aviators with combat and command experience, for not only explaining technical and military terminology but for proofreading and upgrading my "mid-century modern" grammar, syntax, and prose. Eric had become one of Davy Jones's and King Neptune's "trusty shellbacks" after crossing the equator himself. Brian, a first-in pilot for two Middle East campaigns, combined my previously separate and randomly ordered chapters into a complete document. The side story about Lucky Lindy is an homage to you "flyboys."

I must thank troopers Bill Ryle and Bob Weber, whom I never met but who kept in touch with Dad and who sent me priceless photos from Australia, New Guinea, and Negros after his passing. Thanks is also due to Dad's association, foxhole and squad tent mates Doc Landes, Max Phillips, Andy Amaty, John Lindgren, George Clay, Harry Akune, Ben Jermolowicz, Pete Komer, Jesse Castillo, George Kojima, Don Abbott, Arnie Williams, Mike Matievich, Pat Patterson, Andy Ando, Ralph Leyva, and Al Viera, whose stories my brother and I heard over and over yet of which we couldn't get enough. I hope I did them justice.

This work would still be sitting in Word files on a PC if not for Bruce Edwards, a colleague in our young-adult years but more recently an author of young-adult books. Bruce not only advised me about writing a proper intro and methods of publication, but graciously and voluntarily print formatted the entire manuscript and offered to publish under his Lambert Hill banner. The cover design is entirely Bruce's: I sent him the Disney drawing, the recruiting poster, and the book title. He did the rest, including editing the old pictures within. Thank you for taking over the daunting, if not downright overwhelming, publishing process.

My brother, Jon, like our father a gun enthusiast, showed me the differences between the Springfield, M1 rifle, and carbine, loaned me several of the books in the bibliography, and forwarded the letters from William Calhoun about his experiences on the carbine test panels.

My cousin, Bill Dockter, and his son, Warren Dockter, Ph.D.—President of the East Tennessee Historical Society and author of several books on Churchill—were enthusiastic from the start about reading each chapter and getting the next "installment" as I finished them. In Bill's words to me, "We stand on the shoulders of giants." His father, Betty's and Dotty's brother, flew bombers from Montana to Watson Lake in the Yukon to be turned over to the Russians for use against the Germans. But that's another story, for Bill or Warren to write.

To my wife of over forty-five years, Claudia, whose dad was the coxswain on an LST in the Philippines, and whose uncle sank a U-boat with his PBY in the Gulf of Mexico, thank you for giving me continual encouragement for this project, listening attentively late at night as I read drafts of chapters to you, asking questions for clarification, and suggesting ways to temper the barracks and foxhole language.

To our children, Kate, Karyn, and Joshua, thanks for reading the disjoint chapters and for your enthusiastic input. You are your grandfather's legacy and thus the reason why he—and all his buddies, for that matter—wanted to get the war over with and get on with their lives. Partly, this book is for your children, and their children, so that when they study about World War II, they can say, "Yeah, I know about that war because my great grandpa was in it, and he and his paratrooper friends told some stories about their experiences in it."

Lastly, I apologize to all those troopers that I didn't get this done in time for them to see it or correct my misconceptions, but I trust that their children, grandchildren, and great grandchildren will remember and appreciate how these men fought and survived the biggest and most destructive war the world has ever known in the hopes that their descendants would not have to. For those whose names are on the crosses, stars, or monument in Manila—and who never got to look into their babies' faces—every man and woman who made it home agreed that you are the heroes.

"TIME WILL NOT DIMINISH THE GLORY OF THEIR DEEDS"
— Gen. John J. Pershing

Bibliography

BOOKS

William B. Breuer. *Retaking the Philippines*. New York, NY: St. Martin's Press, 1986. Island by island, detailed accounts of Army and Navy advances from Mindanao to Luzon. Reads like a novel.

Dwayne T. Burns. *Jump into the Valley of the Shadow*. Philadelphia, PA: Casemate Publishers, 2006. Autobiographical account of 506th PIR by an original member of the Band of Brothers.

Gerard M. Devlin. *Back to Corregidor*. New York, NY: St. Martin's Press, 1992. Synopsis of American acquisition of Corregidor Island and its capture by Japanese Imperial Army, early operations of the 503rd PIR, and details of planning and carrying out the assault on Corregidor by the Rock Force.

Gerard M. Devlin. *Paratrooper!* New York, NY: St. Martin's Press, 1979. From DaVinci's drawings to the Test Platoon to the occupation of Japan. Thorough treatment of the formation of US Airborne units and their many battles in every theater of WWII.

Lt. Gen. E. M. Flanagan, Jr. *Corregidor The Rock Force Assault.* Novato, CA: Presidio Press, 1988. Background on Fortress Corregidor—its acquisition, fortification, and defeat—and details of operations of the 503rd in the Pacific before and after the jump on Corregidor. Written from many first-hand accounts.

John J. Gobbell. *The Last Lieutenant.* New York, NY: St. Martin's Press, 1995. Historical novel about the fall of Corregidor and advent of resistance in the Philippines. Excellent description of pre-war defenses and the battle to stall the Japanese invasion.

Bennett M. Guthrie. *Three Winds of Death.* Chicago, IL: Adams Press (503d Parachute RCT Assoc), 1985. Brief history of the Army Airborne and first-hand account of the 503rd regiment's formation and operations. Primary source for a number of authors on the battle for Corregidor 1945, by a member of the original cadre and Company H.

Douglas MacArthur. *Reminiscences.* USA: Time, Inc., 1964. The General's personal reflections on his life, especially his lengthy and distinguished military career.

William Manchester. *American Caesar*—Douglas MacArthur 1880-1964. Toronto: Little, Brown, & Co. Ltd., 1978. Biography, from Army brat to general and beyond. Quotes from contemporaries flesh out his personality.

Kevin Maurer. *Rock Force.* USA: Penguin Random House, 2020. Detailed description of the actions of several individuals and Calhoun's platoon in particular during the battle for Corregidor.

Written in novel form from many firsthand interviews and accounts.

Barrett McGurn. *Yank the Army Weekly*—Reporting the Greatest Generation. Wheat Ridge, Col: Fulcrum Publishing, 2004. By one of its correspondents, the story of the founding, growth, and publishing process for the magazine, and his assignments and experiences in the PTO.

Patrick K. O'Donnell. *Beyond Valor.* New York, NY: Touchstone, 2002. Firsthand accounts from paratroopers, glider men, and Rangers in Africa, Italy, and northern Europe. Includes battle synopses and maps.

Patrick K. O'Donnell. *Into the Rising Sun.* New York, NY: The Free Press, 2002. Firsthand accounts from a number of paratroopers, infantrymen, and Marines on many island and SE Asia campaigns. Includes battle synopses and maps.

Bill O'Reilly and Martin Dugard. *Killing the Rising Sun.* New York, NY: Henry Holt and Company, 2016. Set in the final year of the war, outlines the buildup and battles in the PTO, the concurrent completion the Manhattan Project, and the subsequent fates of the Japanese warlords.

Col. Edson D. Raff. *We Jumped to Fight*. New York, NY: Vail-Ballou Press Inc., 1944. Story of the US Paratroopers (in particular 2/503 - 2/509) from training through battle in North Africa (Operation Torch and Central Tunisia) by their famous commander in the field. One of the first books about airborne operations.

Gordon L. Rottman. *US Airborne Units in the Pacific Theater 1942-45.* Oxford, United Kingdom: Osprey Publishing, 2007. Paperback covering training, tactics, weapons, organization, and synopses of Army and Marine Parachute operations in the PTO.

Gordon L. Rottman. *US Army Paratrooper in the Pacific Theater 1943-45.* Oxford, United Kingdom: Osprey Publishing, 2012. Paperback covering training, equipment, weapons, organization, staging overseas, and brief descriptions of the campaigns.

Rafael Steinberg. *Return to the Philippines.* Morristown, New Jersey: Time/Life Books, 1977 (World War II Series). The fall of Bataan and subsequent operations in the PTO.

Harold Templeman. *The Return to Corregidor.* New York: Strand Press, 1945. Short synopsis of the battle, by the Red Cross Director for the 503rd. Company rosters of the entire RCT engaged in the battle, and photos of the paratroopers by states.

Leroy Thompson. *US Airborne in Action.* Carrollton, TX: Squadron/Signal Publications, 1992. Paperback history of Airborne program, training at Fort Benning, actions in North Africa, the ETO, and PTO.

Keith Wheeler. *The Road to Tokyo.* Morristown, NJ: Time/Life Books, 1979 (World War II Series). Details the final surge towards Japan and the battles on Iwo Jima and Okinawa.

Maj. Richard Winters. *Beyond Band of Brothers.* New York, NY: Dutton Caliber, 2006. Autobiographical overview of Winters'

Army career and perceptions from Basic Infantry Training, through OCS and Parachute School, and the 506th PIR's battles in Europe.

Arthur Zich. *The Rising Sun*. Morristown, New Jersey: Time/Life Books, 1977 (World War II Series). Chronicles expansion of the Empire through Asia up to Midway.

Historical and Pictorial Review of the Parachute Battalions, United States Army. The Army and Navy Publishing Company, 1942. "Yearbook" distributed to the alumni of the Provisional Parachute Group before leaving Fort Benning.

WEBSITES

Boundingfire.com. WWII Games available (including Corregidor and other island battles); requires separate ASL parts.

Corregidor.org. Site contains The 503d P.R.C.T. Heritage Battalion Online (the original Association's site), packed with articles and books written by 503rd troopers.

Fortwolters.com. Info about and photos at the old IRTC.

In the 503rd.org. Database for 503rd PRCT. Verify or add names of members. Contains "Static Line" (Airborne Association) articles and photo collections.

KHLF.com (Karl H Landes Flavors)

Periscopefilms.com. Parachute Jump Training 1943. Training film from WWII on YouTube.

www.biblio.org/hyperwar/USA. Robert Ross Smith. *US Army in World War II*. Washington DC: Dept. of the Army, 1963. Vol 2 Part 16. The War in the Pacific:Triumph in the Philippines. Detailed battle descriptions and maps.

ARTICLES

Maj. Thomas Hardman. Drop on Corregidor. *Air Force, the Official Service Journal of the US Army Air Forces*, May 1945

James P. Lowe. Nadzab (1943): The First Successful Airborne Operation. Louisiana St. University: MA Thesis, Dec. 2004

MacArthur's Elite; 503d Parachute Infantry Regiment (author/ publisher unknown)

Mulgraveshire Historical Society, Gordonvale, Australia

Parish Book of All Saints Church, Gordonvale, Australia

Maj. Thomas Sheehan, USMA '91. WWII Vertical Envelopment: The German Influence on U.S. Army Airborne Operations. MMAS Thesis, June 2003.

Elizabeth Dockter Turner, 1941-1945. Scrapbook of news articles and mementos of World War II.

About the Author

Born in Pasadena and raised in Anaheim, California, Jim Turner taught math for forty years, mostly in Orange County schools but with a brief spell in Saudi Arabia. A succession of part-time, weekend, and summer jobs included the Disneyland Magic Shop, which paid off in membership at the Hollywood Magic Castle and marriage to a pretty Disneylander from the Midwest. He and Claudia, who is a choral music teacher as well as his best friend and soulmate, have three adult children and four grandchildren. Now retired, they enjoy driving America's highways, visiting other countries, singing in church choir, and volunteering for charities. Jim's lifelong penchants for writing and military history culminated in this book.

Made in the USA
Middletown, DE
21 January 2023